Not a Job for a Nice Jewish Boy

NOT A JOB FOR A NICE JEWISH BOY

Dan Cohn-Sherbok

BELLEW PUBLISHING
London

In memory of Digger

First published in Great Britain in 1993 by
Bellew Publishing Company Limited
8 Balham Hill, London SW12 9EA

ISBN 1 85725 069 9

Phototypeset by Intype, London

Printed and bound in Great Britain by
Hartnolls Ltd

Author's Note

Although this memoir is based on fact, it is a fictionalized account of events. In nearly all cases, characters are composites of several individuals and it would thus be a mistake to attempt to identify figures in the book with real persons. In addition, in order not to cause offence, I have altered the names of all persons, places and institutions, with the exception of those of my immediate family.

Contents

Prologue

'So, nu, you must be Ruth and Bernie's boy.'

'Yes,' I said.

'Listen, let me tell you, your father – he's a magician. You see this wrist . . . I broke it, maybe in ten places. And your father's a genius. He put it back together. It's perfect. I can tell you, he's a wonderful man, your father.'

This conversation took place in a jewellery store near the Brown Palace Hotel in Denver. It was December 1969. I had returned from rabbinical school in St Louis to spend the winter vacation with my parents. The woman who had accosted me was a friend of my grandmother.

'Nu, you're home for the holidays? What a pleasure for your parents. You're staying in Denver for a while, then? Perhaps you should meet my granddaughter. She's home too for the school vacation. Such a lovely girl. She's majoring in dance at the University of Arizona. She and her mother are coming to meet me here.'

'Well, actually,' I said, hoping to avoid this confrontation with its inevitable consequences and difficulties, 'I really have to go. I just came in to collect my watch. You see, I broke it skiing last week.'

'Ah, so you're a skier. Now, tell me, you're studying to be a doctor like your father? You want to be a surgeon, too?'

'No, actually . . . I'm not.'

'You don't want to be a doctor . . . with a father like yours you don't want to follow in his footsteps?'

'Well, actually, I'm not very good at science. And I'm a bit squeamish. And to tell the truth, I've never wanted to be a surgeon.'

'You're studying to be a lawyer, then . . .'

'No, not a lawyer either.'

'Not a doctor, not a lawyer, then maybe a businessman? You want to go into business. You'll be a great success, I'm sure.'

'Actually, Mrs Schwartz, not a businessman either. I'm studying to be a rabbi.'

'You want to be a rabbi? I don't understand. Your father is a successful doctor and you want to be a rabbi?'

'I do . . . I've always wanted to be a rabbi.'

Mrs Schwartz fiddled with her necklace. She was uneasy and confused. 'You want to be a rabbi,' she said. 'But it's not a job for a nice Jewish boy! Why would you want to be a rabbi? Listen, I think my grand-daughter's going to be very busy this holiday. What a girl! The telephone never stops ringing. Beck Steinberg's boy . . . Josie Goldschmidt's grandson . . . it never stops . . . A rabbi . . . no, I don't think so.'

And Mrs Schwartz gathered up her purchases and left the shop without a backward glance.

Chapter 1

Wanting to be a Rabbi: Growing up in the All-American Dream

'You can't wear those shoes,' my father said. It was a week before my bar mitzvah, and the worry of the moment concerned my clothes. I was thirteen years old. I had memorized my Torah portion. I could recite my speech in my sleep. My mother had ordered all the food. The caterers were scheduled for the party. Even my eczema was less itchy than usual. But no decision had been reached about how I should be dressed.

'They're my favourite shoes,' I insisted. 'I always wanted a pair of blue suede shoes. Honestly, there's no point in buying black shoes. I'll never wear them again.'

My father glared over the *Denver Post*. 'No son of mine is going to his bar mitzvah thinking he's Elvis Presley. Those shoes go back to the store tomorrow.'

'But I like them,' I protested. 'They'll look great.'

'They look terrible. And you won't wear them. That's the end of the matter.'

I never did take them back. When Bar Mitzvah Saturday came round, I put them on. There wasn't anything my father could do about it. In silence we drove to the Temple. He didn't speak to me, but that wasn't unusual. Instead he shook his head. But it was my bar mitzvah, and I was determined to do it my way.

The Temple in Denver is located in the Jewish section of the city. Surrounded by a gigantic parking lot, it looms over the neighbouring suburban houses. The stained-glass windows of the sanctuary – in abstract designs – dominate the building. On the morning of my bar mitzvah, 1 February 1958, the lot was filled with cars. Proudly, my father slid his Jaguar into a reserved space near the entrance. The service would not take place for half an hour, but already friends and relations had arrived. As we walked to the rabbi's office, my parents were waylaid. Seeing so many smiling faces, my father's mood changed. This was an occasion for him as well as for me, an opportunity to show off his only son, to impress guests with his affluent hospitality. My mother glowed. She was Secretary of the Temple Board; the Temple was her second home. This was her big day too.

We knocked on the door. No answer. Where was Rabbi Frankel? My parents looked at each other. After several anxious minutes, he appeared. 'Sorry to keep you waiting,' he said, opening the door. 'I was in the toilet.' My parents sighed audibly with relief. He hadn't forgotten. We took a seat in his office as he explained the final details. My father would sit on the right of the ark; I would sit next to the rabbi. The rabbi would help me if I made any mistakes. He patted me on the shoulder. 'Don't worry, Danny,' he said. 'You'll do fine.'

The rabbi robed. He was a tall, pock-marked man with a typically hooked nose and straight white hair brushed back over his ears. I knew my parents were important members of the Temple and had considerable influence. It was in the rabbi's interest for my bar mitzvah to go well. Most bar mitzvah boys are terrified, but I was confident if a little apprehensive: I didn't want to let my parents down, especially after the blue-suede-shoes episode. I followed the rabbi and my father through a narrow hallway to the sanctuary. We entered through the back and took our seats. I looked at the congregation and saw my grandmother sitting next to my mother. The former, in a matronly black dress, radiated pleasure and pride; the latter looked strained and anxious. Near them was my uncle, and several rows behind sat various cousins. Dotted through the audience were friends from school.

Behind me, the choir began singing. The service started. In a trance I followed the prayers. After an interminable time the Torah Scroll was taken out of the ark. I was called to read my portion. I read it – no mistakes. Then the Haftarah. Again, no mistakes. The Hebrew part was over – so far, so good. But there was still my speech. Out it came as I had memorized it, word for word. It was not my own creation – rather the anguished product of my mother's labours. I thanked my parents; I thanked Rabbi Frankel; I thanked my bar mitzvah teacher; I thanked each and every one of the congregation for coming. I spoke about my grandmother and her late husband. I quoted from my Torah portion. And then it was over. My bar mitzvah had ended as I believed it would. I was a success!

At the reception held in the Temple hall I was mobbed. My grandmother headed the throng. 'Danny, darling,' she said, 'you were wonderful.' My mother hugged me. She looked profoundly relieved. The burden of my bar mitzvah had been lifted. Her son had triumphed. She could hold her head up among her friends. She simply kissed me. My father shook my hand. He looked almost pleasant. 'Well done, Dan,' he said. Then my friends surrounded me. They patted me on the shoulder. Everyone was happy. And hungry. The crowd moved towards the refreshments. But a hush descended on the room when the rabbi entered. Quickly he recited the Sabbath Kiddush. Guests then surged forward towards the tables, which were groaning with food. In the centre was a huge swan carved in ice; from its beak, drops of water dripped on the table. There were piles of chopped liver, mounds of smoked salmon, stacks of knishes and oceans of cocktail dips. And that was just the first course. Eventually, the company broke up into groups, seating themselves at tables festooned with flowers.

I sat with my parents and my grandmother. Guests came up to our table and congratulated me. They complimented my parents.

'You must be proud,' the rabbi's wife said. 'He did a wonderful job. His Hebrew was very good. Even the rabbi was impressed!'

My mother's sister, swathed in mink, came to sit next to me. 'Danny,' she said, 'you were great.'

We were joined by the conductor of the Denver Symphony Orchestra and his wife – my parents' best friends. 'Hello, Aunt Selma and Uncle Saul,' I said. Selma kissed my cheek, being careful not to smudge her lipstick, while Saul gripped my hand. 'Your speech brought tears to your mother's eyes,' Selma said. 'Have you ever thought of being a rabbi? I think you have just what it takes.'

From the vantage point of our table I surveyed the crowd. Plates piled high, they were having a splendid time. My parents glowed. My grandmother was radiant. I was happy. I was also the most important person in the room. It was my bar mitzvah, and I had triumphed. I began to take Aunt Selma's question seriously. Perhaps I *would* be a good rabbi. At the age of thirteen, I was sure I could do a better job than Rabbi Frankel. My parents always said he was mediocre. My performance was *not* mediocre.

As everyone ate and drank, the photographer took pictures, and unbelievable quantities of roast beef, vegetables, gravy, chocolate cake, meringue gateau, passion fruit sorbet and crème brûlée disappeared. Eventually guests began to leave. They came over to my parents and thanked them. Again I was congratulated. I'd never been kissed so many times. Finally, only my parents and I remained. On the tables half-empty plates and glasses were left to be cleared away. The reception hall was silent. We made our way back to our car. The parking lot was empty except for my father's Jaguar. We were exhausted. In silence, we drove home.

Over the years, I have often looked at the photographs of my bar mitzvah. Although I can no longer recognize most of the faces, I can clearly remember the atmosphere. For my parents, it was a joyous event. It was a time of hope and promise, a day to remember. For me, it was the turning point of my young life. On my thirteenth birthday I decided what I wanted to do: I wanted to become a rabbi.

And why not? From what others had told me, and from what I knew myself, I was a good speaker. I could stand in front of a congregation without fear. I enjoyed the adulation. Indeed, I relished the praise. Being a rabbi was a respectable job. I could serve the Jewish people. I could gain prominence in the community. Possibly I could even achieve national recognition as a famous preacher. Other rabbis had done it; there was no reason I shouldn't emulate them.

I wasn't shy about telling my family and friends of my new ambition, but even to myself I did not confess that my desire to be a rabbi was mixed with worldly ambition. I had no desire to follow my father's footsteps and become a surgeon. I had no interest in the law, or in business. What I sought instead was the elation of standing before an awestruck congregation, making them listen to me. I cannot truthfully say I was called to be a rabbi. I was seduced into it.

As time passed, my father became increasingly concerned at my aspiration to be a rabbi. How could his only child enter such a profession? The sons of his medical colleagues were, without exception, heading for medical school. It was simply unthinkable that the son of a successful surgeon should become a rabbi. This was a career for the less advantaged. Convinced that my judgement was askew, my father was determined to show me the attractions of medicine.

One Saturday afternoon after I returned home from religion school for lunch, my father said: 'Why don't you come with me to the hospital? You'll find it interesting. I have to perform an operation on the leg of a skier who took a very bad fall.' I was delighted with the invitation. It was not often that he took any notice of me, and I was keen to show interest and win his approval.

When we arrived at the hospital we went straight to surgery. My father greeted the nurses, changed into operating clothes, put on rubber gloves and scrubbed up. I changed as well and was fitted with a mask. We entered the operating room. The lights were intense. My father was joined by an anaesthetist and several nurses. I was told to stand back. The first incision was made. Clamps were applied to the wound to stop the bleeding. The bone was exposed. I began to feel sick. The room started to spin. I gasped for air. A doctor standing nearby tried to grab my arm, but I collapsed with a thud on the floor. Coming to, I was helped out of the room. The doctor gave me a cup of water. I went to the men's room and was spectacularly sick, then I sat down outside the operating theatre with my head in my hands. Eventually, my father emerged. The operation was over. It had been a success, but I was a failure.

'Come on, Dan,' my father said without looking at me. 'Let's change.' No words were spoken about my performance, but both my father and I now knew that I would never be a doctor. No one employs surgeons who vomit in the middle of operations.

That evening I overheard my parents discussing my future.

'I couldn't believe it,' my father said. 'He fainted. The nurses were more concerned with him than with my patient. It's a disgrace.'

'You can't blame him, Bernie,' my mother said. 'It's not his fault if he can't stand the sight of blood.'

'But it's so feeble. I never felt that way. I always knew I'd be a surgeon. In medical school we had to dissect bodies. He can't even look at an incision, much less make one himself.'

'He's sensitive,' said my mother. 'Look at the trouble he has with his eczema.'

'He's got to shape up,' insisted my father.

'Well, at least he knows what he wants to be.'

'A rabbi! What kind of a job is that? You can't make a living being a rabbi.'

'He'll never be rich,' said my mother, 'but at least he won't starve.'

'He costs a lot of money. He likes the best of everything. I've never heard him object to our Jaguar. As far as I'm concerned, he can dig his own grave.'

'Well at least he'll be able to recite his own funeral service,' replied my mother.

My father, however, was in no mood for flippancy. Throwing down his coffee cup on the kitchen table, he stormed out of the room, slamming the door behind him.

The next day my father refused to speak to me. He left for the hospital without saying goodbye. It was Sunday, and I was dressed in my football uniform for my weekly practice with the local club: the Bombers. I knew I was supposed to enjoy the game, but I didn't. The coach had put me in as centre. I was to hike the ball to the quarterback. Every time I did this, the other side rushed over to tackle him. I was crushed in the onslaught and ended up under a mass of bodies. What was the point of this torture? That Sunday I couldn't do anything right. The coach shouted at me. 'Come on Danny, get up. Don't just lie there like a beached whale.' My mother, watching from the sidelines, was stricken with shame. Her son, the successful student leader, was not going to become an eminent doctor like his father, neither did he show any talent as an athlete. How could he possibly be a credit to his parents?

From Junior High School I graduated to High School. During the summer, I worked as a counsellor at the Temple religion school camp, the same camp where, as a little boy, I myself had been a camper. Located in the Rocky Mountains, it was constructed next to a picturesque stream. One of my earliest memories of being a camper there was of the rabbi coming to inspect our cabin. I was nine years old. The rabbi looked in the bathroom, then peered at the beds. Looking at my sleeping bag, he asked: 'Whose bed is this?'

The counsellor pointed at me. 'It's Dan Cohn-Sherbok's.'

Glaring at me, the rabbi said, 'It's grubby. Full of dirt. He's a very dirty little boy.'

This was hardly pastoral. I was sure I could do better, both as a counsellor and, someday, as a rabbi.

One of the older counsellors at the camp was a college student from the East Coast who was studying philosophy at Harvard. In his cabin he put up a Harvard banner, and on Friday nights he wore a Harvard tie to the Shabbat service. I was impressed. He was more sophisticated than anyone his age I had ever known. I was fascinated by his stories of student life in Harvard Square. We frequently discussed the advantages of an Ivy League education.

'Dan,' he said, 'you don't want to go to Colorado University. It's the sticks. Denver is a hick town. The Rocky Mountains are great, but Colorado is awfully far from anywhere.'

'I know. My father wants me to go East,' I said. 'He went to the University of Pennsylvania. I think that's where he wants me to go.'

'But it's the garbage can of the Ivy League!'

'My father wouldn't like to hear that. I'd like to go to Harvard. But I'm not sure I'll get in.'

'Of course you will. Your grades are good enough.'

'I don't know. But you're right. I really don't want to stay in Colorado. It's a great place to grow up. The skiing's fantastic. But I've got to have an Ivy League education. My father always makes fun of my mother because she went to Denver University: he says it's a Mickey Mouse school.'

I wouldn't be able to bear such criticism. And it would be quite something to be a rabbi who had gone to a prestigious Eastern college. These conversations convinced me I had little choice. If I was going to be a success, this had to be a major goal. It was the Ivy League or bust!

In addition to such educational aspirations, I continued to pursue a political career in High School. In my sophomore year I was elected Vice-President; the next year I became President of the Junior Class. Given that there were nearly 2,000 students in the school, this was a considerable achievement. My parents were terribly proud. Their son would never become a bone surgeon, he was a failure at football, he suffered from eczema patches, but he did have leadership potential.

Yet during my junior year I realized that there were barriers to my acceptance in certain circles. One of the girls I dated was the daughter of prominent upper-class parents who lived in the best area of the city and belonged to the city's grandest country club. Their house was built in mock-Georgian style; surrounded by acres of lawn, it had a tennis court in the back yard as well as a swimming pool. After we had gone to the movies one evening, this girl suggested we have a drink at their club, assuring me I could go as her guest. By this time I had my own car, and so we drove there. Apprehensively, I went inside. The club was full of well-dressed, affluent adults as well as a few teenagers.

'You know,' I said, 'I've never been here. It's quite a place!'

'You mean your parents don't belong to a country club?' she asked.

'No. Not even the Jewish country club.'

'Why not?'

'Well,' I said, 'my father doesn't play golf. And my mother doesn't like swimming. So I don't think they thought there would be any point.'

'But you'd like it, wouldn't you?'

'I think I would. But to be honest, I'd rather be a member here.'

'I don't think that would be possible. It's ridiculous, but they don't take Jews, or blacks either. I can't see why.'

We sipped our Cokes. Here was a real barrier. No matter what I could achieve at High School, where I went to college notwithstanding, such a club would always be out of bounds. No Jews! The American dream stopped at the entrance to this elegant upper-class world.

America is, in theory, a classless society. My High School was based on meritocratic principles. But in the outside world real limits to social advancement existed. As a Jew, I could proceed only so far. The barriers were apparently insurmountable. But I wondered whether it would be possible for me to leap over this social hurdle if I took on the role of Jewish representative to the Gentile world. Could a rabbi with an Ivy League education and a sufficiently large inheritance mix with upper-class Gentiles? Even if I couldn't actually *join* a prestigious country club, couldn't I become the club's Jewish mascot? This was, admittedly, not the most enviable position, but it was certainly better than nothing.

As Head Boy, my final year in High School should have been fulfilling. Instead, it was beset by difficulties. Increasingly I became conscious that I was the target of hostility. Friends drifted away. My eczema patch got worse. It became harder and harder to get a date. For the Senior Prom I invited a girl I barely knew. All my former girlfriends had lost interest in me. When I picked her up, it was clear that she had been drinking. Her speech was slurred, and she had difficulty walking in a straight line. By the middle of the evening, she was completely incoherent. I had to carry her to my car. Before midnight I deposited her on her doorstep, rang the bell, and waited for her parents to emerge.

'Sorry,' I said, 'Julia's drunk.'

'This is terrible,' her father said. 'Why have you done this?'

'Actually, she did it herself. I'm completely sober. I haven't had anything to drink except orange juice. I just couldn't control her.'

Her mother glared at me. 'You're the Head Boy,' she said. You're supposed to set an example. I trusted you with my daughter, and now look what's happened.'

'But I . . . I . . . didn't get her drunk,' I protested.

The next week Julia and her friends launched an onslaught on my parents' house. At dawn they festooned the trees in the garden with toilet paper. Before they departed they serenaded me at my bedroom window.

My father was not amused. 'Clean it up!'

The rest of the day I spent up a ladder, attempting to pull down swathes of pink toilet paper.

The final social event of the year was a party held at our house. As Head Boy, it was my responsibility to organize a farewell dance for the retiring student council. My parents greeted all the guests and chaperoned the party. There was plenty to eat, and everyone appeared to have a good time. The next morning, however, my father stormed into my room. 'So these are the student leaders,' he yelled. Holding a condom in front of my nose, he shouted, 'Just what's this?'

'Gosh,' I said, 'it's a condom.'

'Whose is it?'

'It's not mine,' I said sheepishly.

'Well, I'm glad to hear it. But who does it belong to?'

'Honestly, I don't know, Dad. I'm surprised anyone would bring one. I don't think there was much chance to use it.'

'I should think not. From now on, no more parties. And don't bother to invite any of your friends here again.'

My final year of High School ended with the May Day Parade. Each class constructed a float, and in a long procession the candidates for May Queen were driven around the school, sitting in convertibles. Together with the Head Girl, I came in the final car. Crowds of students standing on the pavement cheered. It was a glorious finish to my High School career, even though I was aware my popularity had vastly diminished.

In June my class graduated. Dressed in academic gowns and mortar boards, all 550 of us lined up to receive our diplomas. We were socially and academically mixed. Some of us were destined for college; others had already secured employment. Students from poor families stood next to classmates from the most affluent sections of the city. It was unlikely that our paths would cross again.

I should have been elated: after months of anxious waiting, I had been accepted at Tewksbury, a small prestigious men's college in Vermont. For both me and my parents, this was a great relie. Yet I was fearful and depressed. My eczema itched almost con stantly. In both Junior and Senior High School I had been somebody. Success had come relatively easily. But would this be so in the future? I was now on my own. No longer could I seek assurance from home. I would have to be self-reliant, thousands of miles away in a very competitive environment.

During the summer vacation I read the required books for my first year in college. In September I packed, unpacked and repacked. Shirts, socks, underwear, trousers, coats, sweaters, scarves and shoes were crammed together in a huge trunk. In addition, I took a separate suitcase for my first few days.

On the morning I was to leave I woke early. I heard my mother crying. She came into my room and hugged me. 'I don't want you to leave,' she said.

'Really, Mom. If you don't, I won't go.'

'No . . . you have to. But I don't want you to.'

My father was less distraught. At the airport he shook my hand.

'Phone us as soon as you arrive,' my mother said.

Slowly I walked to the gate. I sat on the plane, took out my handkerchief, and blew my nose. Looking out of the window, I could see my parents waiting for the plane to take off. I put on my seatbelt, and in a few minutes the plane was airborne. Sitting next to me was an attractive girl my own age. I tried to recover my composure.

'Are you going East to college?' I asked.

'I'll be a freshman at Vassar,' she said.

'I'm going to Tewksbury.'

During the flight we talked about High School. I told her I had been Head Boy. She said she was from California and had changed planes in Denver. I liked her. I asked if I could write to her at Vassar. I felt better already.

In Chicago I changed planes. Walking through the vast airport, I felt lonely. I wondered if I wouldn't have been happier staying in Colorado rather than travelling thousands of miles. Several hours later, I arrived in Albany, New York, and, as instructed, took a cab to Tewksburytown, Vermont. I checked in to the Tewksbury Inn, where my father had made a reservation for me. In my room I phoned home.

'Hi,' I said, 'I've arrived.'

'It's so good to hear your voice.'

'It was a long journey. I'm exhausted.'

'What's the Tewksbury Inn like?' my father asked.

'It's really nice.'

It was good to speak to my parents. I felt less desolate. But as I ate dinner alone in the restaurant, the same feelings of despondency returned. I was so far from home. Could I make it here on my own? As a Jewish boy from a public High School in the West, I was a foreigner. The Tewksbury Inn, with its New England colonial architecture and antique furniture symbolized the world I was so anxious to be a part of. But could I really fit in?

The next day I walked across the campus to the freshman quad where my dormitory was located. When I found my rooms, I discovered that my two room-mates had already staked out their territory. They had taken the best beds and desks. They were drinking beer. It was only ten in the morning.

I shook hands with them both. 'I'm Dan,' I said.

'I'm Sam,' the taller one announced. 'Have a beer.'

'I'm Harry,' added the other. He was dressed in pyjamas.

'Thanks. But it's a bit too early for me. How long have you guys been here?'

'We got here yesterday,' Sam said. He took out a pack of cigarettes, lit one, blew smoke in my direction. 'Want one?'

'No thanks. I don't smoke.'

'Well, Dan,' Harry said, 'I see from the college list that you're from Denver. Did you go to prep school there?'

'No, public High School. It's the best High School in the city.'

'Is that right?' Harry said. 'We both went to Deerfield. We're from New York. Have you ever been there?'

'Not yet. But I hope I'll be able to make a visit this Christmas.'

'Do that,' Sam said. 'In the meantime, you ought to unpack. Where's your stuff?'

'I left it at the Tewksbury Inn. I stayed there overnight.'

'Well, Dan,' Harry said, 'you'd better get a move on. We're supposed to go to a meeting of all freshmen at twelve.'

These were my room-mates. As I walked back to the Tewksbury Inn, my spirits sank. They were preppies, from one of the best Eastern prep schools. They were friends. I was the outsider. Was this what Tewksbury would be like?

At noon I joined my classmates in Chapter Hall. The President of the College welcomed us. We were privileged to be at Tewksbury, he emphasized. We were the future leaders of the nation. He had great hopes for us. I looked at the hundreds of students around me. They were dressed in sports jackets and blazers. Some were already wearing the college tie. Somehow, I doubted I would become their class president.

After dinner, I went back to my room. I sat on my bed and began to write a letter to my parents. Hearing screaming from the quad, I rushed out to see what had happened. Masses of students carrying waste-paper baskets full of water were rushing at each other. It was the biggest water fight I had ever seen. For hours, students drenched with water refilled their waste baskets and renewed the attack. 'Come on, Dan,' Harry said. 'Fill up your waste basket.'

I didn't participate. It was harmless, rowdy fun, but I was dismayed. I had so much wanted to go to an Eastern college. I had imagined it would be fiercely academic and highly intellectual. Water fights I had not anticipated.

As the year progressed, matters deteriorated. In the spring my classmates had a food riot in the freshmen's hall. When the kitchen ran out of food, they threw plates and glasses. Most of us hid under the tables. When it was over, several students were injured. The dining hall was wrecked. To pay for this damage, all members of the class were fined three dollars each. Indignant, I refused to pay. When the class president came to collect, I protested.

'Look,' I said. 'I didn't approve of the food fight. And I don't see why I should be forced to contribute.'

'We're all in this together,' he said.

'I'm not.'

'Don't be stupid. It's only three bucks. And if we all pay, the problem is solved. We're counting on you, Dan.'

'I don't see why I should be fined for something I didn't do. You should charge those who got us into this mess.'

'I can't discover who was responsible. We're all responsible.'

'Well, I'm not,' I said. 'And I'm not going to let those who *were* off the hook.'

My stand did not make me popular. My superior airs were intolerable. I didn't seduce girls and I loudly disapproved of those who did. I didn't get drunk. I didn't smoke. Not surprisingly, my room-mates became so incensed with me that they requested I be given a room on my own. Unfortunately, it was situated next door to the dormitory bathroom. Every weekend I heard student after student being violently sick from drinking too much. The corridor smelled of regurgitated beer. To add to my discomfiture, those next door to me had their girlfriends stay overnight, and I was constantly awakened by their loud music and passionate sex.

Instead of joining in the fun, I decided I could endure no more, and I trotted off to see the Freshman Dean. I explained that I was unhappy. I didn't know what to do.

'You're overreacting,' he said. 'Why shouldn't your classmates let off steam? They work hard all week.'

'But they're drowning in drink and sex! You don't have to endure people being sick all the time. You can't imagine what it's like.'

'A long time ago I was a freshman here,' he said.

'Was it the same?'

'Of course. And I got drunk just like your classmates.'

'You did?'

'It happens every year. It always has. It's a Tewksbury tradition.' I was not amused. My eczema itched intolerably.

I returned to Denver for the spring vacation. I was so relieved to be in familiar surroundings, even my father seemed friendly. My mother's cooking was delicious. I relished the peace of my own room. After the boisterous and smelly environment of the dorm, it was bliss. I phoned some of my old school friends. They were glad to see me. This was a welcome change from the hostility that had surrounded me at Tewksbury. I didn't want to return. But there was no choice. I couldn't give up. At the end of the holiday I packed my bags, kissed my mother, shook hands with my father, and went to meet the enemy.

On my return I spent my entire time studying – losing myself in my books. In June I made the return journey from Tewksbury-town to Albany, and then to Denver. My parents had found me a job in a friend's ice-cream factory. I was to get up at four every morning, and load vats with ice-cream until two in the afternoon. I lasted one day. Even though I managed to get out of bed in time for work, I had nearly collapsed by eleven o'clock. I knew I'd never be able to survive such a regime after a miserable year at Tewksbury. My second day I resigned.

My father was furious. 'Money doesn't grow on trees,' he snarled. 'It costs me a lot of money to send you to Tewksbury. The least you could do is earn something over the holidays.'

'I'm sorry, Dad,' I said. 'But it's too much for me. I'd never last. Tewksbury was really hard. I've got to have a break. I'll kill myself loading containers full of ice-cream. It's a horrible job.'

'Is that the real reason?' he asked.

'Yeah,' I replied. Yet secretly I knew that if I had to get up at four in the morning, my social life would be ruined. After living a completely celibate life during my freshman year, I wanted to make up for lost time.

Through my parents' contacts, I managed to get a job at a clothing store. Every day I tried to persuade those who came into the shop that they needed shirts, socks, trousers, sports jackets and ties. I told them they looked great in whatever they put on. To my astonishment, I discovered I was quite good at selling: nearly every week I sold more than anyone else. I did have a pang of conscience about attempting to get customers to spend money on hideous garments just because we happened to have them in stock.

In September I returned to Tewksbury. Nearly all of my class had joined fraternities, but I was determined to stand aloof. I lived in a single room in a dormitory reserved for those who had no desire to be part of fraternity life. I resolved to live a solitary existence and avoid my classmates. I worked steadily and my grades improved. In class I said little, but I was dismayed by some of my teachers. In English literature, the Professor told obscene stories in an attempt to liven up Shakespeare. I was shocked and told him so.

After one particularly smutty lesson, I asked if I could stay behind and have a word with him.

'Look, Dr Hannibal,' I said, 'I don't like the way you explain things. It isn't necessary to use four-letter words all the time.'

Dr Hannibal scooped up his papers and moved towards the door. 'I don't think you understand Shakespeare very well,' he said.

'Perhaps I don't,' I replied. 'But that's not the point. If you want us to appreciate Shakespeare's plays, using scatological language hardly helps.'

Fingering his Phi Beta Kappa key, which dangled from his waistcoat, Dr Hannibal sneered. 'I graduated Summa Cum Laude from Columbia,' he said. 'And I have a PhD from Harvard. Who are you to tell me how I should teach Shakespeare?'

During the winter vacation, I stayed with a friend from High School who was in his second year at Harvard. He lived in Eliot House. After being cooped up in Tewksburytown with its one main street, Cambridge was paradise. Radcliffe girls were everywhere. The streets were filled with splendid shops and restaurants. There were students from all over the world. If only I had been accepted at Harvard, rather than Tewksbury! But it was too late. Disconcerted, I returned to rural Vermont.

By this time, I had decided I would major in philosophy. This, I believed, would be a suitable preparation for later study in rabbinical school. Unfortunately I didn't like the philosophy teachers. Imbued with existentialist ideas, they were frequently incomprehensible. In one particularly bewildering class, the professor babbled on about Hegel. To me it was gobbledy-gook. How could I take this seriously? Hegel, he explained, believed that the Absolute unfolds itself in history. I had no idea what this could possibly mean. What Absolute? How could it evolve through time? It made no sense.

I raised my hand. 'Sorry, sir,' I said. 'But I don't follow this. I simply can't figure out what Hegel is talking about. What do you mean by the "Absolute"?'

My classmates sniggered.

'Dan, have you read the assignment for today?'

'Yes. That's just it. I'm baffled.' My eczema began to itch.

'Are you saying you don't think Hegel knew what he was talking about?'

'Well . . . I suppose I am, sort of.'

'So, you, a second-year undergraduate, think you're a better philosopher than Hegel?'

'I didn't say that. All I mean is that I don't understand what we've been reading.'

'Perhaps,' he said, lighting his pipe, 'that's because you're not quite as good a philosopher as you think.'

I cringed. That was hardly a Socratic dialogue. I wondered if I ought to change my major.

In the Easter break I went to New York and stayed at the Tewksbury Club. Located near Grand Central Station, it was an ideal base for exploring the city. Every evening elderly Tewskbury men crowded around the bar and told stories about their days at the college. They were much friendlier than my classmates.

One night when I was having dinner by myself in the restaurant attached to the bar, a sozzled Southern gentleman slouched into a chair at my table. 'So,' he drawled, 'you're here on a visit from the college. What year are you, boy?'

'I'm a sophomore,' I said.

'Are you having a good time?' he asked.

I mumbled a non-committal reply.

'We always are on the lookout for new members of the club. How would you like me to propose you?'

I was flattered. I readily agreed.

After several months, a letter arrived from the Tewksbury Club.

I eagerly opened it. I had been accepted for membership. It was all so easy – at last I was accepted into elite society! Even though my sponsor didn't know me, I was thrilled.

On my return I pondered how I would endure the next two years. Was there any escape? I went to see the Dean to ask about going to Europe for my junior year. There was little hope that I could go to the Sorbonne, since I was not a French major. But a solution to my problem did exist. One of my classmates who was studying classics had applied to spend a year in Greece. The Dean suggested this might be a possibility for me as well, since the classes there would deal with philosophy as well as ancient Greek literature and history. I sent in the required forms, and several weeks later heard I had been given a place.

But how could I persuade my parents to let me go? I phoned them and explained that this would be an excellent supplement to my study at Tewksbury. My father was not convinced.

'It costs a great deal of money to send you to Tewksbury,' he pointed out. 'The education is superb. I don't think you'll gain anything by going.'

'But it would be a great experience. I've never been to Europe.'

'You can go some other time. Right now you should get the best education you can. The classes there won't be up to much.'

'But, Dad,' I pleaded, 'I really want to go.'

I didn't explain the real reason for wanting to leave Tewksbury. I was sure it would be the only way I could face the future. I remained resolute. At last my father gave in. I was free, at least for twelve months.

During the summer I returned to Denver and studied modern Greek with a former friend of my parents who was of Greek origin. It wasn't easy, but at least I could carry on a simple conversation. At the end of the summer my parents drove me to the airport. My mother wept in the car. 'Please be careful,' she said. 'Don't forget to write us every week. And call us if you need to.' My father looked impassive. I hugged them and boarded the plane. Saying goodbye did not become easier with experience.

Arriving in New York, I took a taxi to where the SS *France* was docked. This was to be my first cruise. On board I found my room, a tiny cabin for four passengers. I unpacked, and made my way to the deck. Hundreds of us waited for the ship to depart. Balloons filled the air. With a lurch we set off.

After four days and nights of eating, swimming and dancing,

we docked in Southampton, where I caught a train to London. I then took a cab to my hotel, located near Piccadilly Circus, and as we rode through London streets I marvelled at the beautiful buildings. Once I had booked into the room, I went exploring. I saw the sights: Westminster Abbey, the Houses of Parliament, Buckingham Palace, the National Gallery, the Tate, the British Museum. It was thrilling.

The next day I went to the Oxford and Cambridge Club, located on Pall Mall. The Tewksbury Club had reciprocal relations with this London club, and I was anxious to see it. When I entered, I presented my Tewksbury Club membership card to the porter. He looked at me suspiciously. 'You're a little young to be here,' he said. 'Is this your card?' Although intimidated by his British accent and bearing, I persevered. 'It's mine,' I replied. 'We are allowed to use the club, aren't we?' Reluctantly he agreed. I walked up the stairs to the library, to find a room full of elderly softly snoring Englishmen asleep in leather armchairs. Later I had lunch at a table by myself in the dining room. I had steak-and-kidney pudding. It was a long way from Jewish Denver!

The next day I left from Victoria Station and crossed the Channel to Paris, where I stayed at a small, cheap hotel near the Gare du Nord. I then travelled by train through Italy, arriving in Greece a few weeks later. In every city I visited I saw all the main tourist sights – I had no idea when I would return.

Once in Athens, I took a taxi to the flat where I was to live. It was located in a fashionable section of the city, near Mount Lecapitos. Every day as I walked to class I gazed in wonder at the Acropolis. The treasures of the National Museum were overwhelming. Amid the remains of the past, my studies came alive. In the first semester we travelled throughout Greece to look at ancient ruins, and I became increasingly fascinated by the ancient world. My eczema scarcely bothered me and my grades were better than they had ever been at Tewksbury. I also managed to meet some Greek students of my own age. As a group we went to tavernas and on long walks through the city. Haltingly, I managed to converse in modern Greek.

Despite my enchantment with Greece, I knew that my real interest was elsewhere. I was, after all, still determined to be a rabbi. I longed for Jewish stimulation, and as a consequence decided to spend the winter vacation in Israel. After term ended, I therefore boarded an El Al plane for the Holy Land. My first stop was Jerusalem. The city glimmered in the sunlight as the bus slowly traversed the hills. At that time, 1964, the city was still divided into an Arab and a Jewish section – the fence that separated these two areas was like an ugly scar defacing the city. From Jerusalem I travelled to Galilee, where I visited the mystical city of Safed, and then toured the sites of Christianity. On my return to Jerusalem I explored Mea Shearim, the Hasidic quarter of the city. During my last few days, I met a Yugoslavian girl, Miriam, who had recently immigrated to Israel with her parents. When she took me home to meet her family, I discovered that her father, like mine, was an orthopaedic surgeon.

Looking me over, he asked why I had come to Israel. I explained that I was on vacation and that I was spending my junior year in Greece. 'Are you planning to make aliyah?' he inquired.

'No,' I replied. 'I want to live in America.'

'And what do you plan to do after you finish college?'

I said that I wanted to study to be a rabbi. Miriam's father looked at his wife.

Puzzled, he asked why I wasn't wearing a yamulkah.

'I'm not Orthodox,' I explained.

'In Yugoslavia,' he said, 'there's only traditional Judaism. The same is true here. I can't understand trying to change things. I'm not religious, but I'm Jewish. Being in Israel makes me more Jewish. Why don't you want to come here to live? This is the only place you can be a real Jew.'

'I don't see why I can't be a good Jew in the States,' I replied. 'Jews didn't always live in Israel. For two thousand years they lived somewhere else.'

'But then they didn't have a homeland. We have one now. This is my home. It should be yours too.'

I didn't want to carry on this discussion. I felt uncomfortable. Why couldn't I be an authentic Jew outside Israel? Through the centuries Jews have lived full Jewish lives in many lands; they were proud to be Jewish; they kept the law; they worshipped in the synagogue; they produced religious literature. I was convinced Miriam's father didn't know what he was talking about. Certainly I was determined to be a rabbi, but I also intended to enjoy the material benefits of living in the United States. This surely was good enough.

During the next semester I continued to study hard, go out with my Greek friends, and immerse myself in the ancient world. It had been an exhilarating year. Back in Denver for the summer, I recounted my foreign adventures to my parents. I contacted old friends. I went to services at the Temple. In addition, I enrolled in the Temple Hebrew class where I learned the rudiments of the Hebrew language. At my bar mitzvah I had been able to read the Torah aloud, but had no idea what the individual words meant. At long last, I could now understand some of the prayers in the liturgy. I felt confident about the future. In just over a year's time I would, I hoped, begin rabbinical school. If only I didn't have to return to Tewksbury for my final year!

In June my parents came to my graduation. We lined up outside Chapter Hall and walked in line to a wooded area, where the graduation ceremony would take place. Unlike at High School, I had not been a student officer. My father looked downcast as we marched by. But at least, I thought, I would have a BA from Tewksbury.

Back in Denver, I was immersed in preparations for rabbinical school. I had been accepted at the Progressive Rabbinical Seminary in St Louis, so my first task was to purchase a car so that I could drive there. My father insisted it be well built.

'What about a sports car?' I asked. At Tewksbury I walked everywhere. Now was my chance to have something I really liked.

'It's not very practical,' he said. 'And it's dangerous. What about something like a Ford?'

I didn't listen – what I had in mind was an Austin Healey 3000 Mark II. This was a low-slung British car with a powerful engine. One of my Tewksbury classmates drove one. Now that I was a Tewksbury graduate, why couldn't I, too?

There was a British racing-green model in the sports-car showroom near our house, and I took my father to see it. He wasn't impressed.

'It's not the right image for a rabbi,' he complained.

'I think it's just the thing,' I countered. 'I want to be a modern rabbi, not an old-fashioned one. A Temple youth group would love it.'

'*They* might,' he said. 'But the adults wouldn't. Let's go look at some sensible cars.'

I was determined, and after weeks of nagging my father gave in. He and the salesman negotiated the price, and several days later I drove it home. It glittered outside our house. The neighbours peered inside it. It was thrilling to drive and I adored it.

During the summer, I continued my Hebrew studies and pursued an active social life. One evening I went to a hang-out that had recently been established for those sympathetic to the beat generation. It was a somewhat seedy-looking coffee house, located near downtown. I saw an old High School friend there who introduced me to a girl who had just returned to Denver from Aspen, where she had worked as a waitress. We talked about skiing. I told her I had just graduated from college and had returned to Denver for the summer holidays. She was suntanned and attractive. I phoned her the next day and we went out. After several passionate evenings, I decided she was the girl for me. She wasn't Jewish, but I couldn't see that this should be an overwhelming obstacle. Conversion was allowed.

Susan, however, was less enthusiastic. 'Let's not make any plans,' she said. 'It's better just to have fun.' I saw her every day, but I was reluctant to tell my parents about my affair. Eventually, however, they found out about Susan from one of their friends, who had seen us together. My father insisted I talk to him. We sat on the patio. 'Dan,' he began, 'you're being very stupid. You tell us you want to be a rabbi, but you go out with a shiksa. Who are you kidding?' I turned away from my father's piercing stare. I hated this inquisition. 'You're making too much out of this,' I said.

'I've spent a lot of money sending you to Tewksbury,' he went on. 'We just bought you an expensive sports car. You're going to seminary for five years. Don't you think you owe us something?'

'I'm grateful,' I stammered. 'But I can't see what Susan has to do with all this.'

'*You* can go off to rabbinical school – but your mother and I *live* in Denver. I don't appreciate hearing you being criticized by our friends.'

'What do you mean?'

'How do you think we know about this? It's going around that you have a non-Jewish girlfriend who is a ski-bum. This just won't do. I won't tolerate it. If you want to live at home, you've got to stop this.'

My eczema began to itch. I went to my room. This was intolerable. My parents viewed themselves as liberals; they were both members of the Democratic Party. They belonged to a Progressive Temple. Nevertheless, they were as prejudiced as the Orthodox. We didn't live in a ghetto. They had sent me to non-Jewish schools and then to Tewksbury. What did they expect?

I heard my mother call me. 'Can I come in?' she asked. Hesitantly, she entered. 'I know what Dad said. He's right. We're both proud of you. We want what's best for you. If you're going to be a successful rabbi, you've got to have a Jewish wife. It won't do you any good going out with all these Gentiles. Why don't you find a nice Jewish girl?'

'Look, Mom,' I said, 'I don't have any plans to get married. And you haven't met Susan. You'd like her.'

'I'm sure she's a pleasant person. But she's not the right type for you.'

Despite my parents' opposition, I continued to see Susan, but at the end of the summer we said goodbye. We promised we'd write to one another, but we both knew that our relationship had come to an end. My parents were right. After all, I was going to be a rabbi.

Chapter 2

Becoming a Rabbi: The Dilemmas of Rabbinical School

In September I filled my car with books, clothes and suitcases and set off for St Louis. En route, I stayed at motels in Kansas and Missouri. Every night I phoned my parents to tell them the progress of my journey. Eventually I arrived at the Progressive Rabbinical Seminary. Located near Washington University, the college consisted of a group of red-brick buildings on a small campus. I parked my car in the parking lot, unpacked and moved into a small room located on the fourth floor in the student dormitory.

That evening I assembled with my classmates for an introductory session. The director of the introductory term explained that we would be working very hard. In the past rabbinic students were locked in the building, he explained. Only on the weekends were they released. We were fortunate, he continued, because the regime had become more liberal. We were now free to go outside! None the less, we would be required to study Hebrew all day and night. Every week we would take exams. It was crucial that we perform well if we were to pass the first year.

Such a nightmarish account caused considerable alarm. None of us had expected to work that hard. I certainly had not. After all, I had just graduated from college – this was no time to become a grind. After the director had spoken, the President of the Seminary welcomed us. I knew what he looked like since I had seen his picture on the cover of *Time* magazine. He stood before us and took out a handkerchief. With tears in his eyes he emphasized the importance of the rabbinate.

'Boys', he said. 'I don't have to tell you that being a rabbi is a wonderful vocation. You will become leaders of our people.' He then recounted his adventures in the Negev, where he had worked as an archaeologist. Throughout he wept. It was certainly moving. Later I discovered that the President always cried whenever he spoke and it always had a powerful effect on his hearers – rich women, in particular, were so overwhelmed at fundraising gatherings that they unhesitatingly wrote large cheques for the seminary. After the session I met my future classmates. Most were from the Midwest, but a few others came from the East Coast. It was a mixed group. Very few had attended prestigious colleges – the majority had been to their local universities. They were utterly different from the preppies of Tewksbury. I was profoundly relieved. I would not have to endure wild, drunken, debauched parties here.

The next day we began class. Our teachers were third-year students at the seminary, and they were determined to make us sweat. I was put into an intermediate group because I had some knowledge of the language. Those in the bottom group couldn't even read the alphabet, whereas most of those in the top group had studied Hebrew in college. The pace was staggering. I spent four hours doing homework the first night. At midnight I had completed the assignment. I put on my pyjamas and went to the communal bathroom, where I encountered Morris Goldberg, a tall, bespectacled student from Australia. 'How ya doin'?' he said.

'I'm exhausted. What do you think?'

'It's not too difficult,' he said. 'I did two years of biblical Hebrew at university. If you think you've got problems, you should see what the guys in the lower class are like. The person next door to me looks like a perpetually frightened rabbit.'

The next three months were torture. Every week we suffered the ordeals of a Hebrew test. In bed I frequently fell asleep subconsciously conjugating verbs. But at last the initiation programme ended and our normal classes began. The pace was slower; I began to relax. My Hebrew improved, and I had time to do other things. Every day in the late afternoon I set out on a three-mile jogging course – I crossed the nearby park and then went around Washington University campus. En route I appraised the female undergraduates. What a welcome sight after years of seclusion in the mountains of Vermont!

The classes in my first year were utterly different from those at Tewksbury. Instead of discussing assigned readings, we were forced to translate texts. The Bible was reduced to syntax. Jewish liturgy and rabbinic sources were studied for their grammatical structure rather than religious content. In my midrash class our teacher – a refugee from Europe – tormented my classmates if they dared come unprepared for class. 'So,' he would say to an unsuspecting student, 'I see you have not worked hard enough on this text! Open the book. Now read – and let us savour your mistakes.'

The philosophy teacher was a notorious religious sceptic and a persecutor of anyone with Orthodox leanings. In our first session, one of the more pious students wore a yamulkah.

'What is that?' Dr Roth asked, pointing to his skullcap.

'It's my yamulkah,' Joe Greenblat replied.

'And just what are you doing, wearing it to class? This is not a yeshivah, you know.'

'I know. But I always wear one.'

'Have you all heard that?' Dr Roth exclaimed. 'Gentlemen, you have among your number an authentic yeshivah bocher. A frummer . . . and I do not tolerate frummers in my class. Off with your kipah.'

Joe Greenblat turned white.

'You will not remove the offending object, then. So be it. But I shall assume, Mr Greenblat, that you do not exist. You are a non-student, a non-frummer. In essence a non-entity.'

The class remained silent. None of us dared to object to this treatment. Greenblat sat smouldering, doing nothing as Dr Roth continued his lecture.

At the end of the year we all took what was called the 'Readiness Exam'. For three days we sat a battery of tests which determined whether we would be permitted to continue. Feverishly we struggled with tortuous translations. Exhausted, I collapsed in the dormitory when it was over. Fortunately I was familiar with a number of the passages from biblical and rabbinic literature which we were required to decipher. I thought I had passed, but I wasn't certain about the rabbinical commentary we had to translate on the second day. If I had failed that, would I be allowed to continue?

Although I did pass the Readiness Exam, this was not the final ordeal of the first year. At the end of the semester, in true Jewish-American style, each of us was required to have an interview with a local psychiatrist. Previously, we had all completed an enormous multiple-choice questionnaire. It was not clear, however, what the psychiatrist was looking for. It was like running an obstacle race in the dark.

I drove my car to his office, which was located in the Jewish suburbs. Lavishly decorated with deep carpets, modern furniture and abstract paintings, it exuded affluence and culture. In the waiting room I glanced through several magazines. Presently, a receptionist announced: 'Dr Levinson is ready to see you now.' I followed her into the doctor's office. 'Where's Dr Levinson?' I asked. 'He'll be here soon,' she said, smiling, and shut the door. I sat in an overstuffed armchair and waited. On the walls were diplomas from various institutions. In the corner was a skeleton.

When the psychiatrist arrived I stood up and shook hands. Small in stature, Dr Levinson suffered from a slight nervous twitch. 'Do sit down,' he gestured. Arranging himself across from me, he lit a pipe. The process of stuffing it full of tobacco, striking a match and getting it to smoke took several minutes. At last he looked up. 'So,' he said. 'You want to be a rabbi?'

'Yes . . . I do.'

He puffed on his pipe. 'How long have you wanted to do this?' he asked.

'Ever since my bar mitzvah. I never really wanted to do anything else. My father's a doctor, but I didn't want to follow in his footsteps.'

Dr Levinson looked at me quizzically. 'You don't like your father?'

'That's not what I meant,' I back-pedalled. 'I just don't want to be a doctor.'

'And why not?'

'Because I'm not interested. I don't think I'd be very good at it. I fainted when I saw my first operation.'

'And you like your father?' Dr Levinson persisted.

'Well, yes, I suppose so. He's pretty tough, and very busy. We don't see much of each other. I haven't really thought about it very much.'

'And your father, he's happy you're going to be a rabbi?'

'Well, not exactly. As a matter of fact, he's not pleased at all. But my parents want me to do what I want to do.'

Dr Levinson was engulfed in smoke. I could no longer see his tic. I coughed. Continuing his exploration of my family relationships, he asked me about my mother.

'You're fond of her, then?'

'Of course. She is my mother.'

'Not all Jewish boys like their mothers,' he pronounced. 'Tell me about her.'

I explained that my mother was a housewife, a local painter, and that I was her only child.

'You're close to her?' Dr Levinson asked.

'I guess so. Actually, I am very close.'

'And your father, he approves of this?'

'Yeah. I guess he does. I've never given it much thought.'

'It's time you did. Do you ever dream about your mother?'

I couldn't see where this conversation was going, but I suspected the worst. What did my mother have to do with my being a rabbi? What was the interview all about? Did this man really think my relationship with my parents had influenced my decision to become a rabbi?

'Dr Levinson,' I said, 'I thought we were going to talk about my suitability for the rabbinate.'

'But we are.' He smiled coyly. 'We are.'

I was baffled. And then astonished by his next question. 'You've had sex?'

'I beg your pardon?' I said.

'Sex . . . in college, you've had sex?'

'Dr Levinson, this is a bit personal.'

'Personal! Of course it's personal. That's just the point. We are talking about the personal.'

'But I'd rather not discuss this.' I was outraged.

'*You* may not . . . but *I* do. And *we* must. So tell me a bit about your sexual experience.' I fiddled with my tie. I didn't know where to look. What was I to say? First my father, then my mother, now sex. But there was no choice. If this was an exam, I had to pass it. But what were the right answers?

Reluctantly, I described various sexual encounters. Dr Levinson watched carefully as I stumbled over these exploits. When I stopped, he asked: 'Is that all?'

'More or less,' I said.

Leaning forward, he eyed me suspiciously. 'When you were a little boy, did you play with other boys?'

'Play? Well yes, I played lots of different games. I played football, if that's what you mean.'

'No . . . that's not what I meant. What I have in mind is something more sexual.'

Peering into his waste basket, Dr Levinson began banging his pipe on the edge. After he emptied it, he reached into his pocket, took out a leather pouch, stuffed more tobacco in his pipe, and then began again the process of lighting it. This gave me some time to think. It was now clear what Dr Levinson was looking for: homosexuals. The Progressive Rabbinical Seminary was taking no chances: they were being rooted out before they advanced far in their studies.

After a lengthy pause, I continued, 'No, Dr Levinson, only girls. I've only played with girls.'

'You sound a little defensive about this.'

'Nope. No boys. I've never touched them.'

This seemed to satisfy him. He changed subjects. 'And visions? have you ever had visions? Or maybe heard voices?'

'No visions, no voices,' I insisted.

'You don't have conversations with God? You don't hear him telling you to do this or that, or to behave in some sort of way?'

'Well, if you are referring to my conscience, I do feel bad or good about some things.'

Dr Levinson's pipe had gone out. His twitch seemed worse. I felt my interview was ending. He picked up a pen and wrote something in a notebook. Then he stood up. 'Well, that's it. Thank you for coming. It's been a pleasure to meet you. Best of luck in your studies.' He opened the door, shook hands and grimaced. The door slammed shut. The receptionist showed me the way out. Dazed, I drove back to the seminary.

When I arrived there, I looked in on Morris. 'Did you go to see the psychiatrist?' I asked.

'This morning,' he said.

'How did it go?'

'I think I passed. What about you?'

'Me too. But I wonder how many of us will get through.'

'I hear George had rather a rough time,' he said.

'Really?'

'Yeah, it's a shame.'

'What did he say wrong?'

'I'm afraid he told the truth,' Morris said gloomily.

Over the years, I have often reflected on my encounter with Dr Levinson. All of us had been sent to a psychiatrist to test our sexual proclivities. Given that we were to become congregational rabbis, such a precaution was understandable. After all, we would become role models for our congregants. Temple boards would want us to be married with children. They would be horrified if we set up house with someone of the same gender – even in the 1960s, such a situation was unthinkable. Yet as time passed some of my classmates did do just that. One of the most pious students later divorced his wife; he now serves as a rabbi to a homosexual congregation in California, has an extraordinarily handsome boyfriend, and is a fervent advocate of gay rights. Despite Dr Levinson's inquisition, some clearly slipped through the net.

The seminary was also clearly determined that religious fanatics would be eliminated. Having mystical visions was almost as bad as having a moustachioed lover. What was wanted were all-American, assimilated rabbinic students who would fit in with congregational life. How different this was from ancient times! Moses, Isaiah, Ezekiel and the other prophets of the biblical period would never have survived an interview with Dr Levinson.

During the summer, I recuperated in Denver from my first year of rabbinical seminary. Sitting outside in my parents' garden, I reviewed Hebrew verb tables and read novels. I phoned up some of my old girlfriends, but discovered to my dismay that they were either engaged or had moved away. None the less, I dated an attractive niece of one of my mother's mutual friends who was visiting for the summer. I picked her up in my Austin Healey, and we went to movies, concerts and the theatre. We both liked each other, but little more. In stark contrast with the relationship with Susan, it was a summer romance with no future.

On my return to the seminary, I was plunged deeper into traditional religious sources. Having mastered the elements of Hebrew, we were expected to read a variety of rabbinic texts (including the Mishnah, midrash, rabbinic commentaries on scripture, and the Talmud) in the original. In addition, my class was subjected to the horrors of Talmudic Aramaic. This language is akin to Hebrew, but has its own peculiar grammar and syntax. Like Hebrew, it is written without vowels. But as distinct from Hebrew texts of the Bible, which are printed with vowels for students, the Aramaic of the Talmud contains only consonants. Although I could translate the text into English, I had no idea how to pronounce it!

During my second year, all students in my class were required to register with the military chaplaincy. This was in preparation for graduation, when those of us who had not married would be required to enter one of the branches of the armed services. The Vietnam War was in progress and there was thus a constant need for chaplains. Those who had families were exempt (this was a major inducement to find a wife). I refused to go along with this scheme: I had no intention of serving in the army, and I also had deep reservations about the efficacy of armed conflict. I wanted no part of it. To the astonishment of the seminary authorities, I declared that I wished to be registered as a conscientious objector.

In the history of the seminary, no one had made such a protest. I was summoned to see the Dean. When I entered his office, I discovered that he had assembled there an array of professors from the seminary as well as rabbis affiliated with the military. This panel was seated in comfortable armchairs in a semi-circle. I was told to sit on a stiff chair in front of them.

'We've had your request,' the Dean began. 'And quite frankly, we are puzzled. You say that you wish to have conscientious objector status. And you state that you want to have nothing to do with the armed services.'

'Yes,' I said meekly.

'We are interested in your reasons.'

I swallowed. The patch of eczema on my leg began to itch.

This, I perceived, was not going to be a pleasant interview. My interrogators stared at me. 'You see . . .' I stammered, 'I am against war.'

'So are we,' the Dean sneered.

'Yes, but Judaism says that peace is all-important. That's what all the prophets declared. The Bible prophesies peace for all nations. You know, "the lion will lie down with the lamb", and all that.'

'I don't think you need to fill us in on the Bible,' Dr Smirnoff said. He was my Bible teacher. 'Dare I say all of us know the Bible a bit better than you. What we are curious to learn is why you, as a rabbinic student, think you can stand out against everyone else.'

'I'm a pacifist!' I blurted out.

'Ah, a pacifist,' Dr Roth announced. 'I am pleased to make the acquaintance of a real-life pacifist. It isn't often that we have one of these exotic creatures here in the college. So, permit me to ask you: just why are you a pacifist?'

'Because I don't think war ever solves any problems.'

'You think it just makes things worse?' he asked.

'Yeah, I do.'

'Force is always wrong, then? Never right.'

'Well, yes, I suppose so. Certainly military force is.'

'Let's take a little example, then.' Stroking his moustache, he grinned. 'Let's imagine that you were at home with your mother. And you heard a terrible noise. And there was the sound of breaking glass. There in front of you stood a known murderer, holding a large axe. He then grabbed your mother and threatened to rape her. Would you stand by and let him get on with it?'

'I can't imagine there would be much else I could do,' I said.

'But let's say you had a little revolver in your pocket. Would you use it?' he persisted.

'I'd try and reason with him.'

'Good. Good. Reason with a mad, axe-wielding rapist! What if he refused to listen?'

'I'd reason more loudly,' I conjectured.

I shifted uneasily. Things were not going well. My eczema itched intolerably. I wondered if I might be thrown out of the seminary. It was clear I needed to change course. 'I see what you're driving at,' I said. 'But what you're describing isn't the same as the armed forces. I don't approve of the military. Wars don't bring peace, they just make matters worse.'

The Talmud professor – a survivor from the concentration camps – looked distressed. Gesticulating at the others, he related his experiences at Treblinka. He had been taken there as a child and separated from his parents. At the end of the war, he was rescued by the Allies, and eventually made his way to the United States. 'You tell us that armies make no difference,' he concluded. 'If it hadn't been for England and America, I wouldn't be here today. And neither would you!'

What answer could I give? The interview ended, and I was told that the seminary would let me know the result. I was certain that no exemption would be allowed. If the war in Vietnam continued, I would be required to serve as a chaplain. Who knew where I would be stationed? Even though chaplins are not required to carry guns or engage in combat, they could be shot at. I was depressed.

When I got back to the dorm, I told Morris what had happened.

'You didn't handle it the right way', he insisted.

'No? What should I have done?'

'You'd never be able to convince those guys,' he explained. 'They're committed to the chaplaincy. I think Roth even got to be a Major when was in the army. Anyway, Judaism isn't a pacifist religion. Think of Joshua – he certainly wasn't opposed to war. The Jews took the land away from the Canaanites by force.' Shaking his head, he continued. 'Our professors won't listen to you or anybody else, especially while there is a war going on.'

'So what am I supposed to do?'

'Why don't you join the Jewish Peace Fellowship,' he suggested.

'What's that?'

'I read about it in *Commentary*. It's an organization for Jewish pacifists.'

'But you said Judaism isn't a pacifist religion.'

'It isn't. But the organization exists anyway. Lots of important people belong. Including Progressive rabbis.'

Following Morris's suggestion, I joined, and received a batch of leaflets. Several weeks later I was summoned again to see the Dean. This time he was on his own. 'I'm afraid we won't be able to help you,' he said.

'But look here,' I gestured, holding up a Jewish Peace Fellowship brochure, 'I've joined this Jewish pacifist organization. Quite a few rabbis belong. If they are pacifists, why can't I get a deferment?'

The Dean took the brochure, read it and dismissed me. I stood outside his door and shamelessly eavesdropped as he made a telephone call. 'Jack,' he said, 'it's Melvin. You remember that student who didn't want to join the chaplaincy? Well, I think we've got a problem.'

Eventually, I received a brief note. The decision, he wrote, had been postponed, and that was the last I heard of it. Among the students, I had set a precedent. Hearing about my victory, others joined the Jewish Peace Fellowship. None of us wanted to serve in the Vietnam War, and the college was quickly populated by conscientious objectors. Overnight it became a haven for draft dodgers.

During my second year, I was employed as a Sunday-school teacher in the local Temple. This was my first teaching job and I regarded it as a foretaste of the rabbinate. On the first day twenty-five teenagers arrived for the first lesson. They did not look friendly.

'Well, kids,' I announced, 'I'm your new teacher. My name is Dan Cohn-Sherbok.' I wrote my name on the board. Turning around, I was horrified to see that one of the boys had jumped out of the ground-floor window. 'Who's was that? I shouted, pointing at the empty seat. The girls giggled. 'It's just Mickey,' one volunteered. 'He always runs away.'

I shot out of the room to find the principal of the school. I explained what had happened. 'What should I do now?' I asked. She told me to return to my classroom as quickly as possible.

I ran down the hall. 'What's this?' I said as I rushed into the room. Some of the chairs were overturned, and two boys were fighting. 'Come on, Alan,' some of the girls screamed. 'Punch him in the face.' Blood was dripping from the smaller of the two. As I tried to separate them, he lunged at me and I caught his arm. 'Get back to your seat. All of you. This is a religion school, not a gym.' Eventually, order was re-established. I told the students that this was no way to behave. I wouldn't tolerate any more fighting. They were all to open their notebooks and copy down what I said. I would dictate notes.

For ten minutes there was silence. Then one of the girls announced, 'Mr Cohn-what's-it, I've got to go to the bathroom.'

'I'm sorry,' I said. 'You'll have to wait until the bell goes.'

'But I can't wait,' she replied.

'Sorry. You'll have to. You should have gone before class.'

'If I don't,' she declared, 'I'll pee all over my dress.'

'Let her go, Mr What's-it,' a freckled boy in the front said. 'Otherwise she'll make a mess.'

What could I do? I let her leave. Then a dozen others raised their hands.

'We've got to go, too,' they said.

'Sorry, nobody else goes. You'll all have to wait until the break,' I insisted.

'But we can't,' they chimed.

I was unmoved. At last the bell rang. On the way out one of the boys sitting in the back of the class stopped at my desk. 'I don't think you'll see Hannah again today,' he said. He was right.

The next Sunday was no better. I shouted at the students. It did no good. I threatened them with homework – they took no notice. I told them to shut up. They made more noise. I said I would report them to the principal: they stuck out their tongues. I said they would never learn about their heritage – they yawned. By the end of the morning I was exhausted, and defeated. My eczema was itching intolerably. What was I doing wrong?

I went to see the principal. 'Mrs Green,' I said, 'I can't control them. They're absolutely horrible. I don't like them, and I'm sure they don't like me. Is this normal?'

The principal sighed. She had run the Sunday school for over a decade, and was used to rabbinical students. 'I'm afraid they're always like that,' she explained. 'They have to come here. Their parents make them, and they'd rather be at home watching television or playing outside. It doesn't matter if they do well in religion school. What counts is ordinary school.'

'But we give grades. And there's a report card,' I countered.

'I know. But half of them never take it home.'

'But *I* wasn't like that in *my* religion school.'

'I'm sure you weren't, but then you decided to become a rabbi!'

She was right. Looking back, I remembered that some of my friends had behaved the same way. They deliberately aggravated the rabbi to see if he would lose his temper. They told jokes in class. They were not enthusiastic about their homework. During my Confirmation, one of the clowns in the class told jokes rather than recite his part of the service. It was naïve of me to expect something different. Although it was reassuring to realize that the chaos in my class was not unusual, what was the point of subjecting myself to such torture?

This exposure to congregational life was supplemented in my second year by a course on Temple administration. In one session, the most prominent rabbi in the city came to speak to us. He discussed Temple finance, curriculum planning and general management skills. In addition, he gave us an account of the role of the rabbi. The congregational rabbi, he explained, performs the same functions as a Christian minister: it is his responsibility to preach, perform marriages and funerals and other life-cycle events, and serve as a pastoral counsellor. No longer is the rabbi the most important person in the Jewish community – rather he is a paid employee of the Temple board.

After his discourse, a number of us asked questions. After a series of queries about the practical details of rabbinical life, Rabbi Greenbaum was asked about his own personal religious beliefs. One of the more direct members of the class asked if he told congregants about what he believed himself.

'Oh no,' he said, 'I wouldn't do that.'

'But why not?' Harold Goldstein asked.

'Well . . . because they wouldn't like to know.'

Goldstein looked troubled. 'What do you mean, Rabbi?' he continued.

'Look, I don't normally discuss my own convictions. But I'll tell you – in confidence.'

There was a long silence. 'You see,' the rabbi continued, 'I don't really believe in God.'

Goldstein gasped. My classmates looked at one another. There was another pause.

'Perhaps you find that shocking. But to be honest, I've never been able to. But I always wanted to be a rabbi. Just like all of you. When I was your age I decided that being a rabbi was the best way to serve our community. And so I came to the seminary.'

'But . . .' Goldstein stammered, '. . . if you don't believe in

God, why become a rabbi? I mean, you have to say prayers, and tell your congregation about God. How can you do this if you don't believe in him?'

'I can see why you're perplexed. But the answer is simple: a rabbi is basically an actor.'

'An actor?' Goldstein echoed.

'Yes. That's the essence of the job. He plays a part in the Jewish drama of ritual observance. When you take a funeral you're there to comfort the mourners. At a wedding your job is to make people happy. At a bar mitzvah your responsibility is to make sure that the spotty adolescent gets through the service. When confronted with a Jewish boy and a Gentile girl, you've got to look disapproving. In all this you've got to play the role.'

'But if you don't believe in the Jewish religion . . .'

'I do, I do.' Rabbi Greenbaum protested. 'I believe in the Jewish heritage. I want to make sure it continues. I want Jewish boys and girls to grow up being proud to be Jewish.'

This was not what any of us expected to hear. But the professor of practical rabbinics was less disturbed by this account than we were. 'Look, boys,' he intervened, 'Rabbi Greenbaum is right. As a rabbi you've got to live up to the part. It's like being in a play. What you believe yourself doesn't matter. The script is written. What is left up to you is to play the part well. If you do, you'll be a success.'

At lunch I sat next to Morris. 'That was amazing,' I said. 'That guy doesn't believe in God, and he fools his congregation so that they become good Jews.' Morris smiled as I castigated Rabbi Greenbaum for his hypocrisy. 'That's a bit uncharitable,' he said. 'How many guys here really believe in God?'

'I don't know. I've never heard anybody talk about it,' I said.

'That's just the point. Probably they aren't too sure what they believe. Or maybe they don't want to think about it. They're not so different from Greenbaum. If anything, he's more honest. I mean, let's get down to it. How's your prayer life going these days?' This was not a question I wanted to answer. I turned the conversation to what was on at the movies that week.

After much brain-bashing revision, at the end of the second year my classmates and I took the exam for the Bachelor of Hebrew Letters. For three days we translated apparently impossible texts from biblical, liturgical and rabbinic sources. This terrifying hurdle was of crucial importance: it was impossible to proceed in the college without passing it. After it was over, most of my class departed for Israel. We were not to learn the results until August.

I took a plane to Rome, stayed overnight at a small hotel near the Vatican, and the next day arrived at Lod Airport. Over the years, I had written to Miriam, the girl I had met years ago whose family lived in Jerusalem. They now had a flat at Tel Hashomer hospital near Tel Aviv. Miriam and her father were waiting for me, and to my astonishment, Miriam had grown about a foot since I had last seen her. She was now taller than me. This was an unnerving beginning to my sojourn in the Holy Land.

Miriam's family was extremely hospitable: they gave me a bedroom of my own and a key to their flat. On the basis of my correspondence with their daughter, they expected I might become their son-in-law. But it didn't take long for Miriam and me to see this was impossible. Miriam was devoted to Israel; I was determined to enjoy America. We had nothing in common.

She was bewildered as to why I wanted to be a congregational rabbi. 'I don't understand,' she said the first night. 'You don't keep kosher; you don't wear a kipah; you don't go to synagogue to pray. How can you become a rabbi if you're not an observant Jew?'

'But I am,' I protested. 'I mean, I'm not Orthodox; but I think the Jewish tradition is important. I'm religious in my own way.'

'If you are, I don't see it,' she countered.

'That's because you don't know anything about Progressive Judaism,' I replied.

'Well, if you're an example of what it is, I'm not interested in finding out.'

I was angry. I had not come to Israel to be insulted. I sulked, just as I had done, as a boy, with my father. It was clear that there was little point in my being a guest with her family for long. The next morning I announced that I thought it would be best if I moved out. Miriam's father looked relieved. The family took me to Tel Aviv to the bus station. I shook hands with them all and boarded the bus.

After a journey of several hours, I arrived in Jerusalem. The sun was shining, and the city glimmered. I checked in to a simple hotel in the centre of the city, across the street from a cinema, and explored. In the years that had elapsed since my previous visit, a great deal of building had taken place; there were new hotels and apartment blocks dotted around the city. Later in the day I phoned a friend from Denver who was staying in Jerusalem for the summer. Although we were from similar backgrounds, he had decided to become an Orthodox rabbi and was studying at Yeshiva University. We arranged to meet at the YMCA.

When I arrived at the arranged time, I spotted him reading a Hebrew newspaper. He had grown a long beard and was wearing a yamulkah. 'Hi, Harold,' I said. Looking up, he smiled. 'It's a long way from Denver isn't it?' he replied. We shook hands. 'Yeah, it's different. But I haven't seen much yet. I just arrived yesterday. How long have you been here?'

'Six months,' he answered. 'I was allowed to spend the second semester studying at a yeshivah in West Jerusalem. So I know the city pretty well by now.'

Walking through the streets we discussed our future plans. 'Do you intend to make aliyah?' I asked.

'I don't think my parents would be very keen if I did,' he said. 'But this is the only place to live. What about you?'

'Well, it's not exactly for me. You must think I'm a heretic, going to the Progressive Rabbinical Seminary.'

Harold chuckled. 'Well now that you mention it . . .'

'Look, Harold,' I went on, 'it's all very exciting. But I can't imagine moving here. I think I'm destined to be a rabbi in a big Midwestern city. What would I do in Israel?'

'You could pick oranges,' he said.

'But surely you're not planning to do that?'

'No, but I'm Orthodox. I'll get a job. The Progressive movement hardly exists here, thank God.'

For the next two months I travelled around the country. This was likely to be the longest period I would spend in the Holy Land, so I was determined to make good use of my stay. I booked tours to the Galilee and the Negev. Together with a group of Christian tourists, I visited the sacred sites of Jesus's ministry. Looking at the Sea of Galilee, I tried to imagine Jesus walking on water. Impossible! On another tour I investigated the trading town of Beersheba, and subsequently descended to the Dead Sea. I climbed up Masada with other perspiring tourists. On all these excursions I took photographs. I wanted to return home amply supplied with lecture material for congregations. I imagined myself standing in front of a screen pointing out the sites of ancient and modern Israel to a rapt audience.

In the middle of the summer, I received a letter from the seminary informing me that I had passed the Bachelor of Hebrew Letters exam. This was a cause for rejoicing. Some had failed, including my friend Morris. He too had come to Israel, but had toured through Europe first with his girlfriend, Sheila. By the time he arrived in Jerusalem, they were not on speaking terms. I met him at the airport and he recounted his troubles. 'She's a bitch!' he exclaimed. I helped Morris with his suitcases as he complained. 'She's completely irresponsible. Damn it – she used up all my money. Most days we didn't speak. But,' he admitted shyly, 'she is good in bed.'

'You mean you made love, even though you don't like her?'

'It's the only thing she can do right.'

'But . . . I don't understand. Why? . . . I mean, if you didn't get along?'

'How else could I have endured the trip?' he asked.

Morris was shocked when his letter from the seminary arrived. 'That's it. I've got to stay in Israel. Maybe I can get the Temple Sisterhood to pay for it.'

'What about the seminary? Will they let you remain here?'

'They'll probably insist,' he moaned. 'I've got to get my Hebrew up to scratch.'

'The student dorm won't be the same without you,' I said, trying to cheer him up.

'Well,' he said, 'it could be a lot worse. A year in Israel will be fun. Perhaps I'll be able to find someone to take Sheila's place.'

At the end of the summer Morris went with me to the airport. I was loaded down with my suitcase, plus boxes of slides. After a long flight I arrived in Denver. My parents met me at the airport and we drove home. My father wasn't particularly interested in hearing my account of Israel, but my mother was more tolerant. She even suggested that I give a talk to her study group – the grandiose name for her set of Jewish female friends who met together every month in each other's houses. For twenty years my mother and nine other women had gathered for what had become a cherished event. No man was ever allowed (except as a guest speaker). I was flattered, and set about organizing my slides and preparing the talk. Eventually I filled two trays with slides and wrote copious notes. Just before I was to return to rabbinical school, the group gathered at our house and after lunch I gave my lecture.

Halfway through I sensed my little audience was becoming bored. One of my mother's friends was asleep, snoring gently. Others did their knitting in the dark. Undaunted, I persisted. 'This shot,' I explained, 'was taken in Safed. In the sixteenth century it was the centre of mystical activity. The great kabbalist Isaac Luria discoursed there on the doctrine of God's nature and activity in the world. And the great halakist Joseph Caro composed his compendium of Jewish law, the Shulchan Arukh . . .'

My mother shifted uncomfortably. This was a bit too serious for her friends. I was not as compelling a lecturer as she had imagined. My presentation was dull and the study group was restless. After nearly an hour she interrupted. 'Dan, I think we ought to break now for coffee and cake.'

I turned off the slide projector. My mother switched on the lights. The study group revived. There were fulsome compliments. But I knew it had been a disappointment. The Jewish ladies of Denver were not particularly interested in the history of Israel. If my mother's loyal friends were bored by my talk, how, I wondered, would future congregations react?

At the beginning of my third year in the seminary the numbers were depleted. About a fifth of the class had stayed in Israel: some were revising their Hebrew; others decided to extend their course of studies for an extra year. After two gruelling years of intense work, we were allowed to select a variety of courses in addition to the required subjects. I had no desire to learn any other Semitic languages, and so I chose classes dealing with modern Jewish fiction.

One afternoon after I had gone jogging, I encountered a classmate in the dormitory with a girl he had brought over for a drink. She was blonde and curvaceous with sparkling blue eyes. I was enchanted. But it was obvious she wasn't Jewish. When I saw him later that evening, I asked him about her – who was she? Was he serious about her? Would he mind if I phoned her? Fortunately he had other interests. He had a girlfriend at home and thus no serious intentions. The next day I phoned. 'Oh, you're the jogger,' she giggled. 'I've never seen a running rabbi. Yes, I'd like to go out for dinner.'

That weekend I picked her up in my Austin Healey. After half an hour I knew I was in trouble. We both knew this was going to be serious. She was studying to be a psychiatric social worker and was a Catholic, the youngest of six children. I was training to be a rabbi. What was I to do? Morris was in Israel, so I didn't have anybody I could talk to. We arranged to meet the next evening. All day I was both elated and miserable. I was determined to end this relationship before it began. I arrived at Jan's tiny apartment in a shabby quarter of St Louis carrying a bunch of red roses. As I entered, I explained why this had to be our last time together.

'It won't work,' I insisted. 'I'm Jewish. I'm planning to be a rabbi. You're not Jewish. You don't look Jewish. My parents would kill me. A congregation wouldn't tolerate it. It's finished.'

She took the roses, put them in a vase, and then sat down next to me on the sofa. 'Honestly,' I insisted, 'this can't continue.'

'Then why did you come?' she asked. 'And why did you bring me roses?'

There was no answer. But I stammered on: 'Look, this is a mess . . . you can see it's hopeless . . .'

'Why don't you calm down?' she said. 'All we've arranged to do is to go out to a meal. Let's do that and forget about the future.'

During the next few months I saw Jan every day. We went out for meals, to concerts, to films, and even to Temple services. We had great fun – but how would it end? As I became more involved, I grew more perplexed. One evening the matron of the dormitory called me into her study. She asked if I wanted a cup of coffee. I could see that advice was forthcoming. 'Dan,' she cautioned, 'I don't want to interfere, but I have heard things.'

Sensing that this conversation concerned Jan, I felt uncomfortable. How could I explain our affair? 'What things?' I inquired.

'People are talking about that girl you're dating.'

'Are they?'

'You haven't made any attempt to hide her – so you've got to expect people to talk.'

'And just what are they saying?'

'You can't go out with a shiksa here, Dan.'

I bridled. Shiksa! What an insult! It's true that Jan wasn't Jewish, but she deserved more than this pejorative description.

'You're studying to be a rabbi,' Mrs Blumgarten continued. 'You have lots of talents. I'm sure you'll be a wonderful rabbi. But no congregation will employ a rabbi with a blonde, non-Jewish wife.'

I could endure no more. Putting my coffee cup down, I walked out. I knew Mrs Blumgarten was doing her duty. She was in charge of those who lived in the dormitory: we were her boys, and she didn't want any of us to go off the rails. Yet I was furious that my relationship with Jan had become the focus of attention. Just who were the people Mrs Blumgarten was referring to?

What was I to do? My parents would not understand. I felt desolate and confused. Surprisingly, however, counsel came from a most unexpected source. One of my teachers was a visiting professor from Israel – Dr Woolf was an international expert on

Hebrew literature, and the seminary was privileged to have him for the year. Although my command of modern Hebrew was limited, he regarded me as one of his best students. Confidentially, he had tried to dissuade me from becoming a congregational rabbi. With a rasping Israeli accent, he teased me about the folly of trying to be a spiritual leader in what he considered the flesh-pots of American suburban life. 'You should become a professor,' he warned. 'So you really want to be the slave of fat, cigar-smoking, plutocratic businessmen and their wives?'

What could I say in response? I had always wanted to be a rabbi. I refused to listen.

One Saturday evening, Dr Woolf entertained my class. My classmates who were married brought their wives; I took Jan. The next week he took me aside.

'Dan,' he said, 'that's a great girl. Convert her and marry her.'

I didn't know what to say. 'But . . .' I hesitated, 'I . . . I don't know. I mean, I'm going to be a rabbi. It would be a problem . . .'

'I don't understand you Americans,' he replied. 'Everything becomes a problem. What's the problem? She'll be a good Jewish wife, and you'll be happy.'

'My parents would never forgive me.'

'Is your own happiness less important than what your father and mother think?'

'But what about my congregation . . . they'd never accept a convert.'

Dr Woolf shook his head. 'It's a pity. You can't see what's good for you. Forget the rabbinate! Teach in a university!'

Dr Woolf was a world-famous expert on contemporary Israeli literature, but I was convinced he knew nothing about American Jewish life. I disregarded his suggestions. How could he possibly understand about my personal happiness?

By the end of the school year Jan and I could no longer put off thinking about the future. She was studying for a Masters degree in social work, and her training was coming to an end. She had to decide where she would get a job. Would it be in St Louis, or elsewhere? On a beautiful spring evening I arrived at her apartment to find her engrossed in a book about Jewish history. I looked suspicious. 'Why are you reading this?' I asked. Jan confessed that she had that week been to see a rabbi about converting to Judaism. I felt terrible. Whatever the official party line, conversion wasn't good enough. Successful rabbis had born-Jewish wives. If I married Jan, I would never get a good congregation. Jan saw my expression. 'I thought you'd be pleased.'

I looked out of the window. 'Look,' I said, 'I'm not really ready to make a commitment.'

Jan was furious. 'I don't think any commitment is required from you – I'm the one who's supposed to make a commitment.'

'I don't mean to Judaism.' I couldn't explain the real problem and took the easy way out. 'I'm just not ready to get married.'

Trembling with rage, Jan stormed out of the room and slammed the door to her bedroom. I heard her crying. I felt miserable. My eczema itched. Yet what was I to do? My career was at stake. I felt pressure from all sides. This was too confusing. The best thing, I thought, would be to go away. But where could I go to escape this dilemma? I still had two more years of seminary to endure.

When the first semester of my fourth year began, Jan had gone off to Boston, where she had a job as a family therapist. I was miserable. Morris assured me I had made the right decision, but I had doubts. What was the point of being a famous rabbi if I felt so empty? 'You'll find someone else,' he assured me. He was now engaged to Devora, a sabra he had met in Jerusalem.

During the second semester I had to choose a thesis topic. Most of my classmates settled for conventional subjects, but I was determined to do something creative: I wanted to write a historical novel about Solomon Maimon, an eighteenth-century Jewish philosopher. I had read his autobiography and was enthralled. I made an appointment to see the Professor of Modern Jewish History and explained what I wanted to do. As I described the project, he leaned back in his chair. 'It's not very scholarly,' he announced.

'Maybe not,' I replied. 'But it would be a real challenge. And I would base the entire thing on Maimon's writings, and secondary sources. I wouldn't just make it up.'

'But you would make some of it up, wouldn't you?'

'Yeah, I would. I mean, it's going to be a novel.'

'Look, Dan,' he declared, 'this isn't a college of creative writing. It's a rabbinical seminary. Our aim is to train rabbis, not novelists. Why don't you write an ordinary thesis like everyone else? Perhaps you could edit one of Maimon's writings, if nobody's done that before.'

That wasn't what I had in mind. I approached several other teachers. No one expressed enthusiasm. At last I went to see Dr Stern, a young new member of the faculty. I explained my dilemma. 'It sounds interesting,' he said. 'I'll supervise you, if you'd like.'

'You will? Great. But why wouldn't anyone else?' I asked.

'Because,' he sneered, 'they're a bunch of stuffed shirts.'

The rest of the semester I collected material. Eventually I packed it into boxes and sent the load to Denver. In June I flew home. After spending several days with my parents, I was driven by my mother to Estes Park, a mountain resort about sixty miles from the city. My father had reserved a small cabin for me for the summer, where I was determined to complete my thesis. I kissed my mother goodbye, unpacked my bags, and put the typewriter on the table. On a wall I hung a calendar. I had sixty days to write an entire book. Looking at the blank paper, I wondered if I could do it.

Every day I got up at about eight, had breakfast, set up my typewriter outside, and began typing. On the ground were scattered all my books. After a week's work I had typed ten pages. I started with Maimon's birth and childhood, and then proceeded to his training as a rabbi. I read what I had written over and over. Was it any good? I didn't have anyone to ask. Then next week I completed approximately the same amount. Each day I noted on my calendar how much I had written. By the end of the first month, I was nearly halfway through. It looked as though I was going to finish on time. I felt I deserved a break.

That weekend, I returned home, and my mother fed me all the things I liked. I was suntanned, and I had grown a short beard. On television I watched a romantic film – and thought of Jan. My sense of contentment evaporated. The next day my mother asked me why I looked so miserable. 'Is it your work?' she asked.

I could bear it no longer. I broke down and told her all about Jan. When I finished, she said: 'We know about her.'

'You do?'

'Yes, she came to visit.'

I was stunned. 'She did?'

'In the spring. She was here at a convention in Denver.'

I couldn't believe it. I still phoned her and occasionally wrote, but she had never mentioned it. 'What happened?'

'She called and asked to come and see us. We had her for lunch. She was obviously after you, and we told her that you were going to be a rabbi and you could never marry someone who wasn't properly Jewish. Dad was pretty blunt.'

'Oh God!' I moaned.

'She's not for you, Dan,' said my mother. 'I'm sure she's a nice person, but she knows you're well off. She's one of six children, for heaven's sake. That's what she's after.'

'How can you say that?' I was furious at my mother's insinuation.

'Anyway,' continued my mother, 'she forgot to take her jacket with her. It's still in the hall.'

Guiltily, I looked in the closet. There it was – an old reefer jacket. It looked shabby beside my mother's furs. I wondered if I should send it to her.

When I returned to Estes Park, I continued to type away, and by the end of the summer I had completed the entire novel: 352 pages, far longer than I had anticipated. I repacked my books, returned home, and a few days later departed for St Louis.

When I arrived, I unpacked in the dorm and sought out Dr Stern. I knocked on his office door. 'Come in,' he said. He was sitting on the floor reading a large folio of the Talmud. He stood up and shook hands. 'Welcome back . . . did you finish the book?'

I handed over the manuscript. 'It's longer that I thought it would be,' I said.

'I can see that. Don't worry. I'll let you know what I think after I read it. But, before you go, just give me a synopsis.'

'Well,' I explained, 'basically it's a biographical novel about Solomon Maimon. He was a Polish Jewish philosopher who lived at the end of the eighteenth century. He was a child prodigy and became a rabbi when he was eleven.'

Dr Stern motioned me to sit down. He lit a cigarette and put his feet up on his desk. I continued, 'Well, he first supported his family by working as a tutor – in his spare time he studied Jewish philosophy and kabbalah. Then he went to Berlin, where he became a friend of Moses Mendelssohn. Later he lived in various cities and published studies of philosophical subjects, including Kant's thought.'

'That's it?'

'No – those are just the biographical details. Maimon is interesting because he was a heretic. He gave up Judaism in a quest for truth.'

'A rabbi and a heretic, huh?'

'Yeah.'

'You don't think you'll go the same way, do you, Dan?' Dr Stern teased.

'Me? . . . no, I mean, I'm going to be a congregational rabbi.'

Dr Stern flipped through the manuscript. 'Lots of words here,' he mumbled. 'A heretic . . . hmmm . . . well, well.' He looked up. 'I'll be in touch.'

Several weeks later I received a note from Dr Stern, accompanied by my manuscript, full of red marks. It read: 'It's not the worst novel I ever read – as a matter of fact, it's not bad. But you make Maimon sound as though he grew up in Denver in the twentieth century. Perhaps these corrections will help. Redo it, and let me have it back in about a month. H. S.'

I did not feel encouraged.

The final year at the college concluded with my ordination. My parents and grandmother came from Denver; other relatives, from Miami Beach and elsewhere, gathered for a family reunion. I booked everyone into the Sheraton Hotel in downtown St Louis. The evening before the service there was a private dinner. Among the group were a number of my teachers. Just as we were sitting down, my father's sister took me aside. 'Danny darling,' she whispered, 'I'd like to make a little speech before dinner. Is that all right?'

'That's very nice of you,' I said.

Later my father accosted me. 'Leona told me you gave her permission to say something. Well I told her no. So there's to be no speeches.'

I was puzzled. But it was my parents' party. 'Oh,' I said. 'Sorry – I didn't know you'd mind.'

'I do. And that's all I have to say.'

Despite my father's instructions, Aunt Leona stood up just before the soup was brought in and announced that she wanted to say a few words. My father glared at his sister. He mumbled something to my mother, but there was nothing he could do without causing a scene. It was Saturday night, but my aunt insisted on reciting the Friday-night blessing over the candles in the centre of the table. I wondered what the rabbis in the room would make of this. Then she embarked on a long rambling speech about how proud she was of me. She handed me my grandfather's tefillin as well as her late husband's Passover Haggadah. When she finished, in the gruffest possible tones, my father made a brief toast, and we began to eat. I glanced at my teachers. I couldn't imagine what they thought of my family.

The next day all my classmates arrived early at the large Temple in the centre of St Louis for photographs. This was to be our last meeting together. We had survived five years of rabbinical school, and would now separate. The majority had found jobs in congregations, but a few of us were embarking on further study. I myself had been accepted to do research for a PhD at Cambridge University in England. While at the seminary I had served several small congregations part-time, and I did not yet feel ready for the full-time rabbinate.

During the service my class sat together. One by one we went forward to be ordained. The President of the seminary – representing all our teachers – put his hands on my shoulders and recited the ancient formula: 'Yoreh, Yoreh, Yadin, Yadin' (Let him teach, Let him make rabbinical decisions). I wondered how I could ever fulfil the latter part of this injunction, since no one ever called upon Progressive rabbis to give legal rulings. While this ceremony was taking place, my relations were leaping up taking photographs. After all of us were ordained, the keynote address was given by a famous black civil-rights leader: he explained that it was our duty as newly-ordained rabbis to press for social reform. When he finished, my aunt (who was confined to a wheelchair) stood up and applauded. The congregation looked on in amazement.

Afterwards there was a large, formal lunch for ordinands and their parents. Various members of the faculty made speeches and the class president responded. As he spoke, my father glanced at me. I wondered if he was disappointed that this wasn't my role. As at my graduation from Tewksbury, I felt I had failed to live up to his expectations. None the less, I had survived five years of a gruelling regime. I was now a rabbi – I had reached the goal I had set for myself so many years ago.

Later in the day I went back to the seminary to pack. I took down all my books from the shelves and began to fill cardboard boxes. I stuffed all my clothes, as well as blankets, sheets and pillows, into large trunks. All of this was to be shipped to England. As I packed, I came across letters I had received at the college. There were a few from girls in Denver, masses from my parents, and several from Jan. While I reread them, Morris entered my room.

'Congratulations,' he declared. 'You beat me to it!' Because he had stayed in Israel for a year, Morris wasn't due to graduate until next June. By this time he had broken off his previous engagement, and was now due to be married to an Australian girl who was completing her studies at Washington University. She had just qualified as a lawyer. She was serious and Jewish and suitable in every way. I had mixed feelings about her and I was pretty sure she did not like me. The wedding was to take place the following day.

'It's hard to believe it's over,' I said.

'It won't be the same without you.'

'Well, you've got Judy to keep you company.'

Looking over my shoulder, he saw Jan's letters. 'You ought to throw those away.'

'Come on, Morris,' I pleaded. 'They're part of my past.'

'It's best not to dwell on it,' he continued.

'I'm not dwelling.'

'Oh yes you are,' he replied. As usual, Morris was right. I missed Jan, and now I was going to leave the country. I wondered if I would see her again. Was I right to go?

The next day I put on a rabbinical gown and, together with one of the teachers at the college, officiated at Morris and Judy's marriage, which took place in the college chapel. Because their families lived in Australia, their parents weren't able to come, but there was a small gathering from the college faculty as well as friends from St Louis. During the ceremony I recited several prayers and made a short speech. Following the service a reception took place in the seminary. I knew nearly everyone there, but standing back from the crowd was a stunning red-head I had never seen. I looked at her; she stared back. Later, she came up to me.

'I'm Victoria,' she said. 'We haven't met, but I know all about you.'

'You do?' I was puzzled.

'Morris always talks about you.'

'He does? To you? I mean, I don't understand.'

Victoria smiled sadly. 'I am, or rather was, Morris's secret girlfriend.'

I was astounded. Morris had never said a word. First he was engaged to Sheila, then to Devora and he finally married Judy. Who was Victoria?

'You see,' she continued, 'I'm not Jewish, and Morris could never marry a shiksa. I was willing to convert, but apparently that doesn't count.'

My head was spinning; Morris had discouraged me from seeing Jan. Repeatedly he had stressed that I would ruin my career. He had told me to find someone else. Yet, all the time he had been in the same predicament. I looked at Judy and then back at Victoria.

'I hope he'll be happy,' Victoria said, reading my thoughts. She stepped closer, looking extremely beautiful, and said quietly and bitterly, 'But I doubt very much if he will.'

In the evening I took a taxi to the airport. As I drove away, I looked back at the seminary. I was now a rabbi – I had achieved my ambition. I wondered what the future would hold.

Chapter 3

Being a Student Rabbi: A Taste of Congregational Life

During my years at the seminary I had served several small congregations scattered throughout the country. Once we had passed the Bachelor of Hebrew Letters exam, as part of our training my classmates and I were allowed to take Sabbath services in these small temples. To decide who would go where, a lottery was held at the beginning of every year. At the start of my third year, I drew Jonah, Alabama. I had never been to the South, so I was excited by the prospect. But where was Jonah, Alabama? In the library I looked it up in an atlas. Located near Birmingham, it had a population of about 10,000. I wondered if there was such a thing as Jewish southern hospitality.

Jan drove me to the airport on my first trip. In the car I did imitations of what I thought the congregants would like. 'Howdy, ya all,' I drawled. 'Welcome to Jonah. Would ya like some southern chicken soup?'

I flew first to Birmingham, and then caught the bus to Jonah. On board I looked around: I was the only white person. As we drove through the Alabama countryside I overheard two elderly blacks engaged in discussion. 'Youse wrong about that,' the first said. 'The good Lord always answers my prayers.'

'I just can't believe it. No suh. It just ain't that way. I pray, and pray, an nothin happens.'

'Well, youse got ta keep on praying.'

'It don't do no good. My little Lindy – she's sick, and she don't get no better nohow.'

'The Lord, he's answering dem prayers. He just ain't said yes yet.'

A theological discussion on the Greyhound bus! But these were not my congregants – I only hoped those who belonged to Temple Shalom would be equally interested in the mysteries of the Divine.

When I arrived I went to the department store where the President of the congregation worked. Located on Main Street, it was easy to find. I asked for Melvin Fineberg. A short, stocky middle-aged man came in my direction. Shaking my hand, he drawled (just as I had imitated): 'Welcome to Jonah, Rabbi; now you call me Melvin. Let's go out and get something to eat.'

I followed him through the store, and as we walked down Main Street he pointed out where other Jews worked. Indicating a small shop on the corner, he said: 'That's Bert Levi's store. He owns the best shoe shop in town. If you ever need some shoes, Rabbi, go see Bert. He'll give you a good discount. And over there, that's Sam Gardenschwartz's furniture shop. I can't imagine you'll need to take back a sofa to the college. But he'll always give you a good deal.' Motioning to the biggest building on the street, he said: 'Jack Goldstone is a big macher in the congregation. He's the president of the local bank. If you want to open an account here, you should go see Jack.'

We stopped at a Woolworth's and sat inside on stools at the counter. 'Well, Rabbi,' Melvin said. 'What would you like? They do real good sandwiches. Or maybe you'd like an ice-cream? I always have three scoops of vanilla with chocolate sauce.'

'Ah, thanks. Just a cup of coffee would be fine.'

'You sure? Well, OK. Hey, Gloria,' he shouted to a slim, attractive waitress. 'The regular. And this here's the new rabbi. Get him a cup of coffee.'

When his ice-cream arrived, the President explained about the congregation. There were forty families; some husbands and wives were converts. There were even a few who had Gentile spouses. 'But we don't ask any questions,' he said. 'There aren't many of us here, so we can't be too choosy.'

'And your services, are they mostly in English? I mean, do you want me to use much Hebrew?'

'Well, we use the Union Prayerbook. And to be honest, Rabbi, we prefer it in English. You could say a few prayers in Hebrew – lots of people like that. And of course the Torah is in Hebrew. But we haven't got any Hebrew scholars so we're not fussy about it. It's much nicer if people can understand what the service is all about. Don't you think?'

'Yes, yes . . . I do . . .' I said. But I couldn't help thinking what my teachers at the seminary would think of this conversation.

What was the point of the Bachelor of Hebrew Letters degree if congregants weren't interested in Hebrew?

The President then took me to a motel, located on the outskirts of the city. After I had registered and deposited my suitcase in the room, he took me to the parking lot. 'Here's your car, Rabbi,' the President said, opening the door of an old Mercedes-Benz. 'I hope you like it – it belongs to Maurice Fine. He doesn't need it any more so he gave it to the Temple for our visiting rabbi.'

'Gosh,' I said. 'This is great. Thanks. But how will I find the Temple?'

'Now don't you worry about that. We'll take you there tonight, and then you can drive yourself in the future. You just relax, and we'll be back to take you to dinner at six. The service begins at eight.'

This was an auspicious start to my rabbinical career: a comfortable motel room, my own Mercedes, dinner with the President. After swimming in the hotel pool, I put on a suit and waited in the lobby. Melvin arrived with his wife and announced that we were going to the local country club. As we drove there, I asked him about the membership: 'Can Jews join? In Denver they can't.'

'We're not a big city like Denver,' he explained. 'So anybody can belong. Of course you've got to be proposed and seconded. But there's no restriction on anybody. Except Negroes, of course.'

At dinner the President instructed me on my duties. 'We're glad the college sends us a student rabbi. Everybody's grateful, so you'll feel at home here. And there's not much for you to do. Just preach the sermon on Friday nights, and on Saturday the members would be mighty grateful if you dropped in to see them at work.'

'They would?'

'Yup. You don't need to make an appointment. When you go downtown, just go in to their stores. They're always happy to see the rabbi.'

'And that's it?'

'Well, you'll need to visit anybody who's in hospital. I'll let you know. There's just one thing I ought to tell you, though. Are you involved in civil rights, Rabbi?'

'Civil rights? Well, not really. I mean, I haven't thought a lot about it.'

'That's good to hear, Rabbi. Now, I'm a liberal guy myself, and so are lots of our members. It's just that in Jonah it don't do any good to make a fuss. The folk down here don't like it.'

The food had arrived. The President and his wife had ordered prawn cocktails, and I did the same. I wondered if they'd mind that their new rabbi ate prawns. But I guessed they wouldn't. 'You see, Rabbi, we're a small Jewish community, and a lot of us are doing real well. We don't want to cause trouble. There's quite an active Ku Klux Klan in these parts.'

I swallowed. 'Ku Klux Klan?'

'Some of the big-wigs in City Hall belong. But they don't bother us. We want to keep it that way. The last rabbi preached sermons about segregation in the South, and there was an article in the newspaper. Some of the members were real upset. Fortunately, nothing happened. But we've got to be careful. I'm sure you understand, Rabbi.'

As I finished my prawn cocktail, I pondered what I had been told. Perhaps this would not be quite as delightful an experience as I had imagined.

Once a month, I visited the Jonah community. Melvin arranged that I had dinner every night with a different family. Invariably the food was the same – matzoh ball soup, fried chicken and vegetables, and home-made pie. But the houses were different: most members lived in modest suburban dwellings, but the richer congregants dwelt in the most exclusive part of the town in sprawling, ranch-style homes. This social division was reflected in the running of the Temple – the President and board members were made up almost entirely of the wealthiest members of the community.

Throughout the year I coached Greg Grossman, the son of the only Jonah millionaire, for his bar mitzvah. On my last visit I officiated at the ceremony. When I arrived at Birmingham Airport, I was met by Jack Grossman's black chauffeur. Ushering me to a large Cadillac, he told me about the weekend's proceedings. 'It's going to be something,' he said. 'There's about fifty out-of-town guests who've already arrived. Right now most of them are at the house. I's supposed to take you there right away.'

En route to Jonah he told me about the guests. 'Grandpa Sternberg – that's Jack's wife's father – he's here from New York. He's an old man now, but he was big in New York real estate. The rest of her family are from the East too; Jack's father – old man Grossman – he's from Mobile. That's where the rest of Jack's family's from.'

'And what do the New Yorkers make of Alabama?' I naïvely asked.

'Your guess is as good as mine. I guess they think of us as small-town folk. But there's nothing wrong with that. No, man. I'd never want to live in a place like New York.'

When I arrived some of the guests were swimming in the pool. Others sat at tables, arranged on a large patio, having lunch. 'Come on over, Rabbi,' Jack Grossman shouted. He was dressed in Bermuda shorts, and his vast bulk filled out a short-sleeved shirt. 'Have a steak sandwich, Rabbi; they were just flown in from Kansas.' Motioning to a black waiter, he said: 'Johnnie, get the rabbi a drink. What about a beer, Rabbi?'

'That's fine . . . thanks.'

Jack gestured that I should sit next to him. 'The whole family's here, Rabbi. From Alabama and back East. That's Mollie's father,' he said, pointing to a tall, moustachioed elderly man seated under an umbrella and wearing white trousers and a long-sleeved shirt. He was reading a large paperback novel. Seated next to him was a voluptuous red-head wearing a skimpy bikini. 'The girl's his niece. Hey, Ruth!' he shouted. 'Come meet the rabbi.'

As she slithered over to our table I tried not to stare. She stretched out a hand with long, red fingernails and smiled. 'I've heard all about you, Rabbi,' she said.

Ruth's bikini hardly kept her suntanned body covered. She fluttered her long eyelashes. I wondered if they were real. Her eyes were intensely green. Were they really that green or possibly helped by coloured contact lenses? There was no doubt, however, that her body was all her own. 'It's nice to meet you,' I said.

'There's the bar mitzvah boy,' Jack announced. I turned around and saw Greg dive into the pool. I hoped his Hebrew would be as good as his diving. 'So, how long are you here for, Rabbi?' Ruth asked.

'Just the weekend. I'm still in rabbinical school and have to go back on Sunday.'

'That's too bad,' Ruth said, twirling her bikini straps. 'I hope you'll have some free time this weekend.'

'Well, I hope so too,' I said.

'Got to go now, Rabbi,' Ruth said, standing up. 'See you later.'

I watched as she trotted back to her uncle.

'That's quite a girl,' Jack whispered. 'Just got divorced a couple of months ago. You ought to get to know her, Rabbi.' I thought about Jan and sighed.

The next day was the bar mitzvah. I arrived at the Temple early. From my office I had a good view of the street. About half an hour before the service, the Grossman family arrived in their Cadillac. Like his father, Greg wore a black suit; his mother was dressed in a tight-fitting red dress. I shook everyone's hand and reassured Greg. 'You'll do fine,' I said. Greg looked unconvinced. Previously I had made a tape of his Torah portion so he could hear how it should be pronounced – I hoped he had practised. Because I was in Jonah only once a month, I had had little opportunity to hear him read, and he had rehearsed the Torah scroll only a few times. Would my first bar mitzvah be a catastrophe?

Soon the Temple filled up with the rest of the Grossman family as well as the usual congregants. I began the service promptly at eleven, but stragglers continued to arrive. By the time of the Torah reading, everyone had settled into seats. First, Greg recited the blessing and then I guided him through his portion with a silver pointer. When he stumbled, I helped him with the pronunciation. At last he finished. He then recited the blessing over the Haftarah, and read it in Hebrew. Again he stumbled, but he persisted. When it was over, Greg's mother beamed. His father patted him on the back. He hadn't done a very good job, but it appeared that his parents were satisfied.

At the reception Jack Grossman welcomed all the guests, and Greg made a little speech thanking me for all I had done for him. I wished I had done more. After the Kiddush, the entire gathering sat down for lunch. I was seated at the top table next to Ruth. She wore a low-cut dress, and I struggled not to look down her front as we ate. 'You were wonderful,' she purred.

'But I didn't really do anything,' I said. 'Greg was the star performer.'

'You're far too modest,' she continued. 'I loved your speech.'

'You did?'

'It was very moving. Didn't you see Greg's mom crying?'

'She cried?'

'It was so sweet. She's awfully choked up about little Greg. By the way, I hope you're coming to the party this evening at the country club.'

'Ah, well . . . I am, as a matter of fact.'

'Good,' she said, stabbing a shrimp. 'I'll see you there.'

For the last time I drove the Mercedes to the country club. When I arrived, a band was playing and the party was in full swing. I greeted congregants, and then went over to the Grossmans' table. Jack stood up and handed me an envelope.

'Rabbi, we sure are grateful for all you've done for Greg. This is just a little present from Mollie and me.'

I didn't know what to say – I had never received a tip before. 'Well, thanks,' I mumbled. 'But it's not necessary . . .'

'Our pleasure,' Jack said.

Later in the evening I saw Ruth. She had squeezed into an even tighter-fitting gown with an even more swooping neckline. 'I hope you'll ask me to dance,' she said.

She clung to me as I tried to waltz to the music. I was not a good dancer at the best of times, and I stepped on Ruth's foot. 'Sorry,' I said.

Ruth giggled, and pressed against me. This was all very flattering, but we were dancing closer than I thought prudent. I looked around the room to see if anyone was watching. After we finished dancing, Ruth put an envelope in my pocket and winked as she headed off for the drinks table.

When I arrived at my hotel, I opened both envelopes. In the one from Greg's father was a hundred-dollar bill, and a letter thanking me for teaching Greg his Torah portion. The other was a note from Ruth which read: 'Danny – when you come East I hope you'll look me up. My number in New York is 987654. I think we could have a good time, don't you? Love and kisses, Ruth.'

I wasn't sure which gave me more pleasure.

In the summer after my third year at the seminary, I was the summer replacement for the rabbi at a Reform Temple in Brownsville, Pennsylvania. Every year when Rabbi Fishman went on his summer holidays, he arranged for one of the students to take his place. The congregation was located in a leafy suburb, and my apartment was nearby.

At the start of the holidays, I drove my Austin Healey to Brownsville and parked in the Temple parking lot. Waiting for me at the entrance was a squat, scholarly-looking middle-aged man dressed in a black suit. To my surprise the rabbi had an English accent. He was from Liverpool, England, and had been a student at Cambridge before he went to the seminary. After finishing his rabbinical studies, he stayed on to do a PhD in Semitic languages. I was impressed!

After showing me my apartment, Rabbi Fishman took me out to dinner at an elegant restaurant.

'I hope you'll like the congregation,' he said, pouring out the wine.

'I'm sure I will,' I said.

Rabbi Fishman smiled. 'At least it will be an interesting introduction to the rabbinate.'

I wasn't sure what to say. Did he like them? What was he telling me? 'Ah . . . is there anything I should know?'

'I've left a list of instructions with my secretary. She'll help you out. Don't worry – I'll only be away for a couple of months.'

'Have you been here since you finished at the seminary?' I asked.

'No. I was a college chaplain at the University of Virginia for several years. Then I came to Brownsville. Quite a change!'

'For the better?'

'It's like marriage,' he grinned. 'For better or worse . . .'

The next morning I got up at seven-thirty to take Rabbi Fishman to the airport. As I pulled out from the parking lot, I heard a screeching of brakes. A large Dodge swerved and smashed into the front of my car. Both of us skidded and stopped. I wasn't hurt, but there had been a ferocious impact; I rushed out to find the other driver white with fear. 'Are you OK?' I asked.

He slowly opened the door and stood up. 'Yeah, I'm all right. We better call the police.'

I knocked on the front door of the house facing the street where the accident took place and asked if I could use the phone. First I called the police, and then Rabbi Fishman.

'Rabbi,' I said. 'I've just been in an accident. I can't pick you up for your flight. You better get a taxi. I'm OK. So don't worry. Have a nice summer, and I'll see you when you get back.'

Trembling, I went outside and looked at my Healey. It was a mess. The side was crushed, and the front fender was turned at an angle. One wire wheel was bent. Glass was everywhere. My status symbol was a wreck.

Eventually, I went back to my apartment to change for work. This was my first day, and already I had failed to pick up the rabbi and had demolished my car. I wondered what would happen next. The secretary phoned Max Gold, the President of the Temple. Later in the morning, he knocked on the door of the rabbi's study.

'Come in,' I said.

The President was dressed in golf clothes and had an easy manner. We shook hands. 'I understand you've had an accident,' he said. 'Why don't you take the day off and come home for lunch?'

'Gosh,' I replied. 'That's very nice of you. But I've just started. Maybe I ought to stay at the Temple.'

'And do what?'

'Well, I could start on my sermon for Friday night.'

'But it's only Monday. Come back with me to my house. You can borrow some trunks. I think you could use a good swim.'

I followed the President to a large, red Bentley parked in the lot. He unlocked the door and I got in. I'd never been in a Bentley before – it smelled of leather and oozed power and money. As we drove to his house, he told me about himself. He was from a poor family, had graduated from the University of Pittsburgh, and made a fortune in land development. Proudly he announced that he had become a multi-millionaire by the age of thirty. When we arrived, he parked the car in the garage and took me out to the pool where his wife was floating on an inflated raft.

'I've brought the rabbi home for lunch,' he shouted. 'He's just smashed up his car and failed to deliver Fishman to the airport.'

Mrs Gold took off her sunglasses. Sympathetically she cooed: 'Oh, you poor dear. I hope you're not hurt.'

'No, I'm OK. Just a bit shaken.'

'I'm not surprised. Why don't you change and come in the water? You'll feel a lot better.'

I went upstairs and put on a pair of outlandish trunks. They were far too big for me and I hoped they wouldn't come off. I'd had enough trouble for one day! I jumped into the pool. Max Gold sat in a lounge chair by the side, drinking what looked like a pink cocktail. 'Hey, Rabbi,' he shouted, 'did you see what's on the bottom?' I looked down. There was a mosaic under my feet. But since the water shimmered in the sunlight I couldn't make out the design.

'It's a Picasso, Rabbi. I had it done last summer. The same design as the Picasso we've got in the living room.'

A Picasso? Surely not done by Picasso himself. I was confused. Mrs Gold paddled over. 'It was Max's idea,' she explained. 'He doesn't know anything about art. What he knows about is money. But last year he woke up in the middle of the night and decided that he wanted to become a collector. The next day he phoned the biggest art dealer in town and told him he wanted to buy Picassos.'

'I've always liked the guy,' Max interrupted.

'He bought three oils and twenty signed lithographs. Then he got a local firm to make up this mosaic based on his favourite.'

'Don't you like it, Rabbi?' Max asked.

'Great,' I said. 'Really great. Let me have a look.' I dived under the water and peered as best I could. I came up for air. 'Tremendous. I've never seen anything like it.'

'Absolutely right,' Max said. 'I'll bet nobody in Brownsville got anything like it.' He chuckled. 'Ha, a Picasso in the pool.'

Lunch consisted of steaks grilled by the housekeeper and a scrumptious chocolate cake. Over coffee I leaned back in my deck-chair.

'This is the life, isn't it, Rabbi?' Max said. 'Have another swim.'

This time Max flopped in, wearing a rubber ring. As he splashed about, he asked me about my career. 'So, Dan,' he inquired, 'where are you going to be a rabbi?'

'Well,' I said, 'I don't know. I still have two more years to go at the seminary.'

'Let me give you a tip,' he said. 'You should aim for Temple Emanuel-El in New York.'

'But that's the biggest Temple in the world.' I was taken aback. 'It's on Fifth Avenue. I don't think I'd have a chance.'

'So?' he said. 'In life, if you don't aim big, you won't get anywhere. Look at me. I didn't have a penny when I started. Now I've got a Picasso in the pool.'

In Brownsville all rabbis were given free membership to the Jewish country club. On the first weekend I drove there in an old Ford which Max arranged for me to have while my car was being repaired. I pulled up alongside a Mercedes-Benz in the car park. A shapely lady in skimpy tennis shorts was opening up the trunk of her car. 'Hey, can you do me a favour?' she called.

'Of course,' I answered. 'What would you like me to do?'

Pointing to a bag of golf clubs, she replied, 'Would you be a darling and carry them for me?'

'Why . . . sure . . .'

'Oh, honey, that's awfully nice of you,' she said, sauntering off to the entrance. 'Just put them in the hall, will you?'

I followed behind, lugging the bag. I wondered if this was to be my role as the visiting rabbi. When I deposited them in the hall, she approached me with a dollar bill in her hand. 'Thanks a lot,' she said.

I was embarrassed and cross. 'Look,' I said. 'I'm glad to help. But I can't accept a tip. I'm the new rabbi.'

She giggled. 'The rabbi! No! You're just a kid!'

'Honestly,' I protested. 'Well, actually I'm a student rabbi. I've taken over Rabbi Fishman's congregation for the summer.'

'You're Fishface's replacement? No kidding! Well, honey, let me get you a drink instead.'

Every afternoon, when I finished my work at the Temple, I went to Meadow Hills Country Club. Often I played tennis with some of the women in the congregation. Once in a while I won, but usually I lost. I simply couldn't keep up with these agile Jewish women who had practised all summer. Frequently the sound of 'Bad luck, Rabbi' rang out from the courts. In addition, I usually had a swim before I went home. There was no doubt that summer camp had been a better preparation for life as a rabbi than rabbinical seminary.

While I was at Brownsville, I went on a visit to Pittsburgh, where my father's sister and husband lived. There I met a girl who came from a well-off family; her father was an executive vice-president of the biggest bank in Pittsburgh. She had been a student at Vassar and was studying for a PhD in history at the University of Pennsylvania. Although I was missing Jan acutely, we liked each other, and I invited her to come and visit me in Brownsville. When I told Elaine Gold about her, she was delighted. 'Ask her to stay with us,' she offered. 'We've got plenty of room, and it would be no trouble.'

'That's very kind. Are you sure?'

'Of course. But remember to tell her to bring a swimming suit.'

When I picked Mimi up at the airport, I explained where she would be staying.

'That's ridiculous,' she complained. 'I don't want to stay with people I don't know. I've come to stay with you.'

I frowned. 'Look,' I explained, 'you can't. Honestly. I'm the rabbi. What would my congregants think?'

'Why should they know?'

'It's impossible to keep this kind of thing a secret. It would get around.'

'We're both adults, for God's sake.'

'It just won't work. I can't. They wouldn't understand. You've got to stay at the Golds'.'

In the car she fumed. When we arrived, Max came out to greet us. He was dressed in madras Bermuda shorts; he thrust out his hand. 'Glad to know you,' he exclaimed. 'Come right in.'

Elaine showed Mimi to her room, and I went out to the pool. I sank into a chair and waited for the women to emerge. Max pulled up a deck-chair. 'Rabbi, she's one hell of a looker,' he said.

'Yeah, she is.'

'And quite a figure.'

I agreed.

'Elaine tells me she's from a wealthy Pittsburgh family.'

I nodded.

'You want my advice,' he said. 'Marry her. Always marry money. Better rich than poor, that's what I always say.' I thought about Jan, who was poor, and felt sick at heart.

That evening Max and Elaine had arranged a party for us. Most of their guests were from the congregation, but a few others were Max's business associates. We started with drinks by the pool with Max as bartender. Then there was a barbecue on the patio. Max, dressed in Hawaii shorts, supervised from the sidelines. 'That'll be two steaks medium-rare,' he yelled to the cooks.

Mimi watched in disbelief. Contemptuous of the entire affair, she sulked in the corner and hardly spoke all evening. After supper, the guests changed into swim gear and jumped into the pool. Max had organized races, and we all joined in. I won the breast-stroke, as Mimi looked on in disgust. When I was awarded a prize – a bottle of French champagne – she audibly groaned.

The next day I came over to the house to take Mimi out to lunch at the country club. She sat in silence as I drove there. After we ordered, she berated me about the Golds and their friends. 'They're horrible,' she sneered.

'Be reasonable, Mimi,' I said. 'They've been very nice to me. The day I smashed up my car, they invited me to lunch. Max got me a car to drive.'

'Big deal!'

'Come on. They're generous people. It was good of them to organize a party last night.'

Mimi refused to budge. 'It was stupid!'

'I don't see why you're so angry,' I said.

'I'm not angry with them. I'm angry with you for putting up with all this.'

'All what?'

Our drinks had arrived. I had ordered iced tea; Mimi had white wine. Sipping her drink, she castigated my congregants. 'You're blind if you don't see how vulgar they are! You went to Tewksbury. You're the son of an orthopaedic surgeon. You're supposed to have some taste.'

'Ah, Mimi, don't be such a snob.'

'I am a snob,' she admitted. 'Did you see that ridiculous Picasso mosaic in the pool? It's dreadful.'

'I rather like it.'

'Oh, Dan, you couldn't possibly.'

'I do. It's . . . cute.'

'Cute!' Mimi exploded. 'It's crass. There's no other word for it.'

The waiter brought our salads. Mimi attacked hers with fury – I couldn't understand why she was so angry. 'OK,' I said, 'they're not cultured. They're rich, and they make a splash with their money. But they're good people.'

'Yuck!' she commented.

'Mimi,' I went on, 'I'm their rabbi, at least for the summer. I've got to get along with all my congregants, no matter what they're like. The rich ones as well as the poor ones.'

'From last night I didn't think there were any poor ones,' she countered.

'The point is that I've got to accept them as they are. And, the Golds are nice. I like them.'

Mimi stared at me. 'You'll end up just like they are . . . a bloated, pretentious, hedonistic slob.'

'Ah come on, Mimi,' I pleaded.

During the rest of the lunch we ate in silence. Mimi was no candidate to be a rabbi's wife, but I suppose she did have a point. By the standards of Tewksbury, the Golds and their friends – my congregants – were vulgar. Nice, but vulgar. I enjoyed their affluence. Who wouldn't? But this was only a summer job. Would I want to be submerged in all this for the rest of my life?

Although I spent most of the summer at the country club and at the Golds' house, I did have numerous duties as the replacement rabbi. I conducted services, visited Jewish patients at Brownsville hospital, and trained bar mitzvah students. Because most of the congregation were away for the summer, I did not see many members. None the less, I did try to interest those who remained in Brownsville. In the summer of 1969 the black community throughout the United States had been agitating for reparations from the Christian community. In several instances, black militants stormed into churches, interrupted worshippers, and demanded financial compensation. I thought an incident of this nature could be an interesting psycho-drama, and approached George Halstead, one of the more liberal members of the Temple. I asked if he would be prepared to pretend to be a black and stage this kind of protest. I explained that he would have to dress in blue jeans and paint his face. He agreed, and the following Friday night, he sat unrecognized at the back of the Temple sanctuary. As I began my sermon, he stood up and shouted: 'Hey man, you listen to me!'

There was a stunned silence. No one moved. 'You Jews were slaves in Egypt,' he declared. 'But now we are slaves in America. We are the ones who suffer under new pharaohs.'

I tried not to smile. This was a great success – no one suspected this was George. He continued: 'You're rich; we're poor. It's time you take care of us.'

I glanced at Max, who was sitting on the pulpit – he looked terrified. There was a rustling near the back, and an elderly matron stood up. 'You get out of here,' she hissed. 'You and your kind aren't welcome.'

Heads turned around. No one knew what to do. I watched as congregants whispered to each other. George raised his fist: 'Power to the people,' he yelled. 'Power to the people.'

I decided I had better explain that this was really George in disguise and that we had planned this display to test the congregation's feelings about social deprivation. At first there was a sigh of relief, then an outburst of anger. A prominent member of the board stood up. 'We have had enough, Rabbi. You're not from here, and you don't know our community. Let's get on with the service.' Others joined in – I could see that my plan to have a discussion about communal responsibility rather than a sermon was impossible. Sheepishly, I proceeded with the rest of the prayers. Afterwards, at the Oneg Shabbat, most of the congregation left without saying goodbye. Max took me aside. 'Dan,' he said, 'come over to my house. We need to talk.'

Despondently I followed Max to his house, parked my car and went inside. Elaine turned on the television, and Max handed me a drink and led me into his study. The walls were covered with Picasso lithographs. Max sat down behind a huge mahogany desk and I slouched in a leather armchair facing him. My eczema began to itch. 'I guess it didn't work,' I said.

Max nodded. 'Look, Dan,' he said consolingly, 'this is your first job. Everybody makes mistakes.'

'But I thought it would be a great idea . . . you've got to admit we fooled everybody and made quite an impact. George was tremendous.'

Max stood up. He paced around the room. 'You can't play with people's feelings like that. They won't stand for it. Why should they feel guilty? They come to Temple to feel good.'

'But, Max, Reform Judaism is prophetic Judaism. We have social responsibilities . . .'

'Maybe that's what they teach you in rabbinical school – but it's not practical in real life.'

The next day Max phoned me at the Temple. 'Dan,' he said. 'I've been getting calls all morning. Lots of people are upset about what happened last night. I told you they wouldn't like it.'

'There's nothing I can do about it now.'

'I know. But some of the older members think you shouldn't continue for the rest of the summer.'

I couldn't believe this was happening. How could my experiment have caused so much trouble? Would I be reported to the seminary? 'I'm only here three more weeks,' I protested.

'That's what I told them. It'll be all right, but this just can't happen again.'

I was growing irritable. 'OK, Max,' I said. 'I got the message.'

'Good. Now, why don't you come for a swim and cool off?'

I carried on as usual for the next few weeks, but hardly anyone came to services. I had the impression everyone was waiting for me to leave. On my last night Max and Elaine had me to dinner, and their maid fixed my favourite food. We sat out by the pool. After dinner I had a final swim and a last look at the Picasso mosaic. Elaine kissed me goodbye and Max gave me a hug. They had been very kind to me and I was grateful, particularly after the fiasco at the Temple.

Several weeks after term had begun at the seminary, I had to return to Brownsville to collect my car – all summer the garage which had collected it from the accident had been waiting for parts to arrive from England. At last it was ready, and I took the train to Brownsville. The Golds had asked me to lunch, and I drove there in my newly-repaired Healey. Over drinks, they told me that Rabbi Fishman had been fired.

'But he just got back from vacation,' I said.

From a portable bar on the patio, Max shouted out: 'Fishman's days were numbered long ago.'

'I don't understand. I thought you liked him. After my catastrophe at the Temple, I thought you'd be thrilled to have him back.'

Max's stomach jiggled as he rattled the cocktail shaker. He was making a special Hawaiian concoction. After pouring drinks into glass tumblers, he sat down. 'Look,' he explained, 'Fishman never fitted in. He was a bachelor – here everybody's married. He's got an English accent that nobody understands. He's got degrees in languages nobody speaks. He doesn't play golf. He doesn't swim. He's never been on a tennis court. He refuses to go to fashion shows. He hates bowling. What kind of rabbi is he?'

'But he's dutiful. I mean, he does all the things rabbis are supposed to do.'

Max refilled his glass. 'What do you think of the Gold-special?' he asked, beaming.

'It's great, Max,' I replied. 'But honestly, what did Fishman do wrong?'

'What did he do right would be a better question,' Max responded.

As Elaine handed out plates, she concurred with Max. 'He's right, Dan. What the Temple wants is a nice person. They're not interested in whether the rabbi can read foreign languages. What matters is the rabbi's personality.'

'And Fishman's got no personality,' Max insisted. 'Listen, I can tell you as president, the guy puts everyone to sleep.'

'He's not like you, Dan,' Elaine continued. 'You like swimming and tennis. You go out with girls. Sometimes you get too serious – like that night at the Temple. But basically you fit in.'

'That's so important?'

Max looked at me with disbelief. 'Honestly, sometimes I don't think you have any brains. I know you've been to college for God knows how long. Probably too long. As I said before, you've got to be realistic about being a rabbi.'

I was still bewildered. I couldn't imagine Rabbi Fishman playing golf with the ladies at the country club – but he did have other qualities. To my mind, he was an ideal rabbi: intelligent and caring. What difference did it make if he didn't want to go to fashion shows or bowling? These were hardly grounds for being dismissed from one's job.

When I got back to the seminary, I telephoned Rabbi Fishman. I told him how sorry I was to hear about the situation, and asked if there was anything I could do.

There was a long pause. 'Thanks,' he said in clipped English. 'Kind of you to ring.'

'Would it help if I wrote to the board?' I inquired.

Again, a long silence. 'Wouldn't do a bit of good,' he said. 'Jolly kind of you to offer. Don't give it any more thought. Good luck yourself.'

I felt an overwhelming sadness as I hung up. What had gone wrong for Fishman? He was a learned, conscientious rabbi. Why didn't they appreciate him? It was all too baffling.

*

At the onset of my fourth year at the seminary I drew Venice, Illinois, as a bi-weekly congregation in the class lottery. On my first visit I flew to Chicago and then caught the train to Venice. As instructed, I deposited my suitcase at the hotel on Main Street and set off for the President's department store nearby. When I entered, a shop assistant greeted me. I explained that I was the rabbi and asked to see Stanley Greenberg. As I waited, I looked at the clothing and shoe departments. Perhaps, I thought, the President might give me a discount on a new suit. Eventually Stanley emerged. 'Sorry,' he said. 'Customers!'

We shook hands, and he took me to the back of the shop where there was a small staff room. 'Coke?' he asked, putting a quarter into a large dispensing machine.

'Thanks,' I said.

He handed me a cold can and a straw. 'How was the trip?' he asked.

'Ah . . . fine. It didn't take too long from Chicago.'

Stanley noisily sipped his Coke. 'Never does. Good service. How's the hotel?'

'It's very convenient. I'm sure I'll like it.'

'Good. It's a nice place. Friendly people. You want another Coke?'

'No thanks,' I said.

Leaning across the table, Stanley glared at me. 'Now listen, Rabbi,' he explained. 'We're quite a traditional congregation. You don't have any ideas about changing things, do you?'

This was not the interview I had anticipated. 'No, I don't think so,' I said.

Stanley looked relieved. 'That's good. The guy we had from the seminary last year upset everybody. We had some resignations, and we don't want it to happen again.' Stanley stood up, buttoned his collar, and pulled up his tie. 'Got to go back to work,' he announced. 'The service is at eight – just call for a taxi and it'll take you there.'

Ushering me out into the street, Stanley slapped me on the back. 'See you, Rabbi. Don't be late!'

It was only five o'clock, and I had nothing to do for the next three hours. This was quite a change from Jonah: no hospitality, no car. I went back to the hotel and watched television in my room. At six-thirty I went to the restaurant, and ordered dinner. On my first Friday night I ate alone in an empty hotel. An hour later, my taxi arrived and took me to the Temple. When I arrived, the organist let me in. She was an elderly woman who had volunteered years ago to undertake this task. While I put on a robe in the Temple office, she disappeared behind a screen to practise. Just before eight, Stanley arrived with his wife, as did about thirty other congregants.

After the service I met the members of the congregation at the Oneg Shabbat, and Stanley's wife Sarah asked if I'd like to come home with them for dessert. I got in the back seat of their Ford, which was littered with newspapers, cartons of cigarettes and empty bottles of beer. In the front Stanley and Sarah gossiped about the members of the congregation.

'Did you see what Selma was wearing?' Sarah asked her husband.

'Yeah, mink,' Stanley grunted.

'It's not even winter, Stanley!'

'Nope.'

'Well, what do you think of that?'

'Nice mink.'

'Oh, Stanley, it's revolting.'

'You wouldn't say so if it was yours,' he said.

Sarah turned around, seeking my support. 'Don't you agree, Rabbi? I mean, it's not even cold yet.'

I wasn't certain what to say. What if word got back to Selma – whoever she was – that I disapproved of what she wore? What was the tactful reply? I shrugged my shoulders and said nothing.

Several minutes later we arrived at the house. Stanley and Sarah lived in a small bungalow in what appeared to be an unfashionable area of Venice. When we entered, Stanley led me into the family room, where we were met by the babysitter, who had been watching television. Stanley explained that he had to drive her home; Sarah went into the kitchen to make coffee. I pushed aside clutter from the sofa and sat down. After some time Sarah came in carrying a tray with coffee cups and cookies. As I drank my coffee, I looked around the room. The taste was atrocious: the walls were covered with reproductions of cowboy paintings; the flowers in vases were fake; the furniture was poor imitation Louis XIV with gold squiggles. The only redeeming feature was a fat, tabby cat asleep on an armchair. I went over to stroke it. It spat at me.

When Stanley returned he put a Mantovani record on the stereo. Listening to the sickly music, I wondered what Mimi would have thought.

'Would you like a cigar, Rabbi?' Stanley asked.

'No thanks,' I said.

Veiled in smoke, Stanley explained about the congregation. Venice, he stated, was a small town with about thirty Jewish families. Most of those who belonged to the Temple were brought up non-Orthodox, but there were a sizeable number of members from more traditional backgrounds. 'But since we can't support a synagogue as well as a Temple, we've got to compromise. We hold Progressive services on Friday night, but Saturday some of the more Orthodox members get together and put on their own service. They haven't got a minyan, but it doesn't matter.'

I was puzzled. 'Do they expect me to officiate?' I asked.

'No, they're happy to do it themselves. As a matter of fact, I think they'd prefer it if you didn't come.'

'But I'm the rabbi . . .'

'Look,' Stanley said, 'you're the rabbi, sure. But these men don't like the non-Orthodox. They think it's watered-down Judaism. To be honest, they don't think much of Reform rabbis either.'

The next day I avoided the service and wandered around town. At lunchtime I went to a small restaurant near the hotel. It was full of people, so I assumed the food was good. I ordered a triple-decker club sandwich and a Coke, followed by cherry pie and ice-cream. Throughout the meal I read a new novel by Philip Roth: *Portnoy's Complaint*. After lunch I went back to the hotel, turned on the television and had a nap. I was awakened by the telephone.

'Hello,' I said.

'It's Stanley, Rabbi. We got to talk.'

I sensed there was trouble. My eczema began to itch. But what could I have done? Perhaps someone had complained about my sermon? I couldn't imagine.

'I'll be right over,' Stanley said.

I went down to the lobby and waited. Looking furious, Stanley entered the hotel and motioned for me to join him. We went to the coffee shop. Before we had a chance to order, Stanley told me that he had just been on the telephone to Jerome Litwin, the treasurer of the congregation. 'He said you ate at Brown's restaurant for lunch.'

'You mean the restaurant down the street?'

'Yeah, that's Brown's.'

'Yeah, I did.'

'And you had a bacon sandwich . . .'

'A bacon sandwich? No, I had a club sandwich.'

Stanley stared at me. 'And what do you think they make it out of, Rabbi?'

I reddened. Stanley was right. It was a bacon, lettuce and tomato sandwich.

'Come on, Stanley,' I said defensively. 'We're Progressive. We don't keep kosher.'

Stanley rolled his eyes. 'Rabbis don't eat pork, no matter how Progressive,' he declared.

'And what were you reading?' he inquired.

I pulled out the novel from my sports jacket. 'It's by Philip Roth,' I said.

Contemptuously he pushed it aside. 'That guy's an anti-Semite,' he declared. 'And it's full of smut. You shouldn't read that kind of garbage in public.' Stanley stood up. 'Don't let it happen again, Rabbi. I mean it. We've had enough trouble with seminary students. We don't want any more.' As Stanley walked out, a waitress came to take my order. When I told her I wasn't hungry, she smiled. 'Don't worry, honey,' she said. 'Come back later when you've got an appetite. Now, have a good day!'

One of the duties of the rabbi in Venice was to visit students at the local college. On several Saturday nights I went to social events arranged by the Jewish Society; continually I was pursued by a stout second-year student. Dr Rubin, the faculty adviser, told me that Rosie had a crush on me. What was I to do? I didn't want to hurt her feelings, but I had no interest in establishing a relationship. Back at the seminary, I told Morris about my problem. 'Avoid her,' he said.

'How can I? She's always around.'

'Then tell her the truth.'

'I can't, Morris.'

'You'll get into trouble if you don't,' he cautioned.

Instead of confronting Rosie with the truth, I inadvertently found a solution. One afternoon when I had nothing to do, I leisurely browsed among the shelves of the college bookshop. In the religion section I noticed a good-looking blonde sitting on the floor reading a book. When I peered over her shoulder to see what she was reading, she looked up and smiled. 'Hi,' she said.

'Hi. I couldn't help but look at what you're reading. I'm the local rabbi.'

'You look a bit young to be a rabbi,' she said.

'Well, I'm not really the rabbi. I'm a student rabbi. I come here every other week.'

Marilyn was a major in religion, writing a thesis on Martin Buber. Inevitably, she was not Jewish. Over coffee we discussed her dissertation. I asked if she was free for dinner on the Saturday of my next visit. We arranged to meet at the Student Union and go out to a pizza parlour near the college.

Two weeks later, I met Marilyn and we went out as planned. During the meal a group of students sat near our table. I recognized several from the Jewish students' group, including Rosie. When she saw me, she looked shocked. As Marilyn and I talked I noticed that Rosie was staring at me. I looked over and smiled; she turned away.

The next day I had arranged to see Marilyn after Sunday school. As I walked through the campus, I came across the faculty adviser. 'Rabbi,' he said, 'we ought to talk.'

'Is there something wrong?'

Dr Rubin nodded. As we walked in the direction of the Student Union, he told me that Rosie had been dismayed and furious to find me with a non-Jewish girl. Her friends had come to complain that morning. They supported Rosie, and said they would not come to any event where I was present.

'But that's ridiculous,' I said. 'I have no interest in Rosie. I never went out with her.'

Dr Rubin paused. 'I know. But look, Rabbi. There's a problem. We need all the Jewish students we can get to keep the society going. Rosie's a troubled girl. But that's not the point . . .'

'Then what is the point?' I asked.

'I don't want to intrude on your private life, but was it wise to go out with a Gentile girl in a student pizza place?'

When I met Marilyn I was incensed. I explained what had happened. Marilyn took my hand. 'Perhaps we ought to meet in a more private place,' she said.

'Damn that Rosie,' I complained.

'Don't be harsh, Dan. She's not a happy girl.'

'Well, I'm not a happy rabbi.'

'Forget about it,' she urged. 'This is just a part-time job, and you don't have to be here more than a year. Why don't we just have a good time together?'

I saw the wisdom in her advice. I only hoped Dr Rubin wouldn't phone the President of the Temple.

On future visits to Venice I avoided the Jewish Society at the college – I hoped my absence might encourage Rosie and her friends to attend. But I continued to see Marilyn. She didn't replace Jan, whom I still missed sorely, but I liked her and it was nice to have someone to go out with. Fortunately Marilyn had a car, so we went to restaurants in neighbouring towns. Since members of the Temple didn't offer hospitality in the evenings, no one minded my absences. When we got back to Venice, Marilyn came up to my room in the hotel. We watched television, read books and talked.

One Saturday night Marilyn stayed later than usual. At midnight the door to the hotel was shut. I assumed that I would be able to let Marilyn out myself, but I discovered it was locked. What were we to do? Reluctantly, I walked across the lobby to the desk and rang the bell. An elderly lady peered out from a small room behind reception. She put down her knitting and asked what I wanted.

'Sorry to trouble you,' I said, 'but I can't get out.'

She eyed me suspiciously. 'You're the rabbi, aren't you?'

'Well, yes . . .' I stuttered.

'Where are you going this time of night?'

I anticipated this might cause difficulties. But what could I do? 'Actually,' I explained, 'I've got a friend here. I'm going to walk her back to the campus.'

She unlocked the door, and Marilyn and I left. 'I wonder what she'll say when I get back?' I asked as we walked along the deserted streets.

'She's not a member of the congregation, is she?'

'No, but still . . . I don't like it.'

'I hope I didn't get you into trouble.'

'I don't think so. But in this profession, you can never be too sure.'

I arrived back after two and rang the bell. Nothing happened. I rang again, and at last the woman who had let us out emerged. She shook her head and unlocked the door. Testily, she told me what time it was.

'Sorry. I didn't mean to disturb you.'

'I don't think your congregation would like to hear about this,' she said.

'What do you mean?' I asked. 'My private life has nothing to do with them.'

'Well, if you were my rabbi,' she continued, 'I wouldn't like hearing you had girls overnight in your hotel room.'

I reddened. 'Look, she wasn't here overnight. That's why we needed to be let out. And I don't see why anyone should hear what I do in my free time.'

That night I couldn't sleep. My eczema itched intolerably. What if this person reported me to the President? Perhaps word would get back to the seminary. The only way out, I thought, would be to tell Stanley myself. By the morning my eczema was red and raw. At nine I phoned him. 'Stanley,' I said, 'I've got to speak to you. It's important. Could you come to my hotel?'

'Now?' he asked.

'I know it's Sunday morning, but I've got to be at religion school at ten. Would you mind?'

'OK, Rabbi,' he groaned.

I met Stanley in the lobby. Fortunately the woman who had the night shift had disappeared. 'I'm really sorry about this,' I explained. 'But something happened last night. It's better you hear about it from me.'

Stanley hadn't bothered to shave. He looked grumpy. 'Yeah, what?' he asked.

'Well, I was with a girl last night . . . and she came over to the hotel . . . and we didn't leave until late. And the woman on the desk wasn't very nice about it.'

'That's great,' Stanley said. 'You can't keep out of trouble, can you, Rabbi?'

'Stanley, nothing happened. She just left late, that's all.'

Stanley stood up. 'It's better you told me. But, look, you're the visiting rabbi. You can't bring back girls to your hotel room, no matter what happens.' A thought struck him. 'Hey, was this girl a daughter of any of the members?'

'No. Just a student at the college.'

'That's a relief. Is she Jewish, at least?'

I opened my mouth and shut it. My eczema continued to itch.

'Rabbi,' Stanley said, 'what the hell do you think you're doing?'

At the end of the fourth year at the seminary my class had a lottery for High Holy Day pulpits. This time I drew a congregation close to home: Temple Bethel in Greenwood, Colorado. High in the Rockies, this beautiful mountain town was a ski resort in the winter and a fashionable vacation spot in the summer.

After term ended, I went to Colorado to write my rabbinic thesis; simultaneously I prepared a set of sermons for the High Holy Days and practised reading the Torah portions. At the end of August I moved out of the small cabin in Estes Park and stayed with my parents in Denver. Several days before Rosh Hashanah, I took the bus to Greenwood and checked in to the Mountainside Hotel. I phoned the President of the Temple at the First National Bank, where he was the manager. 'Come over for dinner,' he said. 'Is there anything you don't eat, Rabbi?' he asked.

My experience in Venice made me wary of what I should say. 'Everything's OK except prawns or pork,' I replied.

'Don't worry about that, Rabbi. We don't keep kosher, but we never have seafood or pork at home.'

I had clearly said the right thing. At least I was off to a good start.

At seven, Dick Rebuck picked me up from the hotel. He drove an E-type Jaguar; I was green with envy. Sliding into the passenger seat, I marvelled at the leather interior – it was even nicer than my Austin Healey. 'This is fantastic,' I said. As we roared off, I explained that I had once had an Austin Healey, but now I drove an old Nash Rambler.

'Didn't you like it?' he asked.

Forlornly, I told him about my accident in Brownsville. Once the Healey was repaired, I explained, I had sold it and bought the Rambler for seventy-five dollars from a rabbinic student in his final year at the seminary.

'Too expensive, huh?' he asked.

'No. It wasn't the cost, really. I just didn't want such a fast car after my accident.'

Covetously surveying the interior of the President's Jaguar, I wondered if I had made a mistake.

Dick and Laura Rebuck lived in a large house nestling on the mountainside. Lined with pine, it was full of Navaho carpets and American antique furniture. A large Saint Bernard was asleep in front of a blazing log fire. Dick introduced me to his wife, and his two children, who were dressed in their pyjamas. When Laura went upstairs to put them to bed, Dick asked if I wanted a beer. I sat on the sofa, and he stretched out in a leather armchair. 'You've got a lovely house,' I commented.

'Glad you like it. We had it built two years ago when I got my promotion at the bank.'

It was dark outside, and I looked at the twinkling lights in the distance. It would be nice to live like this, I thought. I wondered if they might need a full-time rabbi.

The President appeared to have read my thoughts. 'Have you ever considered returning to Colorado?' he asked.

I wasn't sure what to reply. My ambition had always been to become a rabbi of a large suburban congregation in a big city, either in the Midwest or on the East Coast. Yet Greenwood did have its attractions. 'Well,' I said. 'I might.'

'You know,' he continued, 'we haven't got that many members.

But we would like to have our own rabbi. You're from Colorado; so you might think about it.'

Was I being offered a job? I wasn't sure.

'Of course,' Dick interrupted, 'we couldn't offer much money. Actually I don't think we'd even be able to raise enough for what the seminary considers the minimum salary.'

'Oh,' I said.

'But there's plenty of skiing. And clean mountain air.'

Such things, I reflected, were free. But without much of a salary, I certainly wouldn't be able to afford an E-type Jaguar and a mountain home. Perhaps this wasn't such a good idea after all.

On Rosh Hashanah my parents and my grandmother drove up from Denver for the service. The congregation was full – nearly 150 people filled the small sanctuary. As at my bar mitzvah, my grandmother beamed with pride while my mother looked apprehensive and my father grave. At the end of the service I gave the priestly benediction, and walked to the back of the sanctuary. There I greeted everyone who had come. I shook hands with the men and kissed the women: I did this with as much dispatch as possible; I didn't relish kissing so many people I didn't know. After everyone left, my family returned to Denver and I joined Dick and Laura for lunch. They had asked several other couples to join them. Dick was one of the few businessmen in the Temple; nearly all the other congregants were faculty members at the local college. At lunch I sat next to a Professor of English and his wife, who taught art history. They asked me about my studies, and we discussed various novels by Jewish writers, including Philip Roth. How different this all was from Venice, Illinois!

During the rest of the week I was entertained by several other congregants who also taught at the college. They all lived in more modest houses than the President, but they were filled with books and interesting souvenirs from their travels abroad: one professor had spent a sabbatical in Africa and covered the walls of his study with multi-coloured masks; another professor collected ancient Greek pottery. I couldn't help but compare these fascinating objects with the Picassos that Max Gold had amassed. I wondered what the members of Temple Bethel would make of the mosaic on the bottom of his pool.

My family returned to Greenwood for the Yom Kippur service, and drove me back to Denver, where I stayed for another week. The night before I set off for St Louis, my parents gave a party in my honour. About a hundred people came to their house, including the rabbi who had officiated at my bar mitzvah. Over the years he had followed my progress; refilling his drink, he took me aside and asked about my future plans. 'So, Danny,' he asked, 'what happens after next year?'

'I'm not sure,' I said. 'I've been thinking about going on to study for a PhD.'

Rabbi Frankel looked concerned. 'You don't want to serve a congregation?' he asked.

'I do. But I don't think I'm quite ready.'

'If not now, when?' he inquired.

'Well, I don't know.' Was Rabbi Frankel leading up to something? Perhaps he wanted me to return to Denver to be his successor. Over the years, he had a number of assistants, but he had made sure that none had stayed for long. I wasn't certain how to approach the subject. 'I've always thought I might want to come back to Denver,' I hazarded.

Rabbi Frankel frowned. He put his hand on my shoulder and leaned closer. 'You can never be a hero in your home town,' he said.

'But I like Denver.'

'Let me give you some advice,' he continued. 'Don't come back. Go some place where nobody knows you. You can make a fresh start that way.'

'The skiing's good in Colorado.'

'It's good back East, too. And anyway, I've already hired an assistant for next year.'

This was a surprise. I hadn't heard anything about it. 'You did?'

'Didn't your mother tell you about it?' he asked.

'No. She didn't. Gosh, I guess it's too late for me then.'

Without answering Rabbi Frankel turned to greet some of the guests. I tracked down my mother in the kitchen.

'Mom,' I said. 'Why didn't you let me know that the Temple was looking for an assistant? I would have liked to have been considered.'

My mother looked horrified. 'You wouldn't want to be the rabbi here!' she exclaimed.

'I would . . . at least I think I might.'

'I don't think it would be a good idea,' she said. 'Of course it would be nice to have you in Denver, but I don't see how we could live in the same town with our son as the rabbi of the Temple.'

'Why not?'

'How could Dad and I endure all the gossip?' she asked.

Chapter 4

An All-American Rabbi: Wrestling with the American Dream

During the first term of my final year at the seminary I received a phone call from Joel Silversmith, the President of Temple Israel, a small congregation in Denver; he explained that they were without a rabbi and asked if I might be able to serve them until the summer. By this time, they hoped, they would have hired a new rabbi. After consulting with the Dean, I was given permission to leave the seminary a semester early as long as I completed a course in Bible by correspondence. I flew home for the winter vacation and initially met with the President and officers of the Temple. At a lavish lunch in a restaurant close to the Temple, they outlined the terms of my employment: I was to perform all rabbinical duties and receive a salary of 1,000 dollars a month. The Temple would supply me with a car, but I would be responsible for housing and all other expenses. I agreed.

The next day, however, the President called me at my parents' house. 'We've got a problem,' he said. 'I'm afraid we'll have to reduce your salary by 250 dollars a month.'

I told him I'd have to think about it, and that evening at dinner I recounted the phone call to my father. 'Don't give in,' he advised.

'But I don't really care about the money – it would be a good experience. Probably they can't afford to pay more.'

'Don't be a fool. They want to get you cheaper now that you've agreed to come.'

Following my father's advice, I phoned the President the next morning. 'I've given your offer serious consideration,' I said. 'But I don't think I really should say yes.'

'Why not?' he demanded.

'Well, you contacted me at the seminary – not vice versa. And when we met you said the salary would be 1,000 dollars a month. You must have done your sums before you made that offer.'

There was silence at the other end. 'Are you still there?' I asked.

'OK, OK. Make it 1,000 dollars a month. But I hope you're worth it.'

This was not the most auspicious beginning. Perhaps I should have complied – it wasn't that much less. When I told my father what happened, he was pleased. 'You did the right thing,' he said. 'They'll respect you more for it.' I wasn't so sure.

In January I started as the rabbi at Temple Israel. Located on the outskirts of Denver, the Temple was a modern building resembling a whale. The rabbi's study was lined in pine and overlooked a small park. I borrowed some of my mother's paintings to decorate the walls and also hung up my Tewksbury diploma. The secretary of the Temple, Barbara Bloom, was a Jewish girl from Denver who had been a few years behind me in religion school; she was in her early twenties and was unmarried. Her office was across the hall. On my first day, she was at her desk when I arrived. 'Hi,' she said. 'You probably don't remember me, but I was at Temple religion school when you were doing your bar mitzvah.'

She was right; I didn't remember. But the President had told me about her. 'Oh, yes, you're Barbara Bloom.'

Barbara beamed. 'Gosh, you even know my name. What am I supposed to call you, Dan or Rabbi?'

'Call me Dan,' I said. 'After all, we went to religion school together.'

Barbara showed me my room, explained how the dictaphone worked, and departed. Even though I closed the door, I was able to hear muffled noises from across the hall. It sounded as though Barbara was talking to someone. I listened. She was on the telephone to her mother. Although I couldn't make out everything she was saying, I did hear several phrases, one of which was: 'He's cute . . . I hope he'll ask me out.' I could see this was going to be a fraught situation.

The next day I made an appointment to see Rabbi Frankel – I wanted to let him know that I had come as a temporary replacement at Temple Israel and I was anxious for his advice. I arrived after lunch at his house. He took me into his study, offered me coffee, and then got straight to the point. 'I've heard you're staying in Denver to be Temple Israel's rabbi. I wished you'd talked to me about this earlier.'

'Why?' I asked.

'Dan, I've had a lot of experience with the members there. You know they broke away from this Temple years ago because they didn't like the new Prayer Book.'

'I'd heard about that,' I said.

'It was very unpleasant, and we lost a lot of income. These people are a lot of trouble. I think you're in for a hard time.'

'But I'm only going to be here for four months.'

'In the rabbinate four months is a long time.'

'I thought it would be a good experience, an introduction to being a rabbi . . .'

Rabbi Frankel refilled my coffee cup and handed me a plate of cookies. 'I hope you're not intending to stay.'

'Stay? No, no. They're going to hire a new rabbi by the summer.'

Rabbi Frankel eyed me suspiciously. 'But if you're on the spot?'

I hadn't considered the possibility. Perhaps Rabbi Frankel was right – on the other hand, the President had made it clear this was only a temporary job. But if everything worked out well, possibly they wouldn't look for someone else. I wasn't sure what to reply.

Rabbi Frankel looked very uncomfortable. 'I remember what you said about becoming my assistant when I heard the news. I can see you might want to come back to Denver. But, as I said before, you'll never be a hero here. You should make your mark somewhere else.'

This was not the interview I had expected. I had intended to ask Rabbi Frankel for some tips about how to handle my congregation, and he was trying to persuade me not to remain in Denver. We clearly had different agendas. It was all most confusing.

The meeting ended sooner than I expected, and the rabbi's wife showed me to the door. Outside, I paused by the window of the rabbi's study and overheard him talking to his wife. 'That boy really bothers me,' he said. 'If he stays in Denver all the best families will want him to officiate at bar mitzvahs, weddings and funerals. His parents know everyone.'

'Don't worry,' his wife said consolingly. 'He'll never stand the people at Temple Israel.'

When I arrived back at the Temple, I noticed a large sign in the front which I hadn't seen before. It read: 'Bingo every Monday night. Everyone welcome!' Barbara was in the hall fixing notices to the noticeboard when I entered. 'Hey, Barbara,' I said. 'I haven't seen that big sign before. Are we going to have bingo here?'

'Oh yes. It should be fun. They just put up the board outside. Do you like it?'

'It's awful – it dwarfs the Temple Israel sign.'

'I think they want to make sure it attracts attention. The members have put a lot of work into this project.'

'But why? I mean, we are a Temple, not an amusement arcade.'

'They need the money.'

'That's the reason?'

Barbara nodded.

From my office I could see both signs on the front lawn. In large red and blue letters was the announcement about Bingo promising 'big prizes'. To the right was a much smaller sign which read 'Temple Israel' and beneath it in very small letters was a quotation from Isaiah: 'Let justice flow down like fountains and righteousness like an everflowing stream.' I wondered how far the two sentiments were compatible.

In my first week at the Temple I appeared on a local television show – the host asked me a variety of questions about Judaism and modern Jewish life. Since the programme was recorded, I watched it with my parents at their house. Although my mother looked apprehensive throughout, she was clearly proud of me. The next day at the Temple, Barbara treated me like a celebrity. In the afternoon, however, I heard someone yelling: 'I resign, I resign.' I opened the door of my office to find an irate man in overalls carrying a sign which read: 'Picket the Studio – Fair Wages for Fair Work.' He was climbing up the stairs. Who could he be? When he saw me he lunged at me with his sign. 'There you are,' he said. 'How could you do it?' he cried.

'Do what?'

'Cross the picket line!' he shouted.

I had no idea what he was talking about. 'Perhaps you'd better come into my office,' I said.

As I sat behind my desk, he menacingly pointed his finger at me. 'You are a disgrace!' he said. 'Didn't you know we were picketing the studio?'

'Studio – what studio?'

'The TV studio. That's where I work. I was standing in the

picket line, and you crossed right in front of me. I was ashamed. My own rabbi.'

I supposed he was talking about the programme in which I had just appeared. I had no recollection of any pickets – I was so nervous I had simply walked from my car straight into the television centre.

'Look,' I said. 'I don't remember crossing any picket line. I've never been to the studio before. I didn't know you were picketing. In fact I don't know who you are.'

'My name's Saul Woulk. I'm one of your members. If you don't know that, you should. And you insulted me. I pay a lot of money to belong here and I expect some support from the rabbi.'

'But we've never seen each other. How could I know you? I've just started.'

'That's no excuse,' he insisted. 'I don't want to be a member here. I've come to resign. And that's that.'

'Mr Woulk,' I said. 'Please sit down. I'm sorry if you're upset. I understand what you're saying. But I assure you I didn't know anything about the picket line. If I had, I wouldn't have crossed it.'

My assailant sat on the sofa and put his sign on the floor. He looked unconvinced. 'How can I know that?' he asked.

'I give you my word,' I said. 'Honestly, I wouldn't have. Please don't resign.'

Sam Woulk scratched his head and looked out of the window. After several minutes, he stood up. 'OK, Rabbi. Just this once. But if you ever do anything like that again, I'll resign. I expect you to be on our side.'

I put out my hand. Mr Woulk shook it reluctantly. 'I'm serious, Rabbi,' he continued. 'It costs a lot of money to be a member of the Temple, and I want my money's worth.'

When he left I made myself a cup of coffee. Sitting at my desk I pondered this confrontation. I had promised to support this aggressive member in any future demonstration. I wondered why he had gone on strike. He had not told me, and I hadn't asked. Were he and his protester friends pursuing a just claim and, worst of all, what causes had I unwittingly promised to support in the future?

One of my tasks at the Temple was to counsel members of the congregation. At the seminary I had taken several courses in psychology and human relations, but nothing had prepared me for my first interview. On the telephone, one of the new members – Jack Steinberg – asked if he could come and see me about a funeral. When he arrived I asked him whose funeral he wanted to discuss.

'Mine,' he announced.

Could I be hearing correctly? I looked perplexed.

'I want to arrange my own funeral,' he continued. 'I plan to commit suicide, and it's very important that the right music is played.' Taking a piece of paper out of his pocket, he listed his favourite hymns.

'But . . . really . . . this is most unusual,' I stammered. 'I mean, you surely don't plan to take your own life?'

Jack Sternberg grinned. 'I do, Rabbi, I really do. Now can we get on with the music?'

No less astonishing was my encounter with the treasurer's wife. After one of the Friday-night services she confronted me. 'How could you have done this to me, Rabbi?' she asked.

'Done what?' I inquired.

'You didn't go to see my mother in the hospital. She had gallstones, and you didn't even pay one visit.'

'But I didn't know she was in the hospital,' I said.

'That's no excuse. It's your responsibility to know about these things.'

'But I do visit,' I explained defensively. 'Every Thursday I go to the Denver Jewish hospital. I visit any patient who puts down on their admission card that they are Jewish. Did your mother say she was Jewish?'

'Don't be stupid, Rabbi. Of course she said she's Jewish. Is she supposed to say she's Catholic? But she wasn't at the Jewish hospital. She was at St Luke's.'

'She was at St Luke's? But that's a Catholic hospital.'

'Of course it's a Catholic hospital. Her doctor's Catholic, and that's where he does his operations.'

'But I don't visit Catholic hospitals,' I said.

'And why not, if there are Jewish patients there?'

'Well, I would, of course, if I knew they were there. But I didn't know your mother was there.'

Mrs Friedman glared at me. 'You should have known. She's my mother and you should have visited her.'

An old lady limped in our direction. Grabbing her arm, my accuser turned away from me. 'Come along, Mother,' she said. 'I've spent quite enough time with the rabbi who didn't come to visit you.'

On another occasion one of my mother's friends made an appointment to see me. When she arrived, I could see that she'd been crying. 'Oh, Dan,' she said. 'I'm so glad you're in Denver. All the other rabbis have been so horrid.'

'They have?'

'It's so difficult,' she explained. 'You know Deborah, my daughter, don't you? Weren't you in the same class in High School?'

'No, she came after I left.'

'Well, anyway, she's involved with a non-Jewish boy. And they want to get married. He's a nice boy, really. He's not what Bob and I would have chosen for Deborah, but they seem very happy. Well, the problem is that I'd like them to have a Jewish wedding and no rabbi will perform one.'

I shifted in my chair. 'Listen, Ann,' I said. 'I'd like to help. I really would. But, you see, I can't. I have no personal objection to officiating at a mixed marriage. But I'd be thrown out of the Denver Rabbinical Council if I did. They have a rule that no member can officiate at a marriage between a Jew and a Gentile.'

'So you won't help either.'

'I would if I could,' I explained. 'But I can't.'

'But I thought you were a liberal . . .'

'I am,' I said sheepishly. 'But my hands are tied.'

She looked at me pleadingly. 'I counted on you, Dan.'

There was nothing I could say. Ann became tearful. I handed her my handkerchief. She blew her nose and wiped her eyes. After snuffling a bit she stood up. 'I so much wanted them to have a Jewish wedding. It would have made all the difference to us. I thought religion was meant to help people.'

'I'm really sorry,' I said. I felt helpless and hopeless. I walked her to her car; as she drove away I realized that she had taken my handkerchief with her.

One of my duties at the Temple was to oversee the religion school. Every weekend about hundred students were delivered to the Temple by their parents. In the 1960s, Temple Israel had been influenced by modern trends in education: rather than communicate facts, the emphasis was on experience. Empathy, not information, was the main concern. After five years at the seminary memorizing Hebrew verbs and translating ancient texts, this was a radical departure for me.

I was initiated into this new approach by the head of the religion school, David Gross. A bald teacher in his thirties, he had studied education at the University of Colorado and was anxious to test out the scholastic theories he had learned in a religious context.

On my first Sunday, he expounded his views. Sitting in my office, he smoked a large cigar and explained his ideas. 'You see, Rabbi,' he said. 'In the past Jewish kids were crammed full of facts which they quickly forgot. There just wasn't any point to this kind of education.'

I could see what he meant. But how could pupils know something, if they didn't actually learn anything? I looked puzzled.

'Look, Rabbi,' he went on, 'the important thing is to experience Judaism . . . not just read about it.'

'But what do the students experience?' I asked.

'They live Jewish history,' he retorted. 'Wait until next week and you'll see what I mean.'

The next Sunday there were no formal classes. Instead, all the children were divided into groups: some were told they were to play the part of slave-drivers; others were to be slaves. My role was to be Pharaoh, and I had to put on a sheet and a crown. Instead of building a pyramid the slaves were forced to stack chairs. Sitting on an armchair raised on a podium, I watched the slave-drivers abuse the slaves. After an hour of shouting and stacking, the slaves were told to gather together and discuss how they felt.

Not surprisingly, they were exhausted and angry. Eventually all the students – slaves and slave-drivers alike – sat on the floor, and David told the story of the Exodus. At noon the parents collected their offspring. I took off my sheet and crown and went up to the rabbi's study. It had been a noisy experience; I was glad it was over. Possibly the students had gained some notion of what it was like to be a slave, but I wasn't sure. After all, they only had to stack chairs for an hour, knowing that they would soon go home for lunch. This was hardly what the ancient Israelites endured thousands of years ago.

To my surprise, another responsibility of the rabbi was to join the kindergarten class on a trip to the circus. One Sunday afternoon at the end of my first month at the Temple, a bus picked up all the children plus their mothers. I sat with one of the mothers as the children sang all the way to the circus. When we arrived, the children piled out of the bus and we all went to the refreshment stand. Mothers bought hot dogs, ice-creams and chocolate bars and, loaded with food, we took our seats. As I ate my hot dog, mustard spilled out all over my trousers. One mother, used to such catastrophes, handed me a box of tissues. I cleared up the mustard as best I could. The children loved the clowns, lions and elephants. But what was I doing here? Why was I the only man at this outing? What about all those Hebrew verbs I had learned? Clearly the modern rabbi had joined the ranks of babysitters. Was this a role I really wanted?

Another duty of the rabbi was to institute adult education classes. For some time this task had been neglected in the congregation and this made the job much more difficult. None the less, I was determined to try. Since I had to complete a course on the Book of Ecclesiastes for the seminary, I decided this would be a good subject for study. I put an advertisement for the class in the Temple *Newsletter*, and in the rabbi's column I explained about this book of the Bible. I emphasized that it is one of the shortest books and is controversial in character. Barbara designed a poster which we mimeographed and placed around the Temple. At each service I publicized the class, and at the board meeting I urged members to come.

On the night of the first class the janitor arranged about thirty seats in the assembly hall with a podium as well as a blackboard. At just before eight I looked outside. The parking lot was empty. At eight, still no one had come. The class was due to begin, but I had no students. Finally, at half past eight, one of the older members hobbled into the hall.

'Have I got the right night?' he asked.

'I'm afraid so,' I said.

We both sat down on chairs in the front row. 'Look,' I said, 'you're the only person who's come. Perhaps we should cancel the class.'

'Would you mind teaching me?' he asked.

I was despondent. One student for an adult education class! At the seminary we all had looked forward to imparting what we had learned to our congregants: this was to be one of the most exciting aspects of the rabbinate. Could I really teach one student? I had never considered such a possibility.

'I'm sorry the others didn't come,' the old man continued, 'but I'd really like to learn about the Bible. But of course if you don't want . . .'

'No, no,' I interrupted, 'I'll be happy to teach you. But instead of sitting here, let's go up to my office.'

In the weeks that followed Josh Kaplan and I met together from eight to ten each Tuesday evening. As we read through Ecclesiastes I told him how rabbinic commentators as well as modern scholars had interpreted the book. For me it proved to be an invaluable stimulus to completing my course for the seminary. On the basis of my reading, I wrote several essays which I sent to my teacher. Josh was an attentive listener, and he seemed to have gained something from the time we spent together. Yet the contrast between his solitary car in the Temple parking lot on Ecclesiastes night, and the full to bursting car park on bingo nights depressed me. What was the point of five years of study in rabbinical seminary if my congregation was primarily interested in bingo?

While I was working at the Temple, I received a call from Frank Cohen, one of the congregants who was a state legislator in the Colorado House of Representatives. 'Listen, Rabbi,' he said excitedly, 'I've managed to get you appointed as Chaplain of the House for two weeks. What do you say?'

I had no idea what my responsibilities would be – but it was clear this was an honour. 'That's very kind of you,' I said. 'I'd be delighted.'

'Great,' he said. 'You'll find it fascinating. Now, all you've got to do is give opening prayers every day. But be sure to make them good ones.'

When I told my parents, they were thrilled. It was obvious that this was the sort of role they had envisaged for me. The next week I set off for the state capital and parked in the visitors' car park. I was to meet Bob in the cafeteria. He greeted me heartily, bought me coffee, and together we sat at a small table next to a group of secretaries. 'I'm counting on you,' he said. 'You're the first rabbi who has ever been a Chaplain of the House and probably the youngest Chaplain ever.'

I fished into my pocket to make sure my prayer was there. This was going to be a more nerve-racking experience than I had expected. Just before ten, Bob took me into the legislative chambers and introduced me to the leader of the House. Joe Montgomery was a tall, grey-haired Republican from a small town in the mountains. To my astonishment he was wearing a grey suit and cowboy boots – I had never seen such a combination before. 'Howdy,' he said, firmly shaking my hand. 'Glad to have you here, Rabbi.' Motioning to two seats behind a large raised podium, he explained we would sit there and that he would introduce me before I gave my prayer. 'Don't worry,' he said. 'I'll give you the signal.'

After I was introduced, I launched into my prayer. There was a hush. When I finished, the House came alive: representatives milled around the chambers talking to each other and their assistants. Bob came up to me and slapped me on the back. 'Well done, Rabbi. Just the thing to get them going.' On my way out several representatives congratulated me. I could see this was going to be much more rewarding than congregational life.

During the next two weeks, I met a number of representatives, and at the end of my time a group of Democrats had a dinner party to say goodbye. At dinner was one of the legislative reporters who was anxious to do an interview for the *Denver Post* about me. 'This is a slack time of the year,' he explained. 'I think we could do something big. Our readers will be interested in a story about a twenty-six-year-old Colorado rabbi.' I wasn't convinced, but I readily agreed. Publicity so soon! I had, in all honesty, done nothing to deserve it. The next day the reporter arrived at the Temple with a photographer. He asked me innumerable questions about my background and future intentions. Imitating the leader of the House, I had purchased cowboy boots and wore them.

The following Sunday I woke up early and went to buy a newspaper. On the front page was my photograph and a huge article. I stood in the drugstore reading it. It detailed my upbringing in Denver, my college and seminary career, and my future plans to be a congregational rabbi. It also gave a digest of the prayers I had made in the House. Instant fame – I couldn't believe it! All day the phone rang as members of the congregation and relatives called to congratulate me. In addition, I received a call from the reporter. 'I hope you liked it,' he said.

'It's great,' I replied. 'But I don't think I honestly did anything to merit such attention.'

'Well, you won't believe this,' he continued. 'But that article has appeared across the nation. It's been syndicated, and so far I've heard it's been in newspapers from New York to San Francisco.'

'But why?' I asked.

'Because,' he explained, 'there aren't many rabbis who wear cowboy boots.'

Such public attention was intensified when *Life* magazine listed ten heroes on its back page: these were individuals who had transgressed normal conventions to make a point. To my astonishment, as well as everyone else's, I was included (with a photograph of me in cowboy boots). My parents were elated; I was thrilled. But not everyone at Temple Israel was pleased. The day after *Life* came on the newsstands I had a call from the President.

'I saw your picture,' he began. His tone was harsh. 'Quite frankly,' he went on, 'I don't see why you were included.'

What had caused such hostility? I couldn't understand. 'But I thought you'd be enthusiastic . . .' I blurted out.

'Enthusiastic about what? About your neglect of the congregation?'

'But I've done all my duties,' I countered.

'Yeah, technically. But instead of hanging around the capital, you could have been recruiting new members.'

'You never mentioned that I should do this.'

'It's obvious, Dan. What do they teach you at that seminary?'

'But Bob asked me to be the Chaplain. He actually didn't give me much choice.'

'Why didn't you ask me about it first?'

'I . . . I . . . didn't think you'd mind,' I stammered.

'Well, I do mind. We pay you to be our rabbi, not the rabbi of the state legislature. Quite frankly, Rabbi, I think you're on an ego-trip.'

An ego-trip! What kind of gratitude was this for giving the Temple such good publicity? I was offended. Yet the President did have a point. I adored the adulation. I was delighted to be the centre of attention. It was like my bar mitzvah, but even better.

The next Friday night the congregation was bigger than normal, and there were a considerable number of people there I didn't know. I had become a local luminary, and this had swelled numbers. Afterwards, however, at the Oneg Shabbat, I overheard people whispering about me. The comments weren't always favourable. Some of the members expressed their unease at such widespread press coverage. Like the President, they appeared to think I was using the Temple to further my career rather than serve the members. Was this the result of jealousy? I couldn't be sure.

Dissatisfaction, I learned, was also expressed in other quarters. When I went to my parents' house over the weekend, my mother told me she had run into Rabbi Frankel's wife at the supermarket: she had seen my picture in *Life* magazine, and was openly hostile.

'What did she say?' I asked.

'I don't remember exactly. But she went on about how Rabbi Frankel had served the community for years, and how he deserved public recognition but never seemed to get it. Frankly, I think she thought *he* ought to have been in *Life* rather than you.'

'But what's he done?' I asked.

'That's funny,' my mother said. 'That's just what she said about you.'

During my second month at Temple Israel the Sisterhood was busy organizing its annual fashion show. Every afternoon the planning committee met in one of the classrooms. As the day drew near, I was invited to attend one of these sessions. There were eight members present, including the President, Maxine Rothberg, a large woman in her fifties. She greeted me when I entered and introduced me to the group. I sat down, and Maxine explained why I had been asked. 'Rabbi,' she began, 'we want you to model a tuxedo in the show.' Me? A tuxedo? How flattering – yet I was reluctant. 'Are you sure?' I asked hesitantly.

The women smiled. 'It would be a special attraction,' Maxine said. 'The girls will love it.'

'What would I have to do?' I asked sheepishly.

Bella Miltman, the secretary of the Sisterhood who was in charge of the show, explained: 'All you'll have to do is walk down the cat-walk, turn around, and return to the front of the stage.'

'Cat-walk?'

'That's the long stage models walk down,' Bella explained. 'Don't worry, Rabbi. It's easy.'

I had never been a model before. My classes in seminary had not prepared me for this role. My eczema began to itch. What was I to do?

Maxine leaned forward. 'Please, Rabbi. We're counting on you.'

'OK,' I said. 'But I don't think I'll be much of an attraction.'

Bella beamed. 'Oh yes you will,' she insisted.

When I left the meeting, I heard the ladies giggle. Perhaps I shouldn't have agreed. But that would have led to even more trouble.

On the day of the fashion show I didn't come in to the Temple until after lunch. By that time Maxine and Bella plus the committee had decorated the assembly hall with flowers. The Temple smelled like a florist shop. At the front of the hall workmen had assembled a raised podium and platform extending outwards, covered in a red carpet. Throughout the hall were round tables. The show was scheduled for three, and already Temple members were arriving carrying clothes in large boxes. I went up to my study and put on my tuxedo. I looked at myself in the mirror in the bathroom; at least it was a good fit. On my desk was a red carnation and a note from Maxine: 'Dear Rabbi,' it read, 'please put this in your buttonhole. See you soon, Maxine.'

At two-thirty I went downstairs. No one paid any attention to me; instead those in the fashion show were preoccupied with their own outfits. Bella was flapping among the ladies making sure everyone was properly dressed. Just before three all those in the show assembled in a classroom next to the hall. Some of the women were in evening dresses; others wore mini-skirts. A few were in bathing suits. I was the only man.

We listened as Maxine welcomed all those present. Then tape-recorded music began and the first groups were introduced. I peered out of the door to watch. Those in the audience were wearing afternoon dresses; most looked as though they had just been to the hairdresser. Everyone had been served fruit punch and small cakes. After loud applause, the first group returned, and the second batch of ladies exited. I continued to gape from behind the door. Eventually it was my turn. I followed two ladies who were wearing full ball dresses.

The moment I appeared the audience began to clap. From the back I heard someone yell, 'Come on, Rabbi.' As instructed, I stood on the stage, and then joined my companions and we marched down the cat-walk. We stopped, turned around, and then headed towards the stage. As the music blared the woman on my left, Sadie Rosenthal, slipped as she caught her high heel in a swath of material festooned on the side of the cat-walk. As she tumbled forward, I tried to grab hold of her arm and went down too. There were screams of 'Help Sadie!', 'Help the rabbi!' Fortunately neither of us was hurt, and together we hobbled off the stage and down the steps into the classroom. Was it for this that I had endured five years of rabbinical seminary?

After the fashion show was over, I retreated to my study and changed back into normal clothes. As I started to work on my sermon, I heard a knock on the door. 'Come in,' I said.

The President's wife stepped inside. 'I'm sorry if I'm troubling you, Rabbi,' she said nervously.

I stood up. 'You're not disturbing me at all,' I responded.

Miriam Silversmith was a shapely forty-year-old woman with dyed blonde hair. She had a deep tan, and was wearing a skimpy blue dress. 'I loved your tuxedo,' she cooed.

'Thanks . . .'

'It's a pity that you and Sadie took a fall. Are you both all right?'

'Fine, fine,' I said.

Sitting down opposite my desk, Miriam crossed her legs and took a cigarette out of her handbag. 'Mind if I smoke?' she asked.

I did mind. But what could I do? – she was the President's wife.

Miriam fished into her handbag, took out a gold cigarette lighter, and lit a cigarette. She drew heavily and slowly let out the smoke. 'Rabbi,' she began, 'there's something you ought to know.'

This was a phrase that always made me apprehensive. It was invariably the prelude to the most unpleasant revelations. What had I done this time?

'Your secretary, Barbara, she's been talking to Joel,' Miriam said.

What had Barbara said about me? She seemed friendly – what secrets had she passed on?

'The thing is, Rabbi . . . she's got a crush on you.'

I swallowed. I had never given Barbara any hint I was interested in her. I had gone out of my way to establish a professional relationship. 'I don't understand,' I said. 'She's a nice person, and a good secretary. But honestly I haven't done anything to encourage . . .'

'I'm sure you haven't,' Miriam interjected. 'But she told Bella who told Joel that she sort of hoped you might take her out.'

'And what did Joel say about that?' I asked.

'Well, Joel doesn't want to meddle. But we discussed the situation and came to the conclusion that it wouldn't be a bad idea for you to take Barbara out for a meal some time.'

'But that would make things much worse,' I insisted.

Miriam stubbed out her cigarette in an ashtray. 'The problem is that if you don't do something like this, she might resign. That's what Bella told Joel.'

'Resign?' I blurted out. 'That's ridiculous. Why would she resign if I didn't take her out?'

'Look, Dan,' Miriam pleaded. 'We don't want to lose Barbara from the Temple. She's a good secretary and we don't have to pay her too much. If we got someone new, we'd have to pay double. It wouldn't hurt you to socialize with her a bit.'

'But I don't want to get involved with Barbara,' I protested.

'Nobody's asking you to get involved. Just take her out once or twice while you're in Denver. She doesn't have many dates, and it would be nice for her. See it as a mitzvah.' Miriam stood up. 'Joel asked me to talk to you about this. He thought it would be better coming from me. You'd be doing the Temple a favour.'

What could I do? Fearful that my intentions might be misunderstood, I wrote Barbara a note asking if she'd like to go to a delicatessen near the Temple for lunch on Monday to discuss Temple business. I left it for her in an envelope perched on her typewriter. The next day I came in late. There was a letter on my desk. Inside was perfumed writing paper with the message: 'I'd love to. Sincerely, Barbara.' I wondered if I could charge the lunch to the Temple.

A week after the fashion show, the Temple held a gala bingo evening. The prizes offered were even bigger than usual, and there was to be a grand jackpot consisting of a new Ford donated by one of the car dealers in the Temple. On the evening the parking lot was full an hour before the doors opened, and a crowd of people gathered outside. As I watched from my study, the telephone rang. 'This is Joel,' the President said.

'Hi, Joel. You should see the crowd outside the Temple. It's amazing.'

'I'm coming over soon,' he replied. 'But, look, Rabbi. We want you to call out the numbers for the grand prize and hand over the keys of the car to the winner.'

'You do? But I don't know anything about bingo.'

'There's nothing to it. Joe Blumenthal is going to call out the numbers and he'll tell you what to do.'

'I don't mind coming,' I said. 'But I don't see it's really the rabbi's job to . . .'

'It's been decided. We want you to do it. So I'll see you later.'

At eight the doors opened, and masses of people flooded into the Temple. I had never seen such a crowd there before. Members of the Temple dressed in outfits suitable for a casino directed them to the hall where long tables had been assembled. In the middle was a machine with bouncing, numbered ping-pong balls. Once everyone was seated, Joe Blumenthal reached into what looked like a suction cup and took out the first ball. As he called out the numbers there was a hushed silence (except for the click-click of plastic tabs on the bingo cards). As more numbers were called, excitement mounted. At last a black woman in the corner of the hall called out 'Bingo!'; the monitors rushed into action to check her numbers against those Joe had read out.

As the evening progressed, I wandered around the hall greeting members of the congregation as well as visitors. I also purchased a hamburger and a Coke from a food counter run by the Sisterhood. Eventually it was time for the high point of the evening: bingo for the grand prize. I was summoned by Joe Blumenthal, and he announced that the rabbi would call the numbers. Reluctantly I approached the ping-pong machine and stood next to Joe. We shook hands, and then he told me what to do. As the balls bounced against the glass sides of a large container, I reached into a suction cup and called out the numbers of the balls that emerged. A record number of bingo cards had been sold for the jackpot, and I watched as players stared at them and clicked the plastic tabs when I called a number on their card. Tension increased as one number was called after another. Finally a vast woman wearing tight-fitting trousers jumped up. 'Bingo!' she cried. There was laughter, then applause. The numbers were checked and confirmed. 'Will the winner please come forward,' Joe announced. I picked up the keys and handed them over when she stood next to me. 'Let's all give the winner a round of applause,' I said. The hall broke into thunderous clapping. The winner kissed me, and more applause ensued.

The evening had been a great success. Over 10,000 dollars had been raised, including money for the food we had provided. Since all the prizes had been donated, this was clear profit; the money would be used to finance the Temple. The members involved were both elated and exhausted. When the last of the bingo players departed, I helped the Sisterhood clean up. The hall was full of litter; paper cups, plates and plastic knives and forks were scattered everywhere. In addition, cigarette butts filled all the glass ashtrays. At last, at midnight, it was clean and everyone departed.

The next day there was a meeting of the Denver Rabbinical Council. This was a body of all the rabbis in Denver – Orthodox as well as Progressive – which met once a month at the largest Orthodox synagogue. As temporary rabbi at Temple Israel, I had been invited to be a member. When I arrived I sensed the other rabbis were uneasy. I sat next to Rabbi Frankel, who handed me an agenda. Pointing at the first item on the agenda, he shook his head. 'Your Temple is in trouble,' he said.

Under 'Minutes of the last meeting' was the topic: 'Bingo at Temple Israel'. I shuddered; my eczema began to itch horribly. What was this all about?

The chairman of the Denver Rabbinical Council was an elderly Orthodox rabbi who attempted to maintain friendly relations between all the different religious groups in the Denver community. After the minutes were approved, he looked at me. 'Dan,' he began, 'we all know you're here for only a few months. It isn't your fault, what's going on at Temple Israel. We realize you're not in a position to change anything. But we aren't happy about this bingo business.'

Rabbi Frankel spoke next. 'We can't have gambling,' he stressed. 'It sets a bad example for all of us.'

Meekly, I tried to defend the Temple. 'Nobody asked me about bingo,' I explained. 'When I arrived, they put up that big sign in front of the Temple . . .'

'A disgrace!' Rabbi Frankel interrupted.

'Well, I agree, but the Temple wouldn't have bingo if they didn't need the money. And it does seem to work,' I said defensively.

Rabbi Frankel grimaced as I said this. He was becoming increasingly agitated. 'That's no way to raise money!' he exploded. 'Those people would do anything.'

Why was Rabbi Frankel so hostile? He was not making this easy for me. Again, I came to the Temple's defence. 'I'm not sure bingo does much harm,' I said. 'Lots of churches have bingo. And it does bring the members together to do something for the Temple.'

The rabbis looked down at their agenda papers – it was clear I had convinced no one. After a short silence, the chairman explained that he had drafted a letter to the President of Temple Israel which expressed the rabbinical council's condemnation. He passed around copies for all the members. It read:

> As members of the Denver Rabbinical Council we wish to express our disapproval of bingo at Temple Israel. Gambling runs counter to the Jewish tradition and is an affront to our community. We insist you stop this activity immediately. If you do not comply with our wishes, we shall be impelled to expel your congregation from the Rabbinical Council.

'I'm sorry, Dan,' Rabbi Levi said, 'but we have no choice about this matter.'

'But I can't sign this,' I explained.

'We realize that. We know you're here on a temporary basis. Don't worry about it.' Rabbi Levi then passed around the original letter, which all the rabbis signed, and we turned to other business.

Two days later, I received a telephone call at the Temple from the President. Barbara sounded agitated when she put the call through. She knew there was trouble. 'Just what is all this about?' the President fumed.

'What's all what about?' I asked innocently.

'This damn letter from all the rabbis. Don't you know about it?'

I hesitated. 'Well, I do . . . I mean, I was at the meeting when it was discussed.'

'Why didn't you stop them? It's extremely insulting.'

'I tried. But they wouldn't listen.'

'At the very least, you should have told me about it.'

'I'm sorry,' I apologized.

'Much good that will do now. Quite frankly, Dan, I don't see how you can continue at the Temple. After this I think the board will have to reconsider your contract.'

'But I've only got a little over a month left.'

'You may not even have that,' he said. He hung up the phone.

Later that week I again took Barbara to lunch at the delicatessen, and I told her that I had been asked to dedicate the annex at my former congregation in Greenwood. This had recently been built by a local architect, and the ceremony was to take place on a Sunday afternoon in two weeks' time. I knew that this would coincide with the Purim celebration at Temple Israel, but I very much wanted to attend. I emphasized to Barbara that it was very important she inform Religion School teacher David Gross that I wouldn't be able to be at the Temple. Barbara nodded as she scrutinized the menu. 'Listen, Barbara,' I said again. 'This is crucial – you know how sensitive David is about the religion school.'

'OK, OK,' she said. Looking up from her menu, she informed the waitress that she wanted a salami sandwich with french fries and coleslaw.

A fortnight later I drove from Denver to Greenwood. The President met me at the Temple and we had lunch at a nearby hotel. Afterwards, we went to the Temple for service. Nearly the entire congregation was present, and at a party following the dedication ceremony, I saw a number of members whom I had known during my short stay there. I felt like a returning hero, since many of the congregants had seen my photograph in *Life* magazine and asked me about it. Later in the day I drove back to Denver. On my return I went to the Temple. A message was placed prominently on my desk: 'Ring David Gross at home. Urgent.'

I dialled his number. At the other end a gruff voice said: 'Yeah.'

'David, this is Dan. I got a message to call you,' I said.

'Oh, it's you. Damn it, Rabbi, where were you?'

'I was at the Temple in Greenwood,' I explained. Instinctively I knew there was trouble. My eczema began to itch.

'What the hell were you doing there? You should have been at Temple. You were supposed to open the carnival.'

'Didn't Barbara tell you I'd be away?'

'She didn't say anything about it.'

'But I told her about it. Are you sure?'

'Positive. She didn't know where you were, either – I asked her at the carnival. Are you sure you haven't got things mixed up?'

'Honestly,' I said. 'Listen, I'm really sorry about this. Was I supposed to do a lot?'

'Well, you are the rabbi. Everybody wondered what happened. The President especially.'

I sighed. 'Did he say anything?' I asked.

'Not anything you'd like to hear,' he replied.

I tried Barbara at home. When she came to the phone, I told her what had happened. 'Why didn't you tell David?' I asked. 'This is terrible.'

There was silence. Barbara sounded shaken. 'You never said anything about it,' she insisted.

'Yes I did, Barbara. We were at that delicatessen, remember. You were ordering lunch and I told you.'

'No you didn't.'

'Look, Barbara, I have a distinct memory of this: I said, "Don't forget to tell David Gross." I said he was very sensitive about the religion school.'

Defensively, Barbara stood her ground. 'You didn't say a thing. And it's wrong of you to blame me.'

'Barbara, I'm not blaming you. But I did tell you. And now there's trouble.'

'You didn't tell me. And I'm not going to take the blame for your not showing up for the Purim carnival.'

'Come on, Barbara,' I implored. But she hung up. What was I to do?

The next day I got a call from the President. 'Look here, Dan,' he fulminated, 'not only did you miss the Purim carnival, but I understand you're now blaming Barbara for forgetting. Things are bad enough.'

'But I *did* tell Barbara.'

'That's not what she says . . . and quite frankly, Dan, it doesn't really matter if you did. The point is: you didn't show up for the Purim carnival.'

'I went to dedicate the Greenwood Temple annex,' I protested.

'You may have forgotten they don't pay your salary. We do.'

'But they were my congregation.'

'They *were*; now we are.'

Later in the day the President's wife phoned. 'Rabbi,' she began, 'I don't want to interfere, but Joel is very upset. Barbara's threatening to resign over this affair.'

'Not again,' I moaned.

'The best thing is for you to apologize, and then maybe you can take her somewhere for dinner.'

'I've already taken her out to lunch – several times!'

'Yes. I know. But Joel's worried we'll lose her. And a new secretary would cost the Temple a lot.'

'And what do I gain if I do this?' I asked.

'I think it would make everyone feel better,' Miriam said.

'But I wouldn't feel better.'

'I think you'd feel a lot worse if you didn't,' she said.

As instructed, I phoned Barbara and apologized. 'Perhaps there was a misunderstanding,' I hazarded.

'On your part, at any rate,' Barbara snapped.

'OK, but the point is – it wasn't your fault. Perhaps I should have been at the Temple for the carnival rather than at Greenwood.'

'I think you should have,' Barbara blurted.

'Listen, Barbara, we've got to work together until I leave. Let's put this behind us. Why don't you come out for dinner this week and we can discuss what I've got to do in the next few weeks here.'

'Dinner?'

'Yeah, what about Wednesday, just after work? We could go to the pizza place near the Temple.'

'The pizza place?'

'Don't you like pizza?'

'I do . . .' Barbara said. 'But if we're going out to dinner, why not something a bit . . . nicer.'

Pizza clearly wasn't good enough. What was I supposed to suggest? It wasn't a date, after all. 'OK,' I declared, 'what about the little Italian restaurant near the Jewish community centre?'

'I love Italian food,' Barbara said.

'Good. Let's go there. On Wednesday?'

'Wednesday's fine. But couldn't it be a little later? I'll want to change after work.'

'Right. Let's make it later. Would seven-thirty be all right?'

'Seven-thirty's great. You'll pick me up at home?'

'I'll pick you up at home. At seven-thirty.'

'That sounds lovely.'

As I put the phone down, I thought of Jan. Where was she? What was she doing? Was she going out with someone else? I missed her terribly, and thought about her every day. But there was nothing I could do. Here I was, stuck in Denver, forced to take Barbara Bloom out to dinner. Was the rabbinate really worth this sacrifice?

At the end of my stay in Denver the members of the Temple board were anxious to appoint a full-time rabbi. Joel told me that one of the reasons I had been hired was to help them in this process. The first step involved contacting the Director of Rabbinical Placement in Washington; he then informed all Progressive rabbis across the country that Temple Israel was seeking a new rabbi. All those interested in applying for this job were instructed to write to the Placement Office. A shortlist was then drawn up by the Director of Placement and sent to the Temple.

When this list arrived Joel called together a meeting of the board, and I was asked to attend as well. The résumés of all the candidates were circulated before the meeting, and we then discussed each in turn. Because there were ten on the list, the board decided that we should arrange to interview the more likely candidates by telephone. Six candidates were informed that they would be called. At the arranged time, we assembled at the Temple. A telephone with a speaker had been set up, and we gathered nearby to listen. Joel called the first on the list, introduced himself and all the members of the board, and launched into the interview. Joel posed various questions and then each of us took a turn. Most concerned the rabbi's previous experience and why he was interested in coming to Temple Israel. Yet the most vital question dealt with each rabbi's attitude to gambling. Would he mind having bingo at the Temple? Not surprisingly, this question elicited a variety of responses. At the end of the session, we reassembled in one of the classrooms to discuss the results.

'Well, what do you think?' Joel asked.

'I liked the voice of that rabbi from Texas,' one of the members said.

Another disagreed – he thought the Texan rabbi sounded unfriendly. A third opted for the rabbi from Michigan who had a large suburban congregation. One of the younger board members thought the rabbi from California would go down well with the youth group. The youth group representative, on the other hand, thought he sounded too trendy. The treasurer was impressed by the financial acumen of the rabbi from Kansas. The Vice-President liked the fact that the rabbi from Chicago had a doctorate.

At last the President voiced his view: 'I'd go for the one from Kansas – he approved of bingo.'

Silence ensued. The board members looked at each other. Some nodded. The elder statesman broke the silence. 'Joel's right. We've got to have bingo if we're to survive. He seemed a nice enough guy and Kansas isn't too far away. His moving expenses won't be too much.'

'Why don't we ask him and his wife to come to Denver for a visit?' suggested Joel. 'He can meet us, and we can meet him. It won't cost that much, and if we like him – then we've found our rabbi. But if we don't, we can ask one of the others. What's his name anyway? Bergman?'

The next day I arrived at the Temple at ten. Barbara met me on the stairs; she looked agitated. 'Michelle Roberts is waiting to see you,' she announced.

'She is?' I couldn't remember making an appointment to see her. Michelle, an attractive lady in her early forties, served as secretary of the Temple board. She had always been friendly to me, but I sensed she didn't get on well with the President and his cronies. When I entered my office, she was seated in an armchair reading a magazine. 'I'm so glad to see you, Rabbi,' she sighed. 'I had to talk to you after yesterday.'

I sat down across from her. 'What is it?' I asked.

'That meeting was a disgrace! I mean, Joel is trying to force this appointment. We didn't get a chance to discuss anything.'

It was true that there had been little debate. But no objections had been raised to asking Rabbi Bergman to Denver. 'Why didn't you say anything then?' I asked.

'There wasn't an opportunity. Joel just fixed it . . . and all because that rabbi doesn't object to bingo. It's ridiculous. This is a Temple, not a casino.'

'But I'm sure Rabbi Bergman is a good rabbi,' I said. 'He has had lots of experience.'

'That's not the point. We are supposed to be a democratic body. I resent the way Joel managed this.'

What was I to do? In only a few weeks I would be returning to the seminary; I had no desire to become embroiled in Temple politics.

'Well, I don't know what I can do, Michelle.'

'Talk to him, Dan,' she insisted. 'You've got to. You are our rabbi – at least for the time being. And you've got to stop us from being railroaded by Joel and his friends.'

Later that day I telephoned Joel and told him about my

conversation with Michelle. I cautioned him about proceeding too hastily. It was vital, I stressed, that everyone felt they had a say in the appointment of the new rabbi.

Joel exploded. 'Damn it, Rabbi, this is none of your business. We've got to live with the person we appoint – you don't. And I resent the insinuation that I'm trying to push things through.'

I back-pedalled. 'I don't want to interfere,' I said. 'I'm just telling you what Michelle told me. I only want to help.'

'I'm the President, not Michelle,' he ranted. 'And what I say goes. Don't pay any attention to her. The board agreed to invite this Bergman guy, and that's what's going to happen. Just stay out of this, Rabbi!'

A week later Rabbi Bergman and his wife arrived, and the members of the board and their spouses held a dinner for them at the Temple. The food was prepared by outside caterers, and I was placed at the top table next to the rabbi's wife. Rabbi Bergman was asked to say a blessing over the food, and the first course was served. Mrs Bergman was a dark-haired, plump woman in her late forties. As we ate our melon she told me about her three children, now in High School. She then recounted at length how successful her husband had been in the various congregations he had previously served. This narrative continued through the main course. Finally, as we started on the dessert, she asked me about the congregation. What were they like, she wanted to know. What was I to say? Should I tell her about adult education, bingo, the fashion show, the religion school, outings with the kindergarten class, my difficulties with Barbara, conflict with the President? I decided it would be more prudent to keep my mouth shut. 'They're very nice . . .' I mumbled. 'Isn't this cherry pie delicious?' I asked, trying to change the subject.

Rabbi and Mrs Bergman were invited to the President's house after dinner along with several of the Temple officers – I was not included. Several days later, the board reassembled and Joel put forward a motion that Rabbi Bergman be hired with a three-year renewable contract. This was seconded by the Vice-President, and a vote was called. The majority of members supported the motion, but a few, including Michelle, abstained. Temple Israel had a new rabbi!

Before I left for the seminary I phoned Jan. 'Hi,' I said. 'It's Dan. I'm going back to St Louis from Denver, and I wanted to get in touch.'

There was a long pause. 'Dan,' Jan began, 'I've got something to tell you. I'm living with somebody.'

My heart sank. 'You are? Who?'

'He's a guy I met in Boston at the hospital. He's a psychiatrist.'

A psychiatrist . . . I was disconcerted. 'What's his name?' I asked.

'You don't know him. His name is Mickey Milman.'

'Is he Jewish?'

'He is. And, Dan, I'm taking conversion classes.'

Jan was going to become Jewish. This was all too much. 'I was thinking of coming to see you after ordination.'

Jan paused. 'No. I don't think that would be a good idea.'

'Oh,' I said. 'Well, I hope you'll write to me.'

'. . . Yes. I guess.'

As I hung up, I felt completely desolate.

Chapter 5

In Australia: A Rabbi Down Under

While I was at Temple Israel I applied for admission as a PhD student at Oxford and Cambridge. To my delight, I had been offered a place at each university, provisional upon a satisfactory interview. In addition, with Morris's encouragement, I had arranged to be a rabbi during the coming summer in Perth, Australia, before starting my studies in England. Morris had been very keen that I visit his home congregation. The plan was to travel to England for these interviews and then make my way to Australia. The day after I was ordained, I boarded a plane for London, stayed overnight there and the following morning took a train to Oxford.

On arrival I went to the college where the Professor of Theology was a Fellow. Although Professor Hemingstone was hospitable, I had a rather uncomfortable discussion with him about the nature of God's revelation. Sitting in his book-lined study, he asked me: 'And why do you think God revealed himself to Moses on Mount Sinai rather than to Jesus in Galilee?'

Since this was an academic interview, the question was legitimate. Yet I couldn't help wonder whether it had an edge. Was he expressing a degree of Christian antipathy to Judaism? I couldn't tell.

The next day I went to Cambridge, where I met the Professor of Divinity. I had been told by an English friend at the seminary that he was rather eccentric – it was not uncommon, for instance, for him to discourse to his students while sitting under a table. On one occasion it was rumoured he conducted a supervision while taking a bath. Hence, I wasn't sure what to expect. When I arrived at his office, I knocked.

From within I heard a muffled sound. And then a bellow: 'Come in!'

When I opened the door, a dishevelled figure wearing a black gown was looking out of the window. 'Sit ye down,' he said. I removed a pile of books from a chair. There was a long silence. Nearly five minutes passed. What was I to do? I coughed. He at once turned around and stared at me. He grimaced. He moaned. And then he strode out of the room. I wondered whether it might be better to go to Oxford.

Eventually he returned, carrying a pile of newspapers. He thrust one at me. 'Do have a paper,' he said. Behind the Professor came a stout lady carrying a tray with cake and coffee. 'Do you like milk with your coffee?' the Professor asked. 'Have some cake.'

'Uh . . . thanks . . .' I stammered. Professor Rowlandson slumped into his chair. He opened the newspapers, stuffed chocolate cake into his mouth and noisily slurped his coffee. When he finished he stood up. For the next half-hour he told me what I'd be doing when I came to Cambridge. I said nothing as he marched around the room gesticulating, knocking papers off his desk. Eventually, he wound down and thrust his hand in my direction. I was ushered out of the room, and stood in the hallway. 'See you in October,' he mumbled.

Perplexed, I went to the faculty office. The same lady who had brought in the cake was typing a letter. She was the faculty secretary. 'Excuse me,' I said. 'I just had an interview with Professor Rowlandson. I hope it went all right.'

She smiled. 'I'm sure it did. Professor Rowlandson was just saying how much he wanted to have a rabbi as a research student. You'll hear formally soon, but I don't think you should worry.'

I was relieved, but where was I to live in Cambridge? The secretary suggested I contact the University Accommodation Officer, whose office was near Queens' College in the centre of Cambridge. I walked down King's Parade, marvelling at the beautiful buildings. Term had finished, but the streets were full – tourists jostled with professors, clergy with middle-aged women doing their shopping. Finally, I discovered the accommodation office, where I was given the addresses of several flats let by local landladies. Taking a map, I walked down Silver Street. After several blocks I came to a large house called 'Queen's Hall'. I rang the bell and a distinguished, white-haired gentleman came to the door. 'Yes?' he said.

‘I’ve been sent here by the accommodation office,’ I replied. ‘I’m coming in October to study for a PhD in theology, and I need a place to live.’

‘We have a flat available,’ he said. ‘Why don’t you come in?’

I was led down a long entrance hall into a large study. In front of the fire was a sheepdog; books were scattered everywhere. The owner introduced himself as Mr Bowen-Montgomery – he was formerly a civil servant who had retired to Cambridge. He sat in a large wing armchair; I sat opposite on an elegant sofa. ‘What are you looking for?’ he asked.

I explained that I only needed something for myself – ideally, it should have a sitting room as well as a separate kitchen.

‘It might do,’ he said.

I followed Mr Bowen-Montgomery into the drawing room. He unlocked a door and led me into a large room at the back of the house. The furniture was decidedly less grand than in his part of the house, but it looked comfortable; the windows overlooked a vast garden shaded by large trees.

‘I like it,’ I said. ‘How much would it be?’

Mr Bowen-Montgomery looked me over. He paused. ‘It’s quite a big flat for Cambridge; I think £12 a week would be about right.’

I quickly did a mental calculation: £12 a week would be about £50 a month. I could easily afford that. Compared with rents in the United States, it wasn’t that much. ‘What about vacations?’ I asked.

Mr Bowen-Montgomery hesitated. ‘Would you be staying here then?’

‘No . . . I don’t think so. But I’d still like to leave my stuff here.’

‘In that case, it could be £6.’

This seemed more than reasonable. ‘That’s fine,’ I said.

‘Good. But if we’re to hold the flat until October, perhaps we ought to start the rent now. Then you can be sure it will be ready for you when you return.’

I hadn’t reckoned that I would have to start paying immediately. But since it was only half the normal amount I thought I could afford it. ‘That’ll be OK,’ I said.

We returned to Mr Bowen-Montgomery’s part of the house, and I paid him until October. He gave me a receipt and a note guaranteeing that the flat would be mine when I returned. He then walked me to the door and we shook hands. ‘See you soon,’ he said.

On my last day in London I went to the English Progressive

Seminary, which was located in the same building which housed the London Reform Synagogue. This seminary was founded after the Second World War by graduates of the St Louis Progressive Seminary who had emigrated to England. Small in scale, it operated on a shoestring. Most of the teachers were local London rabbis. It had only about fifteen students and, unlike its American equivalent, was not officially recognized by any institution of higher education. None the less, both staff and students were proud of their college.

When I introduced myself to the secretary she took me to meet the Dean of the College, an elderly European rabbi who had written several books about Jewish theology. I had read them at the seminary and I had been impressed. We had a chat about my trip to England and my plans to study at Cambridge. He was about to go to lunch and asked me if I would like to join him. On the way to a nearby restaurant, he told me about his teaching at the college, and the latest book he was writing. Over lunch I told him about my interview with Professor Rowlandson and the flat I had rented. 'If you don't mind my asking, how much are you paying?' he asked.

'Twelve pounds a week,' I said.

He whistled.

'Oh dear,' I said. 'Did I pay too much?'

'It wouldn't be that much in the States,' he replied. 'But here – it's a lot.'

Sheepishly, I confessed that I was also paying half that amount in the holidays just to retain the flat.

The Dean frowned. 'Who did you rent it from?' he inquired.

'He looked respectable enough. He's a civil servant who retired to Cambridge. He didn't look dishonest.'

'The English never do,' he said.

I decided to take my time travelling to Australia to exploit the opportunity to visit Asia, so after my brief stay in London, I set off for a stopover in Athens. I checked in to a small hotel not far from the Acropolis, and walked along the familiar route to the street where I had lived on my junior year abroad. Standing in front of the neighbourhood launderette was the elderly woman, dressed in black, who used to do my washing. She waved at me, and I crossed the street to speak to her. Haltingly I asked her about the students who were currently on the college programme; she told me they no longer stayed in the same flat. It was unnerving to chat to her in modern Greek as I had done years ago – she looked just the same, but so much had changed in my life. No longer was I an outcast among rich college students; I had become a rabbi!

From Athens, I took a flight to Teheran. It was scorchingly hot, and so I wore Bermuda shorts. Everywhere I went, people stared at me – it was obvious that such exposure was seen by them as indecent. After several hours of sightseeing, I returned to my hotel to change into long trousers. Even though the Shah was in power and secularism had deeply affected Iranian society, Islamic customs clearly did not permit such Western habits.

Several days later I flew to New Delhi. At the airport, I got into a taxi cab driven by a Sikh. I told him the name of the hotel where I had made a reservation. Before we set out, another Sikh got into the front. Then two other Sikhs got in the back – I was wedged between them. As we sped along the highway, I was certain this would be my last journey anywhere. Convinced that these four fierce-looking bearded men in their turbans were intent on murdering me, stealing my travellers' cheques and money, and then dumping my body out of the car, I panicked. How could I get out alive? As they chattered in Punjabi to one another, I trembled. What a way to end my rabbinical career even before it had begun! After what seemed an interminable time, however, the taxi driver pulled up at Claridge's Hotel. I couldn't believe my good fortune: I was still alive. I felt terribly guilty for harbouring such suspicions.

India was even hotter than Iran. Once I registered at the hotel, I put on my swimming trunks and jumped into the swimming pool. In the blazing heat, the cool water was refreshing. Yet as I splashed about, it struck me that if I swallowed water in the pool I might come down with some terrible disease. Having survived the ordeal of the taxi ride, would I now die from an innocent swim.

This premonition of an early death appeared likely to be fulfilled on my arrival at Kabul, Afghanistan. I had made a reservation at the Hotel Intercontinental, but as soon as I settled in my room, I came down with an explosive bout of diarrhoea. Convinced that my final hour had come, I sought out the hospital doctor. I was white with terror. What a fate – to die alone in the poshest hotel in Afghanistan! Would my parents come to collect my body? Such thoughts raced through my mind as the doctor looked me over.

'You're fine,' he said. 'Just a case of tummy trouble.'

'Are you sure, Doctor?' I asked. 'I've never had such stomach pains before.'

As he wrote out a prescription, he smiled. 'Don't worry – you'll be fine in a jiffy. Just take some of this straight away. But be careful what you eat. No vegetables or fruit. Only boiled food.'

My next stop was Singapore. This was the last stage of my journey through Asia, and as a special treat I stayed at the Raffles Hotel. On arrival I was given headed writing paper with my name on it. In my room I wrote to several professors at the seminary: I hoped they would be suitably impressed. Later, sitting in the bar drinking a gin sling underneath huge fans, I felt truly cosmopolitan. Yet whenever I thought of Jan now living with a Jewish psychiatrist, I was plunged into gloom.

I was travelling to the other end of the world – would I meet someone who could take her place?

When I arrived in Perth, I was met at the airport by Rabbi Brimstone and his wife Janice. Barry Brimstone was a short, stocky South African who had studied at the seminary in St Louis; he had gone to Australia after his final year and for ten years had served as the assistant to Rabbi Joshua Friedlander. According to my friend Morris, who had grown up in the congregation, Rabbi Friedlander was the most eminent rabbi in Australia and Barry resented being overshadowed. Morris had warned me to be wary of this conflict. Before I left the seminary, he had anxiously requested information about the Perth rabbinical situation – it was his ambition to serve as the third rabbi there.'I'm sending you to spy out the land for me,' he teased. But I sensed this was no joke.

Barry and his wife warmly welcomed me to Australia, and drove me to their house, where I was to stay my first night. The Brimstones lived in a moderately affluent part of the city in a large Victorian house – I was to sleep in Barry's study, where a single bed had been placed alongside a bookcase. I ate dinner with Barry, Janice and their two children and then watched television with the family. At ten everyone went to bed. By myself in Barry's study, I felt acutely lonely. The Brimstones had been exceedingly hospitable, but Perth was so far from the world I had left behind. Perhaps, I mused, it would have been better to spend the summer in Denver, or even in Cambridge. If only Morris hadn't been so anxious that I make this trip!

The next day Barry took me to the flat which the Temple had rented for me. Although it was more than adequate, it had been painted a hideous insipid, bilious green. There was nothing I could do to cover it up. After unpacking, I resolved to spend as little time there as possible. Barry then took me to the Temple, where I met Rabbi Friedlander. He was rotund and jovial with a slight stoop. 'How good of you to come!' he said as he shook my hand. 'I understand you've just been to Cambridge.'

'I was there for an interview; in October I'm going to start on a PhD.'

'Wonderful. Wonderful. Now take off that coat of yours and sit down.'

Rabbi Friedlander sat behind his desk; I was seated across from him in an armchair. Barry had gone off to his office, and we were alone. 'You know,' he said, 'I was at Cambridge too. Trinity College. Just for a year, of course, when I was doing my doctorate in Berlin – just before the war – I spent a year there as a visiting research student.'

'I didn't know,' I said.

'Oh yes. It was so lively, so gracious. All those splendid buildings. And magnificent conversation. You'll love it, too.'

Rabbi Friedlander recounted his exploits during his time at Cambridge, and pointed to his PhD certificate hanging on the wall. 'It's from Berlin, but I wish it was from Cambridge. How lucky you are! A Cambridge PhD! That should go down well in American congregations.' He winked.

The rest of the morning Barry introduced me to the staff at the Temple, and then went through a list of my duties. I was to preach every weekend at one of the three Perth Reform Temples, help in religion school, visit the sick in hospital, and generally make myself useful. Driving me home, he asked about my conversation with Rabbi Friedlander.

'He's very nice,' I said. 'He obviously loved Cambridge. How does he remember all the detail? It must have been forty years ago.'

Barry drove in silence. Just before he dropped me off he spoke: 'I've heard that crap for ten years now. Quite frankly, I'm sick of it. There are other places in the world than Cambridge, you know.'

During my first week at the Temple, Rabbi Friedlander and Barry arranged a meeting to discuss my responsibilities as well as the schedule for the High Holy Days. We were to assemble in Rabbi Friedlander's study. I arrived before Barry, and was ushered by a secretary into his office. Rabbi Friedlander was on the phone – he motioned to me to sit down. 'I'll be happy to be there, Sir John,' he said. 'It will be a great honour.'

When he put the phone down, he explained that he had just been asked to say the invocation at a state occasion when the Queen would be present. He was clearly thrilled. 'Now, Dan,' he announced, 'you must call me Joshua.'

'If you'd like,' I said.

'Have you seen Barry?'

I told him I hadn't.

'He's always late,' he said. 'It's a bad habit . . . be sure to be punctual. A rabbi should always be on time.'

Several minutes later Barry arrived out of breath. 'Sorry,' he apologized. 'I got caught in traffic.'

Barry collapsed into an armchair across from Joshua's desk and fished into his briefcase. He pulled out reams of paper before he found a tattered list. 'I've done a High Holy Day schedule,' he declared.

I looked at Joshua and then at Barry. Who was in charge? Barry handed Joshua and me copies. Joshua looked over the list and scowled. 'Barry,' he said, 'you know I always preach in the Temple on Kol Nidre.'

'I thought it would be nice to have a change,' he hazarded. 'Since Dan is with us, it would be good for the congregation to hear him.'

Joshua glared at Barry. 'There will be plenty of time for that!'

What was I to say? I certainly didn't want to alienate Rabbi Friedlander, but I was reluctant to interfere with Barry's plans. Holding the list, Joshua's hand trembled. 'What's this? Dan is to read the Torah on Yom Kippur as well! Barry, this simply won't do – it's the senior rabbi's role!' Joshua threw down the list on his desk. 'I simply won't have this. I'm sorry, Dan, but I must insist.'

'I don't mind . . .' I stammered. 'Honestly, I just want to help in any way – '

'I don't see why you can't give Dan more of a role in the service,' Barry interrupted.

'It has nothing to do with Dan,' Joshua insisted. 'It's a matter of seniority. And that's all I have to say about this matter.'

The atmosphere was icy after this outburst. After half an hour's discussion, Joshua dismissed us. But as I was about to leave, he called me back. 'Dan,' he said, 'I want to talk to you.' He shut the door and put his hand on my shoulder. 'I'm truly sorry,' he said kindly. 'It's your first day here, and you shouldn't have to hear all this. But you see, Barry has been my assistant for ten years. Ten years of wanting to see me into my grave.'

I listened without speaking. Joshua sat down and stared out of the window. I remained standing. 'It isn't easy waiting to become the senior rabbi . . . but that's no excuse . . . Barry shouldn't drag you into this.'

I mumbled something as he stood up. 'Sorry to flare up. Of course, you must play a full part while you're here. I don't want you to think you're not wanted.'

'I understand . . .' I stammered.

Rabbi Friedlander smiled. 'I'm sure we'll get along splendidly, Dan. I just wanted you to know what's going on.' He opened the door and put his arm around my shoulder. 'Why don't you come over for lunch on Saturday?' he said. 'Come after the service. I'd like you to meet Laura, my wife. And we can have a chat about Cambridge.'

Later in the day Barry drove me to a garage, where I was to collect my car. On the way he discussed my duties, but said nothing about the morning meeting with Joshua. When I got inside the Ford the Temple had rented, Barry knocked on the window. I rolled it down. 'Take care of yourself,' he said. 'Don't forget to drive on the left side of the road. We don't want to send you home in a coffin,' he jested. As I drove off, I wondered just what he meant.

The first week I was at the Temple I was asked by the Perth Jewish Young Adult Club if I would give a lecture at their monthly meeting. After the fiasco of my adult education class in Denver, I decided I ought to choose a lively topic. I suggested: 'The Jewish View of Sex.' In preparation for this event I read several books on the subject and perused the relevant sections of the Code of Jewish Law. From my studies at the seminary I knew that traditional Jewish law was highly prescriptive, but I was amazed by the intricacies of this legislation. In theory Jewish men were to follow a highly regulated, puritanical code of sexual behaviour. All this was light-years away from modern marriage manuals! Did Orthodox Jews really put all this into practice? I had my doubts.

In my confusion I made an appointment to see the rabbi of the largest Orthodox synagogue in Perth. When I entered his house I put on a black yamulkah that I had taken with me. Rabbi Hellman led me into his study and sat down in a large armchair. 'Would you like some tea?' he asked.

'That would be very nice,' I said. 'It's awfully good of you to see me. The thing is: I'm supposed to give a lecture at the youth club, and I thought I ought to check over some details beforehand.'

As I spoke, Rabbi Hellman fiddled with an electric kettle. Eventually it boiled, and he poured water into two mugs with tea bags. He handed me a mug and a plate of biscuits.

Somewhat hesitantly I told him about my topic. 'You see,' I explained, 'I find it hard to believe that modern Orthodox Jews really follow all this law. I mean . . . I know men aren't supposed to touch women. But I've seen Orthodox rabbis kiss their congregants after the service. How can they do this if the law says they shouldn't?'

Rabbi Hellman looked at me intently. 'Are you married?' he asked.

'No, I'm single. I just finished my training at the Progressive Seminary at St Louis.'

Rabbi Hellman smiled. 'How old are you, if you don't mind my asking?'

'I'm twenty-six.'

'That's not so young,' he said.

'Well, I guess not. But the thing is, these laws are a real mystery to me. I was brought up in a Progressive Temple, so I don't know whether Orthodox Jews really follow all these laws or not.'

Rabbi Hellman persisted with his questions. 'You've just arrived, I gather. Have you met any Jewish girls since you've been here?'

'Not really. But I hope I will. Anyway, about this law – is it true that Orthodox Jews really do think about the Torah when they make love? I do find this hard to believe.'

The telephone rang as I was speaking. Rabbi Hellman answered it and for several minutes engaged in an animated conversation about the arrangements for a bar mitzvah. When he put the telephone down, he leaned closer. 'I can understand your interest in this matter,' he said reassuringly. 'You'll feel much better when you get married. There are some lovely girls here – perhaps you'd like me to make some suggestions?'

I left Rabbi Hellman's house with a list of available Jewish girls, but I was no clearer about whether Jewish sex law was followed in the modern world. I only hoped no one would ask me any questions about their contemporary relevance.

On the night of the lecture the hall was packed – about a hundred young men and women crowded in cramped quarters to hear me speak. I lectured from notes for about forty-five minutes; this was followed by half an hour of questions. Afterwards a small group crowded around to pursue the discussion. A curvaceous girl with long red hair offered me some fruit punch. As I conversed with those who stood around, I glanced at her. She looked like a Jewish version of Jan. I was captivated. I hoped she would remain behind until the others left and so I kept talking to her. Eventually we were alone.

'I'm Margie,' she said. 'I really liked your lecture, Rabbi.'

'Call me Dan,' I said. 'Is this your first time here?'

'No, I've been before. But I'm especially glad I came this time.'

'So am I,' I said.

Perth ceased to be a lonely place once Margie became part of my life. Since she worked as a receptionist near the Temple, we were able to have lunch together nearly every day, and she showed me round Perth. On one of her visits to the Temple I introduced her to Barry – he looked disapproving and cut the conversation short. Why couldn't he have been more cordial? Was he jealous that I had such an attractive girlfriend? Several days later, Joshua was in his office and I took Margie around to meet him. He greeted her warmly and later took me aside. 'That's quite a girl,' he said. 'Where did you find her?'

'She was at the lecture I gave for the youth group,' I replied.

'Ah – the one about sex.'

'You heard about it?'

'I came across Rabbi Hellman at a Zionist meeting: he told me you went to see him.'

'It was the oddest conversation – I wanted to find out about the Orthodox view of sex. But instead of answering my questions, he gave me a list of available Jewish girls.'

'So I understand. But you won't need that list now!'

The next Friday when the Perth Jewish newspaper appeared, there was an article about my talk. The headline read: 'Judaism and Sex'. It contained a synopsis of my talk and a brief description of me, plus a photograph. Since I hadn't seen either a reporter or a photographer at the lecture, I was totally surprised. In the evening I was to take the service with Barry at the main Temple. When I arrived, Barry was waiting for me in the hall holding the paper. 'Dan,' he said. 'I think we ought to talk about this – I assume you've seen the article.'

I followed him into his office. Barry sat behind his desk and motioned for me to pull up a chair. 'Look,' he said admonishingly, 'this kind of thing doesn't do the Progressive rabbinate any good. Why did you choose this topic?'

I shifted in my chair. Was this to be an inquisition? 'I can't see anything wrong in lecturing on the Jewish view of sex. It's part of the tradition. Didn't you study about Jewish sex law in the seminary?'

'What we study in the seminary has nothing to do with it. We have difficulties enough with the Orthodox without giving them ammunition against us.'

'But I went to see Rabbi Hellman to make sure I was giving a true picture of the Orthodox view.'

Barry put his head in his hands. 'Why did you do that?'

'Because I thought I ought to get things right . . .'

'Well, you've certainly got everything wrong. Don't you know that Hellman despises anything Progressive?'

'He was very nice to me – he actually gave me the names and addresses of available Jewish girls. And Joshua told me he talked to him at some Zionist meeting. I can't see what you're so upset about.'

'You can't go around giving lectures on such controversial topics – we've got to live here and pick up the pieces. Why didn't you talk to me about this first?'

'Joshua didn't seem to mind.'

Barry shook his head. 'Joshua's not the only one who should be consulted; I'm the rabbi here too. So from now on, make sure you check things out with me too. Now, let's get this service over with.'

Later that evening I took Margie out for dinner at a restaurant near the Temple and told her about my conversation with Barry. 'I've just arrived,' I said, 'and already he's making things hard for me.'

Margie took my hand. 'I think he's just jealous about your being in the paper.'

'But I'm sure he's been in the paper a lot,' I said.

'Probably, but you're new. I expect he doesn't like it.'

'I don't understand it. I get along very well with Joshua.'

'I'm afraid that's part of the problem. Why don't you have something to eat and try to forget about it?'

I looked over the menu, but I didn't feel hungry. Unless I utilized all my diplomatic skills, would my stay in Perth be ruined by Barry Brimstone?

Although I was dismayed by Barry Brimstone's hostility, my relationship with Joshua flourished. Over the next few weeks he asked me to lunch after Sabbath services. His wife Laura was an excellent cook; their hospitality contrasted sharply with Barry's increasing aloofness. After a scrumptious meal on one of these occasions, Joshua took me into his study to show me his doctoral thesis. As he took it from the shelf, he sighed. 'I wish it had been published by a major publisher,' he said. 'It had only a limited circulation.'

'I'm afraid my German isn't very good,' I confessed as I turned over the pages.

'No matter,' he said. 'Now, Dan, I did want to talk to you about your future. Do you know what you want to do after Cambridge?'

I shrugged my shoulders. 'I'm not sure. I've always wanted to be a congregational rabbi, but I don't know where yet.'

'You're not interested in teaching at a university?'

'I don't think so. It's hard to get an academic job.'

'But with a PhD from Cambridge? In the States it would be an advantage.'

'Yes . . . but that's not really my intention. I want to go into the rabbinate.'

'Do you think you'd ever consider coming here . . . I know it's a long way from home, but . . .'

I was puzzled. In my first few days at the Temple, Joshua told me Barry was to be his successor. Had he changed his mind? Was this a serious offer? I hesitated.

'You see,' Joshua went on, 'we might have room for another rabbi.'

'But what about Barry?' I asked.

'Of course Barry is due to take over when I retire. But between us, nothing is certain. The board hasn't made a firm decision. And I don't expect to retire for some years now. So, there are opportunities here – anyway, think it over.'

I was flattered by Joshua's encouragement. The thought of possibly succeeding him did have its attractions – he was the head of a federation of three Perth Temples and the most respected rabbi in the city. I doubted if I could have such an opportunity in the States at my age. But what about Barry? Surely he would stop me if he could – it could become an ugly conflict, and I had no assurance of success. None the less, I was anxious to discuss with my parents the possibility of settling in Australia. The day after my conversation with Joshua I phoned them. After telling them the latest news and hearing about life in Denver, I brought up the subject. 'There's something I want to ask you about,' I said. 'I've been thinking about what I want to do after Cambridge. What would you think of my returning here? Australia's far away, but Perth's an interesting place with a large Jewish community.'

Both of my parents were on the phone. My mother spoke first: 'Do you really like it, Dan?' she inquired.

'Yeah, I do. I've only been here a little while, but I do.'

'It's your choice,' my father said. 'If that's really what you want to do, Mom and I would understand.'

'You really wouldn't mind? I know I wouldn't be close to home . . .'

My mother broke in. 'The important thing is that you're happy. And if that's what makes you happy . . .'

'Well, I don't know yet. I just thought I'd ask.'

There was a silence. 'Dan,' my mother continued, 'if this is what you really want then it's OK as far as we're concerned.'

'Thanks,' I said. 'It's awfully good of you. Anyway, I don't have to make up my mind for a long time.'

'It's good you're thinking of these things,' my father advised. 'Your studies at Cambridge will be over quicker than you think.'

When I put down the phone I felt both heartened and confused. It was generous of my parents not to put up a fuss at the thought of my becoming a rabbi in Australia – most parents would have been appalled by the idea of their son living on the other side of the world. After all, I was their only child. Why did they acquiesce so easily? My mother had indicated quickly enough that she didn't want me to live in Denver when I was at Temple Israel. In that case, her primary concern had not been my happiness but her reluctance to endure gossip. Why did my happiness become relevant only when I considered living far away from home?

When I recounted the conversation with my parents to Margie, she was troubled. 'If I were your parents,' she said, 'I wouldn't be happy to have you so far away.' Margie was voicing my own feelings. Why didn't my parents object? Wouldn't they want me to live nearer? I simply couldn't understand. Previously they had been preoccupied with my development; they still had aspirations for me to become a successful rabbi. But why was I to do this 10,000 miles away from Denver? Over the next few weeks I pondered this dilemma.

One evening Margie and I went to a Greek restaurant. After we ordered dinner, I told her about my perplexity. 'You know, Margie,' I concluded, 'I sometimes think that I'm not their son.'

'You don't think you were adopted?'

'Not really. But what kind of parents would want their only child to live so far away?'

Margie thought about the question. As she ate her Greek salad, she looked consolingly at me. 'This isn't easy for you, is it?'

'I suppose they can't really like me very much.'

'Perhaps,' she said. 'But why? Don't you get along?'

'I always thought I did. But my father and I don't have much in common. And I don't think he ever approved of my becoming a rabbi.'

'And your mother?'

'I always thought we were close. And she didn't mind about my being a rabbi. In fact she was pleased about it.'

This conversation was reminiscent of my interview with Dr Levinson, the psychiatrist, when I was at the seminary. He too had probed my feelings about my parents. But I hadn't thought about it since. Was there something more to his questions than I had thought at the time? As I reflected about this, I mulled over my feelings towards my father. Throughout my upbringing, he had been either indifferent or hostile. We shared no interests; I had none of his scientific leanings; and we didn't look alike. Could it be that I wasn't in fact his son? There had never been a hint of this; but it would help explain his feelings.

When I expressed these doubts to Margie, she reassured me. 'Don't think so much about it,' she advised. 'When you see them again, I'm sure you'll feel better. And they'll be thrilled to have you at home.' I wished I could share her conviction.

While I was considering these problems, I was confronted by another unsettling aspect of the Perth rabbinate. The Temple religion school was headed by a middle-aged schoolteacher, Solomon Finkelstein, who had decided to become a rabbi and was due to study at the seminary in St Louis the following year. Because I was the visiting rabbi, I was assigned to the Confirmation class in his school. At our first meeting, he made it clear that he resented this arrangement, and his hostility increased as the weeks passed. Eventually he stormed into the classroom where I was teaching and demanded that I meet him afterwards. When I entered his office, he was seated at his desk, and I remained standing. 'Dan,' he said, 'I think it would be better if I took over your class.'

'But Joshua told me I was to teach them,' I countered.

'Joshua isn't head of the religion school. I am. And as director, I should be their instructor.'

'But I'm a rabbi,' I objected. 'And a rabbi ought to be in charge.'

Haughtily he announced: 'You may be ordained. But I think of myself as a rabbi, and I will be ordained soon, anyway. So from now on, it's my class.'

When I told Joshua about this confrontation, he was displeased. 'I've told you to teach that class,' he said, 'and that's the end of the matter. I'll let Solomon know, so don't give it another thought.' He took out a piece of paper, wrote a note, put it in an envelope and then sighed. 'These young men are impossible. Barry wants me to retire; Solomon can't bear any competition . . . I fear for the Temple when I'm gone.'

'Is Solomon supposed to come back to the Temple after he finishes at the seminary?' I asked.

'That's the plan at present – but it all depends. How long until you finish at Cambridge?'

'At least three years,' I said.

'Good,' he said brightly. 'That's two years before Solomon will be ordained.'

On Friday night I was to take the Sabbath evening services with Barry; he read the Torah and I preached a sermon. Afterwards I went to his house for dinner. After we finished and the children had been put to bed, he asked if I would like to look at his rabbinical thesis: it dealt with modern educational methods and he hoped to publish it. It had been a long week and as I read the first few pages I yawned. I continued reading, but soon nodded off into sleep. After half an hour I awoke with a start. Barry stopped reading his newspaper and looked at me. 'Is it that boring?' he inquired.

'No, no,' I said defensively. 'It's really interesting . . . I just had too much to eat.'

Barry looked upset. I thought it best to leave, and excused myself. On the way home, I thought about the evening – how could I remedy the situation after dozing over Barry's treasured dissertation? Our relationship, I feared, was at an end.

When I wrote to Morris, I didn't mention Joshua's interest in my returning to Australia; instead I related my feud with Barry and conflict with Solomon. I also told him about Margie. In reply he urged me to be careful not to get involved with synagogue intrigue. 'Keep your head below the parapet!' he wrote. 'And let me know everything that's going on.' The first part was good advice, but how could I do this with Barry and Solomon gunning for me?

In another of his letters Morris asked me to sound out Joshua about the possibility of his returning to the Temple. I was always aware that this was Morris's intention, and I was surprised Joshua had never mentioned Morris in his plans for the future. Several days later, Joshua asked if I would go with him to the hospital on one of his visits. In the car I asked him about Morris.

'He's a friend of yours?'

'We started off at the seminary together, but he stayed in Israel for the third year. So I finished first – but he was my best friend.'

'He was?'

'Yes – but of course he's married now. And I don't know when I'll see him again.'

Joshua frowned. 'I remember Morris very well. You know he grew up in the Temple; I did his bar mitzvah and confirmed him.'

'Did you encourage him to go into the rabbinate?'

Joshua drove in silence. Eventually he spoke: 'I can't say I did. He wasn't the best student, and I could never see him as a rabbi.'

I was surprised. Morris had never given me any hint of this. 'Then you don't expect him to return?' I asked.

'Dan, I don't want you to repeat this to Morris. But I don't think he belongs in Perth.'

'But I'm sure that's his plan . . . I think that's one of the reasons he was anxious that I came here for the summer. He's concerned to know what's going on.'

Joshua glanced at me. 'Are you in touch?' he inquired.

I nodded. After we parked in front of the hospital entrance, Joshua spoke fiercely: 'It would be a tragedy if Barry and Morris took charge of the Temple with Solomon as the third rabbi,' he said. 'I haven't worked all these years for that to happen. You're needed here, Dan . . . don't forget that.'

During my stay in Perth I was invited to visit Melbourne for a weekend to conduct religious services at the Temple there. Joshua and Barry agreed to cover for me, and I booked a flight. I was met at Melbourne Airport by the President of Temple Beth Shalom, who took me to an hotel. He explained that the rabbi would collect me for dinner at about six. At the appointed time Rabbi Sidney Goldfarb, squat, moustachioed and with a foreign accent, arrived at the hotel and drove me to his house. His wife greeted me at the door and led me into the living room. The Goldfarbs' home was decorated in bright colours with abstract paintings on the walls. The furniture was modern in design and knick-knacks were placed everywhere. Mrs Goldfarb confessed that she was a terrible cook; she hoped I wouldn't mind having an omelette. Rabbi Goldfarb recited the Kiddush and a blessing over the meal, and we sat down for dinner.

'You're enjoying Perth?' Sidney asked.

'People have been very nice to me,' I replied.

'And Joshua and Barry? They're looking after you?'

I was reluctant to confess my difficulties with Barry and mumbled an ambiguous reply.

'You know,' Sidney confessed, 'Joshua and I haven't got on for years.'

No one had informed me. Warily I waited for an explanation.

'I'm afraid Joshua is a terrible social climber – he's far too involved with the goyim.'

'But he's very well respected in Perth,' I countered.

'Yes, yes, I know. But that's just the point. His aim is to get a knighthood; Sir Joshua and Lady Friedlander – quite an ambition!'

'Are you sure about that?' I asked.

'No doubt about it. Everyone knows.'

'Do you know Barry very well?' I inquired.

'Barry's got his eye on the main chance, too. But in his case it's not a knighthood – it's Joshua's job.'

I asked if he knew Solomon, too. 'Oh yes,' he replied. 'He was here for an educational conference at the Temple. An aggressive lad – thinks he's already a rabbi. But he'll learn. Now do eat up your omelette. We don't want to be late for services.'

After the service the President asked if I would like to join him and some officers at the Temple for dessert. Rabbi Goldfarb excused himself. 'Have a good time,' he said. 'I won't be at the service tomorrow morning, but do keep in touch while you're in Australia.'

Three of the Temple officers and I went to a hotel in the centre of Melbourne and in the dining room the President gestured to me to sit next to him. I ordered hot apple pie and ice-cream as well as a cup of coffee.

'A very American choice,' the President teased.

'Well, I am an American,' I said, smiling.

'So you are. So you are. But tell us, Rabbi, do you have any concrete plans for the future?'

I explained that I was due to go to Cambridge in the autumn.

'And after Cambridge?' the President asked.

'Well, I'm not sure. But I do want to have a congregation.'

'Would you ever think of coming back here?' asked the treasurer. 'Rabbi Goldfarb is to retire in a few years' time, and we are anxious to find a suitable successor.'

Was this a job offer? It appeared to be one. 'Well, I don't know,' I said. 'Melbourne is delightful . . . but I've only just arrived.'

'No need to make up your mind now,' interrupted the President. 'We just wanted to mention the possibility.'

The next day I was invited to the treasurer's for lunch after the Sabbath service. We drove there in a black Bentley; he lived in a ranch-style house perched on a hill overlooking the city. His wife was a tanned, well-groomed blonde. She wore the largest emerald ring I had ever seen, and throughout the meal she batted her eyelashes in my direction. After lunch the treasurer and I sat on the patio.

'I hope you'll think over what we said last night,' he said.

'I will. It's very generous of you to think of me.'

'Well,' he continued. 'It isn't easy to attract a rabbi to Australia, and since you're already here . . . but I hope you won't be put off by the kind of salary we can afford.' The treasurer took a calculator out of his pocket; he punched it several times and then announced a figure. He was right – it was far below the normal salary of a beginning rabbi. 'I'm afraid that's all we could afford,' he said, 'but of course I haven't included travel and moving expenses. And I think we might even be able to help with housing.'

I hesitated. The treasurer eyed me suspiciously. 'I hope the Temple in Perth isn't also trying to hire you. Have they made you an offer?'

'No, nothing like that,' I replied. 'It's just that I'm not able to make any definite plans at present.'

'Of course. But, Rabbi, we're serious about this. We might even be able to increase the offer. Do let us know before you go back to England.'

After I returned to Perth, I wrote a letter to Morris about my encounter with the officers at the Melbourne Temple. Since I knew Morris was anxious to be hired as a rabbi in Perth, I was reluctant to pursue Joshua's suggestion that I become his assistant; in addition, Barry's hostility added to my hesitation. But taking over as Rabbi Goldfarb's successor posed none of these problems. However, within two weeks I had received a long explosive response from Morris. He was outraged that I would ever contemplate settling in Australia. He appealed to my moral sense: Australia was his home; he had always planned to return. As an American, on the other hand, I had unlimited opportunity as to where I could function as a rabbi. Why, he asked, did I want to stand in his way? It was his aim to work initially under Joshua and Barry, but eventually he intended to take over Rabbi Goldfarb's Temple. In conclusion, he pointed out that I still had at least three more years of study at Cambridge, but he had to get a job in a little less than a year, and he had a wife to support. What he needed at this stage from me was information about the Perth rabbinate, which was the reason he had encouraged me to go to Australia in the first place. He needed help in his career. 'Please,' he wrote, 'don't betray our friendship!'

Morris's letter put an end to any intention I might have had to live in Australia. If I went to Perth as Joshua's assistant, then I would have blocked Morris from being a rabbi there; alternatively, if I became Goldfarb's successor, I would have undermined Morris's long-term plans. The only other option would be to return to Perth as a third rabbi under Barry and Morris when Joshua retired. But such a situation would be intolerable. Thus, when I next wrote to Morris, I told him he had nothing to fear. I would abandon my ambition to come back to Australia after my three years at Cambridge.

While this correspondence was taking place, I received a letter from my parents. They told me they had decided to sell their house and had purchased a lovely bungalow with a large garden in one of the most exclusive parts of Denver. Because they now had less space, they had decided to get rid of all the furniture from my bedroom in their former house. But, they explained, they had bought a sofa bed, which they would put in my father's new study for whenever I returned to Denver. Why, I wondered, were they so determined to displace their only child from their home? My childhood furniture had been sold, and there was no room set aside for me. Did I matter so little in their lives?

Near the end of my stay in Perth, both Margie and I were invited to dinner by the President of the Temple. Margie, however, was reluctant to go. 'Look,' she said, 'you're the rabbi, and he's your boss. I'll just be in the way.'

'That's not true, Margie. He asked you, too. It'll be fun.'

'Not for me.'

'But why?' I asked.

Margie pouted. 'Please, Dan. I don't want to go.'

'But I really want you to come,' I urged.

Reluctantly, Margie gave in, and I arranged to pick her up on the night. I arrived at her house at seven. Although we had been going out all summer, I had never seen her house; we met either at the Temple or after her work finished. But I knew from the address that it was in one of the less affluent parts of Perth. Margie opened the door and asked me in. She was wearing a short red dress and black stockings. I didn't know much about women's clothes, but somehow it didn't look quite right for dinner at the President's. She introduced me to her parents. Her father, short and balding, limply shook my hand. Her mother – a small, faded woman with dyed blonde hair – asked me to sit down. Margie and I sat together on the sofa across from her parents. Mr Gluck spoke first: 'Margie tells me you're going back to England soon.'

'Yes, in just a few weeks,' I replied.

Mrs Gluck smiled brightly. 'Have you had a nice stay in Perth?' she asked.

'Yes, it's been really interesting, especially nice with Margie as my guide.' I looked at Margie – she appeared nervous and apprehensive.

'I think we ought to go,' she said. The Glucks stood up – the interview was over almost before it had begun. As we were leaving, Mr Gluck put his hand on my arm. 'Take good care of her,' he said. 'She's a good girl.'

On the way to the President's house, Margie looked miserable.

'What's wrong?' I asked.

'Nothing,' she mumbled.

I stopped the car. 'Come on . . . what is it? Is it about us?'

She nodded. Tears came into her eyes.

'Look, Margie,' I said. 'I really like you. But I'm going off to Cambridge. I don't think I'll be able to come back to Perth. There isn't a job for me here.'

Margie turned aside. 'I know,' she said.

'And I don't think I'm ready to make a commitment,' I continued.

Margie began to cry. I felt a cad – repeatedly, I had stressed to Margie that I wasn't in a position to settle down. I hoped we could just have a good time while I was in Australia. I was fond of her, but I knew I didn't feel the same passion I had once felt for Jan. I handed her my handkerchief. She wiped her eyes and blew her nose. 'Has my mascara run?' she asked.

'Just a bit,' I said.

By the time we arrived at the President's house, Margie had regained her composure. The President, Charles Schwartz, and his wife, Shirley, lived in a large house in the best suburb of Perth. I rang the doorbell and a maid came to the door. She took our coats and led us into the living room where an elegant group was assembled. Shirley greeted us and introduced us to several people. Margie clung to my hand as we chatted. She looked shy and ill-at-ease, compared with the other expensive-looking guests.

After several minutes Barry and his wife arrived and joined the throng. I recognized a few members of the Temple and introduced them to Margie. About half an hour later, Shirley announced that dinner was ready and we made our way to the dining room. I was seated at the end of the table far away from Margie, who was flanked by two distinguished-looking men. On my right was an exquisite brunette wearing a silk dress and a profusion of diamond jewellery. I glanced down at Margie; she looked shabby and cheap in comparison. As my neighbour nibbled her bread roll, she introduced herself. 'I'm Sylvia,' she said. I told her my name and explained that I was the visiting rabbi at the Temple.

'You're the rabbi?'

Pointing to Barry, who was speaking animatedly to Shirley seated on his right, I said I was one of his rabbinical colleagues. 'But I'm only here for a few weeks more,' I went on.

'Pity,' she said and turned to her neighbour.

I ate my soup in silence. Looking across the table, I caught Margie's eyes. She smiled wanly. She did not look as if she was enjoying herself.

The next day Barry and I met to discuss the High Holy Day services. We sat in his office, and went through the schedule. As we finished, Barry turned the conversation to Margie.

'That girl you took to the President's last night – you've been seeing her a lot.'

'Yeah,' I said.

He looked at me slyly. 'Does she figure in your future?'

I shifted uncomfortably. 'We haven't really made any plans,' I answered.

'You don't intend taking her away, then?'

'It hasn't reached that stage, Barry.'

'Or perhaps you're thinking of returning?'

'No, I don't think so.'

Barry relaxed. He took out a cigarette and lit it. 'Dan,' he said, 'let me give you some advice. You should be careful about that girl.'

What business was this of Barry's? 'Look, Barry,' I said, 'I really don't see why I should discuss Margie with you.'

Barry put his feet up on the desk. 'OK, if that's what you feel – but you really ought to listen.'

What was Barry going to say? I didn't want to hear, but I thought it would look defensive if I walked out. Since I didn't budge, he continued: 'I'm sure she's a nice person . . .'

'She is,' I interjected.

‘But she’s not for you.’
‘Why not?’
‘Did you notice what she was wearing last night?’
‘Yeah,’ I retorted. ‘A red dress.’
‘Dan, it wasn’t suitable for that kind of party. It was at the Schwartzes’ house, after all. She didn’t fit in. I don’t want to sound snobbish, but she’s just not suitable for a rabbi’s wife.’
Who was Barry to make such a judgement?
Barry continued: ‘I’m not criticizing her . . . it’s just that she’s not got the right kind of background. It’s not her fault, but you’ve got to be realistic . . . Look, you’re the son of a doctor; you’re going to Cambridge; you’ve got a good future in front of you. Take my advice – don’t mess around with a girl like that. She wouldn’t help your career.’
‘But why not . . . she’s Jewish.’
‘She may be Jewish. But that’s not enough. A successful rabbi’s wife has got to fit in. Take it from me, Dan, she doesn’t.’
I stood up to go. ‘I think that’s enough, Barry . . .’
‘And, Dan,’ he went on, ‘there’s one other thing: think about why she’s interested in you.’
This was too much. I walked to the door.
‘I really think you ought to hear this,’ he said. ‘I know her parents – they own the laundry where I take my clothes. They’re good people, but they’re not very well off. You’re the only child of an American surgeon – that girl knows a good bet when she sees one.’
Furious, I stomped out and slammed the door. I was incensed. Barry had no right to intrude on my personal life. I resented his comments. I went to my office and sat at my desk. In my anger I reflected on this unsolicited advice, and it struck me that I had once had a similar encounter with my mother about Jan. Both Margie and Jan were classed as unsuitable because they were from relatively poor backgrounds; their interest in me was said to be primarily financial. Could this really be? And what about my reluctance in both cases to make a commitment? I had rationalized my unwillingness with Jan because a rabbi couldn’t marry a non-Jewish wife. With Margie, I had thought it was because I didn’t feel the same way about her as I had about Jan. Was it possible that at bottom I didn’t think that either was good enough for me? Were my motives as crass as that? I was confused and upset.

By the end of my stay in Perth, I was anxious to leave. I knew

I would miss Margie as well as Joshua and his wife, but I longed to begin my studies. At the airport, I kissed Margie and promised to write. The plane journey was interminable – eventually I arrived at Los Angeles and boarded a flight to Denver. I was to stay with my parents for a few days before setting off for Cambridge. My mother was waiting for me at the airport; my father, she explained, was working in the garden. As we drove home, I related my experiences in Australia – there was so much to tell, but so little time. Exhausted, I went straight to bed and slept until just before dinner. During dinner I continued my narrative; throughout, my father looked impatient. As my mother poured coffee, he announced that there was a television programme he didn't want to miss and left me and my mother alone.

'He doesn't seem very interested,' I said indignantly.

My mother didn't speak. After a silence she said: 'How long do you plan to stay?'

'Until Thursday,' I replied.

'It's nice to have you home, Dan,' my mother said meekly.

'Dad doesn't seem to think so,' I declared.

'We love you, Dan. But now that you're grown up, it would be nice if you had a place of your own.'

'What do you mean?' I asked.

'You know . . . wife and family . . .'

'I'm not quite ready to settle down yet,' I said.

'Yes, I know. But you can't always be a student.'

Defensively, I explained the significance of having a doctorate in the rabbinate. My mother listened patiently. 'I agree,' she said at last. 'Dad and I just want the best for you. You should have somewhere where you belong.'

I was annoyed. This was hardly a homecoming. 'You haven't exactly made me feel welcome,' I said. 'I don't even have a room of my own here.' That afternoon I had slept on the sofa bed in my father's study. Everything there had been arranged for his convenience: his desk stacked high with papers was placed in the corner, and the bookshelves were filled with his medical books.

'But you don't live here any more,' she said.

'That's not the point. I am your son – don't you want me here?'

My mother bristled. 'It was your decision to go to Cambridge, you know.'

'That's true . . . but you didn't even want me to live in Denver . . . remember what you said when I asked you about taking over from Rabbi Frankel?'

'How could Dad and I live in the same town with our son as the rabbi?'

This conversation wasn't getting anywhere. The time had come for me to broach the subject that had bothered me all during my stay in Australia. I glared at my mother. 'Am I really your son?' I blurted out.

My mother looked away; her lip trembled. My heart sank. 'So I'm not your son after all! Was I adopted?' I asked.

'No, Dan, you've got it wrong. You're my son. But Dad isn't your father.'

I was shattered. Had my mother had an extra-marital affair? But then who was my father? Before I spoke, my mother explained: 'You're the product of artificial insemination.'

This was not what I had anticipated, and I immediately felt guilty for having suspected my mother. Artificial insemination? Was it possible? Open-mouthed, I listened.

'You see,' my mother explained, 'I didn't get pregnant, and when it was tested, Dad wasn't producing live sperm. So when he was doing a residency in Iowa, we went to the University of Chicago Medical School. That's where you were conceived.'

'Out of a test tube?'

My mother smiled. 'Sort of.'

'And who knows about this? Why didn't you tell me?'

'We kept it secret from everyone, even from my mother. There wasn't any reason to tell. You're our son, and that's all there is to it.'

'But who is my father?'

'We don't know . . . we were only told he was good-looking and a medical student.'

'Was he Jewish?'

My mother shrugged her shoulders. 'I don't know . . . we didn't ask for someone Jewish.'

The next day my mother came out to the garden where I was reading a book. She sat on the lawn. 'Dan,' she said. 'I don't want this knowledge to upset you. I was planning to tell you when Dad died. And I don't want you to discuss it with him, ever. But now you know – don't let it ruin your life.'

'It won't,' I said.

My mother took my hand. 'Perhaps now you can see why having you here is difficult. Dad never really came to terms with your birth. I didn't know he would react that way. It's not your fault; it's his.'

'You mean he doesn't think of me as his son?'

My mother hesitated. 'You are his son; everybody thinks of you that way. But Dad never really accepted it.'

With this revelation I was relieved to depart from Denver. I knew that I could never again be comfortable in my parents' home. Yet at the same time, I felt strangely liberated: no longer would I feel compelled to follow my father's advice or comply with his wishes. No doubt my mother would tell him that I now knew about my birth and he would cease to regard me as his responsibility. And I too would no longer view him as my father – rather, as an irascible old man who always resented my presence and was glad to get rid of me.

My mother drove me to the airport, kissed me goodbye, and I set off for London. On arrival I took a train to Cambridge and went directly to my flat. Mr Bowen-Montgomery was mowing the lawn and he greeted me as I came up the path, lugging my suitcases. 'Did you have a nice journey?' he asked.

'Exhausting,' I said.

'Well, you'll find the flat exactly as you left it . . . except about ten boxes of books arrived and they were put in your sitting room.'

'Thanks,' I said.

Turning to his plants, Mr Bowen-Montgomery snipped off several dead flowers. 'Come and see me when you can . . . then we can settle up your account.'

On the doormat was an envelope written in a spidery script. It was addressed to me – or at least a 'Dan Cona-Sherbet' – who could have written? I ripped it open; it was a letter from Professor Rowlandson. He had arranged to see me two days previously. I left my luggage and set off for the Divinity School. I walked as quickly as I could, filled with dread at the consequences of failing to appear for my first supervision. The sun was shining and the lawns were full of flowers. As I turned into King's Parade, I passed an elderly gentleman loaded down with newspapers. 'Dan!' I heard a voice cry out from behind me. It was Professor Rowlandson. As I turned I saw a tourist approach him and ask for a *Times*. 'It's not for sale!' he bellowed. 'Damn tourists,' he said as we walked together in the direction of the Divinity School. 'Would you like a paper?' he asked.

Chapter 6

An Anglican Rabbi: Being a Rabbi at Cambridge

Professor Rowlandson put his newspapers in a big pile on his desk when we entered his office. 'Sit ye down,' he said. Where was I to sit? Every chair was stacked with papers; I carefully removed a pile from an armchair and sat down. Professor Rowlandson staggered to the window and looked out. 'So good to see you, Dan,' he said with his back to me. For several minutes there was silence. At last Professor Rowlandson spun around, picked up several pencils, and began sharpening them with a penknife. When he finished he held a pencil in each hand and stormed out of the room. Again I was left alone, but this time I waited for nearly half an hour until he returned. In the meantime I wandered around the room looking at the stacks of papers and books. In one pile I found unopened letters, including one I had sent from Australia; another pile consisted of manuscripts, and in a third were half-written letters. How could Professor Rowlandson make sense of it all? I had a sinking feeling that perhaps he couldn't. When I heard a roar in the hall outside I quickly made for the armchair.

'Ah, Dan, there you are,' Professor Rowlandson said as he came into his office chewing both pencils. As he waved his arms, he told me how glad he was to have me back in Cambridge. He asked about my stay in Australia, but before I could answer he launched into a monologue about the Cold War. What did this all have to do with my research? Perhaps he thought I should work on some aspect of this topic. The 'conversation' then lurched to another monologue about science and religion in the nineteenth century. What was the connection? And what did this have to do with me? Eventually the telephone rang, and Professor Rowlandson dismissed me with the suggestion that we should meet in two weeks' time to discuss my work. Work? But what was to be my work? This had not been clarified. Dazed, I staggered out of the Divinity School into Trinity Street. As I walked back to my flat I pondered how I should spend the next two weeks before my next supervision. Should I read about the Cold War, or perhaps look into the nineteenth-century debate about religion and science? Surely Professor Rowlandson didn't think I should write a thesis about either of these topics: it was all most confusing.

When I arrived back at my flat, Mr Bowen-Montgomery was still dead-heading flowers; I waved and he looked up and smiled. I noticed that there was a whisky bottle on the ground near his garden secateurs. It took me hours to unpack my books; when at last I finished arranging my flat, I made my way to the college where I had been assigned as a student member. Penshurst College was about three blocks away, situated in a wooded part of Cambridge. When I entered, I introduced myself to the college porter, who directed me to the Senior Tutor. I knocked on his door and a short elderly gentleman with a clipped British accent opened it. Dr Fitzwilliam was a lecturer in African history and his office was full of masks and African statues. I introduced myself and we shook hands.

'So you're the rabbi?' he said.

I explained that I had just returned from Australia, where I had been officiating in a Progressive congregation. As I spoke, I spotted a very large sculpture of an African man with an enormous penis in the corner of the room. 'Gosh,' I said. 'What's that?'

'Ah that,' said Dr Fitzwilliam. 'It's an Ebo god. A fertility god, actually. Do you like it?'

'Well . . . yes . . . I do.'

'You know,' he said, 'my cleaner's never got used to it. Won't touch it, actually.'

'It's a bit dusty,' I said.

'Ah yes . . . dust thou art and to dust thou shalt return. So it is with us all. I understand Professor Rowlandson is to be your supervisor. How are you getting along?'

I told him about the first meeting and confessed I was perplexed.

'Don't worry,' he assured me. 'It'll be all right. The thing is to find a thesis topic.'

'A thesis topic? Should I have one already?'

'It's a great help, but if you don't, you'll have plenty of time to decide. By the way, would you like some sherry? It's almost time for dinner.'

Sherry? Was this normal? Did the English always drink sherry at six o'clock in the afternoon? If this was the custom, I'd have to get used to it.

In my first week I bought a black academic gown and an old bicycle with a wooden basket. Cycling along the streets I glanced at myself in shop windows; there was no doubt I looked the part of a Cambridge student. At the end of the week I went to my first High Table dinner in the college. Both fellows and research students wore gowns; as we stood around drinking sherry before dinner I thought back to the dinners in the seminary. I wondered what Morris would make of this. After we filed into hall, the Master of the College said a Latin grace; we then sat down to a three-course meal in darkened, candle-lit surroundings. At the end of dinner there was an elaborate dessert, then fruit, nuts and port.

Despite the quaintness and elegance of Cambridge life, I was lonely. I had left Margie thousands of miles behind, and my relationship with Jan was over. In addition, my parents and the familiar world of the United States were far away. Apart from the few people I had met at the college, I had no friends. On my first Saturday night I was acutely gloomy. To relieve my misery I bicycled through empty streets to a disco dance at the Graduate Centre. When I entered the room where the disco was being held, I spotted someone I had met the day before: Friedrich was a Jewish graduate student from Germany who was in Cambridge for the year.

'Hi, Friedrich,' I said. 'You're not dancing?'

In the background music blared – it was hard to hear. 'No,' he said. 'I'm just watching.'

'Do you know anybody?' I asked.

'Just you,' he replied.

I went to the bar, ordered a Coke, and rejoined Friedrich. 'Should I ask someone to dance?' I asked.

'Go ahead,' he said. 'You've got more courage than I do, but then you're an American!'

As I walked to the other side of the room, I surveyed the girls standing near a table littered with drinks and food. I approached a blonde girl wearing a pink sweater; I thought she might be an American. 'Excuse me,' I said. 'I wondered if you might like to dance.'

She looked at me severely, and said in a posh English accent: 'No thanks.'

That was it: my first rejection. I didn't know what to say – this had never happened before. It was downright insulting; the least she could do was dance one dance! I walked back to Friedrich.

'No luck?' he said.

I was embarrassed. I drank my Coke and left. As I bicycled back to my flat, I felt morose and troubled. My eczema itched. Why had I come to Cambridge? Wouldn't it have been much better to stay in the States? I could have gone somewhere like Columbia for graduate work where there were thousands of Jewish girls anxious for a date. Instead I was stranded – for three years – in a foreign country with no family or friends.

As time passed I became increasingly distraught. I had no idea what I should be doing. Term had begun, and I resolved to attend lectures in philosophy and theology. I assumed that I might in this way gain some idea what my thesis topic should be. One of the philosophy dons was a distinguished female academic who had been one of Wittgenstein's pupils. I attended her lectures, but I did not know what she was talking about. Wrapped in a greenish, ancient gown and engulfed in cigar smoke, she lectured on the nature of mind. The students seemed to understand what she said, but I had no idea. Another series of lectures was given by a famous logician. Although they were designed for first-year undergraduates, I was lost.

After two weeks of this confusion, I had my second supervision with Professor Rowlandson. When I arrived at the Divinity School, the secretary accosted me. In the distance I thought I heard the sound of a muffled roar coming from Professor Rowlandson's office. 'I'm sorry,' she said. 'Professor Rowlandson won't be able to see you today.'

'No?' I said.

'It's dreadful, really – but he's in one of his states.'

'Is he OK?' I asked.

'There's nothing wrong, really. I'm sure he'll be fine tomorrow.'

When the secretary departed I walked to Professor Rowlandson's door and listened. It was not my imagination – there really were lion-like roars coming from the room. What, I wondered, was going on?

During the first few weeks of term, the College Rowing Club advertised for members. While in Perth, I had joined the Powerhouse Rowing Club to learn how to row – every week, I had gone out in a small boat with another rower and a coach. It had been exhausting, but I did manage to learn the essentials. Thus, when I saw this notice, I contacted the President of the club. I explained that I had recently learned the rudiments of rowing; he told me to meet him and the other members of the crew at the Boat Clubhouse.

This was located on the river not far from the Commons in the centre of town. I rode there on my bicycle and changed into a tracksuit. As we assembled by the river, the coach rode up on a bicycle carrying a large megaphone. Eight of us carried the boat to the river and were allocated positions. I was put on the left-hand side near the stern. We put in our oars, and the cox gave instructions. We started off slowly. Some of the rowers were experienced; others, like me, were novices. As we rowed, the boat rocked from side to side.

Eventually, we slowed down and the coach shouted from the footpath where he had been cycling. 'All right,' he said. 'That's enough. You all look terrible.' Looking at me, he shook his head. 'You, number seven, you've got to take a much longer stroke.'

We started again. I pushed my oar forward as far as it could go. As I pulled back, the oar stuck in the water (this was known as 'catching a crab'). The boat shook and came to a halt. 'Sorry,' I muttered to the other members of the crew. I pulled my oar back in line, and again we limped off. By the end of the session, we were exhausted – I could hardly walk up the stairs to change. None of us spoke – it was a bone-rattling, humiliating experience. Too tired to ride, I pushed my bicycle to the flat, collapsed in a chair, and went to sleep.

For weeks I tried to master the art of rowing. Some of the original members of the crew dropped out, overcome by exhaustion or research. Others took their place. We were, without doubt, the worst boat on the river. Continually the coach yelled at me from the footpath. 'A bigger stroke!' he shouted into his megaphone. I struggled, but with little success. As term progressed the cox looked depressed and the coach exasperated. Soon we were to race in the Michaelmas Bumps – this involved lining up with other boats on the river and trying to bump the boat directly ahead without getting bumped from behind. The day before the race I cycled to the river. The President of the club was waiting for me. 'Dan,' he said, 'I'm afraid we've got to drop you from number seven.'

This was a shock: I knew I wasn't very good, but no one else was much better. 'Do you want me to row in another position?' I asked.

'I'm sorry,' he said, 'but we need a replacement. Perhaps you can row in the Lent races.'

Despondently, I pushed my bike back across the Commons and sat down on the grass. The sky was grey, and I felt desolate. Nothing seemed to be going right: my eczema itched; I had no notion what I should write a thesis about; I didn't have a girlfriend; and I had been dropped from the college crew. Why had I come all the way to Cambridge to endure such discouragement?

The next day my spirits revived when a letter arrived from the President of the Cambridge Union Debating Society: I had been invited to be a speaker in a debate about the relevance of traditional religion in the modern world. The main speakers included the philosopher A. J. Ayer and the literary critic George Steiner. I was elated! The President explained that he had heard of me from Professor Rowlandson; the Union, he went on, would be pleased to have a rabbi speak on this topic. I wrote back immediately to accept.

On the night, the speakers assembled for dinner at the Blue Boar Hotel, close to the Union building. All the men wore dinner jackets; the women were in long dresses. The main speakers sat next to the President at one end of the table – I was seated near the other and next to a seductive undergraduate named Lavinia. Inevitably, she wasn't Jewish. I had heard of her: she was renowned in Cambridge student circles as a ferocious debater. I wondered if we would be on the same side. During dinner she told me that she was reading theology. I explained that I was one of Professor Rowlandson's research students; I confessed I had as yet no idea what my PhD thesis would be about. We then discussed the peculiarities of all the theology professors – Professor Rowlandson in particular – and then proceeded on to the topic of God's omnipotence. As she ate her duck à l'orange Lavinia expounded her view of divine power. 'If God is omnipotent,' she said, 'then he can do anything.'

'Anything?' I asked.

'Anything,' she insisted.

'That can't be right,' I said. 'It doesn't make sense to think that God could do what is logically impossible, like making a round square.'

'Just why not?'

'Because even God can't do what is absurd.'

'How do you know that? We're only human, but God is beyond

our comprehension: his ways are not our ways – at least that's what Isaiah thought.'

As dinner progressed, we continued this debate, totally ignoring our other neighbours.

What an extraordinary conversation! I had never met anyone like her before. She articulated the most outrageous opinions in the most refined manner while at the same time breathing undiluted sex appeal. She was a formidable opponent. As we walked to the Union, I felt a bit fearful about how I would perform. The President opened the debate in the usual formal manner; the main speakers went first; and then it was our turn. I spoke; I thought I did rather well, but immediately afterwards, my contribution was quietly demolished by Lavinia to uproarious laughter and applause. I didn't relish being ridiculed, and told her so afterwards.

'Sorry,' she said, smiling. 'Do you think I overdid it?'

'Look, Lavinia,' I said. 'I'm new here; I'm an American. I'm not used to this. It isn't very respectful.'

'Oh my,' she giggled. 'You are a cross-patch! Why don't you come back for some coffee?'

Together, we bicycled to her college. Lavinia went first, and I watched her wobble through the empty streets. Even though she was a tremendous debater, her bicycling skills were non-existent. After we deposited our bicycles outside the college, she led me down long Victorian corridors to her room. Over coffee we resumed our discussion of the nature of God, but after an hour I was firmly ushered out. Men were allowed to remain in undergraduate rooms only until midnight. Before I set off, I asked if I could see her again.

Over the next few weeks, Lavinia and I met nearly every day, either in her college or at the university library. In the library tea room, we consumed vast quantities of home-made scones, and then went our separate ways into the stacks. I had at last formulated the topic of my thesis: it would be an exploration of the nature of Jewish petitionary prayer. The point of the investigation would be to discover whether it really worked. Lavinia suggested I should incorporate the findings of a controlled experiment, such as praying for the patients of one hospital but not for those of another. I thought it was more prudent to base the thesis solely on theological reflection. Thus, during this time, I looked for whatever had been written on the subject.

One afternoon Lavinia told me that she would be going to

London for the weekend. 'Why don't you come for tea with Mummy?' she suggested.

'Tea . . . are you sure?'

'Mummy adores Americans,' she said. 'You see . . . several years ago, we had a Rhodes scholar stay in the house. He lived with us every vacation.'

'A Rhodes scholar?' I asked, intrigued.

'Ben's the son of my parents' friends – his father's a lawyer in Virginia. He went to college at somewhere called Tewksburg.'

'You don't mean Tewksbury, do you?'

'Yes, that's right: Tewksbury.'

'I went to Tewksbury.'

'You did? You never told me that. Ben's older than you, you won't have known him. You must come. Mummy will be delighted.'

'What's your mother like?' I asked nervously.

'Like me, only more so,' she replied.

Lavinia's mother lived in an elegant part of London near Kensington Gardens. Apprehensively, I rang the bell of her flat; after several seconds a buzzer sounded to let me in. The entrance hall was lined in oak and the brass surround of the elevator was highly polished. When I arrived at the third floor, I opened the gates to find Lavinia waiting for me. I wore a suit and a floppy brown hat that I had bought in Cambridge. 'Come on in and meet Mummy,' she said. 'And do take off that appalling hat!'

I followed Lavinia down a long passage. At the end, her mother was arranging tea in the kitchen.

'Mummy,' she said, 'this is Dan.'

Mrs Heath was a thinner and slightly more wrinkled version of her daughter. 'Ah . . . the rabbi!' she shrieked. 'Come in, darling, I've heard so much about you.' Handing me a tray filled with tea cups, saucers and biscuits, she guided me into a large sitting room. Lavinia followed, holding a silver teapot.

As Lavinia's mother poured tea, I looked around the room. On the walls were large portraits of distinguished-looking gentlemen in battered gold frames. Scattered throughout the room were pictures of cats, family photographs in silver frames as well as books and magazines. The furniture consisted of a mixture of elegant antiques and hideous plastic chairs and tables.

As Mrs Heath poured tea, she asked me about my studies.

I explained that I was one of Professor Rowlandson's research students.

'He's the one who chews pencils, Mummy,' Lavinia remarked.

'Pencils?' Mrs Heath asked quizzically.

'Honestly, I've seen him do it. Doesn't he, Dan?'

'It's true. Actually two at a time.'

'But surely the dons get enough to eat . . .'

'Of course, Mummy, but it's a habit. He can't help it.'

After we had consumed all the biscuits on the plate, Mrs Heath opened up a tin which contained chocolate cake. 'Now, I hope you'll have some of this cake, Ben,' she said.

'Mummy,' Lavinia sighed, 'it's Dan, not Ben.'

'Oh, I'm so sorry . . . you see Ben lived with us when he was at Oxford. He's an American, just like you.'

'Dan went to Tewksbury, just like Ben,' Lavinia interjected.

'He did? Well, how nice. Do have some of this cake; I bought it at the Prisoners' Aid jumble sale.'

How was I to take it out of the tin? What was I to put it on? And what was I to eat it with? I had never been presented with sticky, chocolate cake without plates, napkins and forks. What was I to do? Uncertain, I reached inside, took out a piece with my fingers, and put it in my mouth. My fingers were gooey with chocolate so I licked them. Was this correct? Was this the English thing to do? I had no idea. In my bewilderment I failed to notice how Lavinia and her mother handled the cake – instead, I was filled with a sense of dread. Had I disgraced myself? This was London; I was from Denver. Lavinia and her mother were posh Gentiles, I was a Jew from the suburbs. Would Lavinia be ashamed of me?

After chatting for about an hour, I explained that I had to catch a train back to Cambridge. I shook Mrs Heath's hand and thanked her for tea. Again, I had a sinking feeling. Was I right to shake hands? The English usually didn't. Was this another faux pas? Lavinia walked me to the door, but before I said goodbye I pulled her into the corridor in front of the lift. 'Look,' I said. 'I'm really sorry if I made a terrible mess of this.'

Lavinia looked puzzled. 'Don't be silly. You were a great hit with Mummy – I could tell.'

'But the chocolate cake – I didn't know how to eat it! I took it with my fingers and then licked chocolate off them.'

Lavinia smiled. 'How else were you supposed to get it out of the tin? And just what do you think you should have done with your chocolate-covered fingers? Wiped them on the curtains? I suppose if you'd had a handkerchief, there could have been an alternative.'

I was profoundly relieved. 'Are you sure . . . I mean I've never had cake without forks and plates and napkins.'

'Poor Rabbi. Life is full of new experiences,' she teased.

Another thought struck me. 'And shaking hands? Was I right to do this? I mean . . . do women shake hands?'

'Poor, poor Rabbi,' she said, kissing me, 'what's a nice Jewish boy like you doing in a place like this?' She shut the door behind me. I heard her laughing down the passage.

For Christmas Lavinia invited me to join her family for lunch. Since nothing was happening at Cambridge during the vacation, I was staying in London in a small bed-and-breakfast hotel. The streets were deserted as I made my way down Oxford Street; only occasionally did I pass anyone. It was bitterly cold as I trudged across Hyde Park in the direction of Mrs Heath's flat. I rang the bell and Lavinia came down to meet me. As we approached the flat, I heard shouts of laughter. In the middle of the passage was Lavinia's brother, Chap, holding a very large glass of transparent liquid. What could he be drinking at noon? 'Chap,' Lavinia said, 'this is Dan.'

Lavinia's brother was a taller, stouter, red-faced version of his sister. 'What about a drink?' he asked.

'And this is my sister, Girl, and her husband Alan. And their daughter Rosie.'

Chap? Girl? Surely these couldn't be their real names. Alan, a bespectacled, tall, balding, middle-aged man in a dark suit inaudibly mumbled a greeting. His dark, curly-haired wife giggled and Rosie stared at me.

Mrs Heath was sitting in the drawing room with a cat on her lap. 'Hello, Dan darling,' she said. Holding up a brown cat by its front paws, she announced: 'This is Mary Magdelene, generally known as Maggers.'

Before lunch the men were instructed to fetch chairs from the flat to put at the dining-room table placed in the passageway. Eventually we sat down to a huge lunch which included turkey, stuffing, sausages, bread sauce, brussels sprouts, roast potatoes and gravy. I was seated between Lavinia and her brother, who consumed vast quantities of red wine. Halfway through lunch he tapped me on the shoulder. 'Hey, Rabs,' he said, 'have some more sausage.' At the end of the meal we all took hold of colourfully wrapped objects known as 'crackers'. I had never seen them before, and wasn't sure what to do.

'Look, Rabs,' Chap explained, 'just pull on the end.' I pulled; we all pulled. Uproarious laughter followed explosions around the table. I was instructed to look inside for a hat and a fortune. As everyone put on their hats, I read my fortune: 'The time is ripe for a change of direction.' I wondered if this was a premonition.

After lunch was cleared, the men were told to help in the kitchen. As he dried dishes Chap had refilled a large glass with more potent-smelling transparent liquid. What could it be? Once all the dishes had been put away, the family reassembled in the drawing room around the piano, which Chap played with much jocularity. First there were traditional carols I had heard only on the radio: 'Hark the Herald Angels Sing', 'Good King Wenceslas', 'Away in a Manger', 'God Rest Ye Merry, Gentlemen'. This was followed by more familiar, less religious Christmas songs: 'Jingle Bells', 'White Christmas', 'Deck the Halls with Boughs of Holly'. And for my sake, the final song was 'God Bless America'. To everyone's astonishment and my embarrassment, I wasn't sure of the words and had to be helped.

The family then sat down to a large tea, and everyone was given presents, including me. Mine were put into one of Lavinia's stockings. I had never had a Christmas stocking before; this was clearly considered an amusing treat. I reached inside to find bars of chocolate, packets of potato crisps, oranges, nuts, paperback books, a pair of socks, drawing pencils and some cologne. I stuffed myself full of Christmas cake, and eventually thanked Mrs Heath and the others for having me to Christmas. Lavinia walked me to the door.

'How was your first Christmas?' she asked.

'Amazing,' I said. 'It was awfully nice of you to have me. Are they always like that? I mean . . . your brother . . . what does he have in that tall glass?'

'Nobody knows,' she replied.

'And Alan, I never understood a word he said.'

'No one ever does. You're lucky if you can hear him.'

'And your sister, Girl. Is that really her name?'

'It isn't like Denver, is it?'

'No,' I said, 'but I think I like it.'

'Well, if I were you,' she said, 'I'd practise the words of "God Bless America". You might also mug up "The Star-spangled Banner". Otherwise my family won't take you seriously.'

Lavinia and I continued to see one another during the rest of the academic year – she frequently helped me with my thesis. At one stage she remarked: 'It's obvious you don't think petitionary prayers work. You need to explain why.'

'Don't you think it might be better to leave it a bit obscure?' I asked.

'Don't be so feeble.'

'But I don't think the examiners will be happy with this conclusion.'

'Your examiners will be even less happy if what you say isn't clear.'

'But Professor Rowlandson is never clear,' I countered.

'He can afford to be obscure; you can't.'

After term ended, I flew to Denver to spend a few weeks with my parents. I wanted to tell them about my experiences, and I thought it would be prudent to let them know about Lavinia as well. I knew this wouldn't be easy. On my first night home my mother served my favourite food; halfway through dinner I brought up the subject of the Heaths.

'I think I ought to tell you about . . . ah . . . my girlfriend,' I said.

My mother looked apprehensive; my father glared at me.

'It's serious?' my mother asked.

'Yes,' I said.

'What's her name, Dan?' my mother asked.

I hesitated. 'It's Lavinia.'

'She has a last name?' my father curtly inquired.

'It's . . . ah . . . Lavinia Heath. Her family lives in London . . . and . . .'

'Oh, Dan,' my mother interrupted, 'I suppose she's not Jewish, is she?'

'Well . . . no . . . she isn't.'

'Dan, you're a rabbi now,' my father rasped. 'It's time you gave up shiksas.'

'Why can't you find a nice Jewish girl?' my mother sighed. 'First it was that ski-bum girl, and then that girl who left her jacket in the closet. And now an English Gentile.'

My father, eyes blazing, cursed. 'Damn it. You'll never grow up. It cost me a lot to send you to Tewksbury, and the seminary. Now I'm paying for Cambridge and you come home and throw this in our faces. I don't want to hear any more of this!' He then stomped out and slammed the door to his study.

My mother was ashen-faced. 'Dan,' she said, 'how can you do this to me?'

'Mother, I'm not doing anything to you or Dad.'

'But you want to be a rabbi, or did.'

'I still do; don't worry. I'll sort things out.'

The next day my mother woke me at seven. 'Dan,' she said, 'Dad is very upset about last night. We're happy to have you in Denver; if it were up to me, I'd have you here for ever. But under the circumstances, I think it would be better if you stayed in a motel.'

I sat up in bed. 'A motel?'

'Yes, there's one nearby. I have phoned them already, and there's a very nice room available. I think we'll have a happier time together this way.'

'But I've just arrived,' I said.

'I know. But otherwise there will be scenes like last night.'

I was beside myself with fury; this was the last straw. 'So you want me to leave?'

'Not leave, Dan, just stay nearby . . . you can come here for all your meals.'

'Thanks a lot,' I said.

As my mother turned to go, she sighed. 'You don't make things easy for yourself, or for us.' And with that she shut the door.

That evening I phoned Lavinia. Her clipped English tones sounded strangely distant and different from the American accents of my parents. I told her about the altercation with my parents and the outcome.

'That's terrible,' she said. 'You should have taken me with you – it would have made all the difference.'

'I'm afraid it wouldn't,' I responded. 'My father will never accept you.'

'He might if we got to know each other.'

Despondently I told her I didn't think this possible. 'He's not easy,' I explained. 'And he knows that I know he's not my real father.'

'But you can't be cast out to a motel,' she insisted.

'At least it'll be more pleasant than sleeping on a sofa bed in my father's study,' I replied.

On Friday night I went to the Temple for Sabbath services, which were taken by Rabbi Frankel's new assistant. At the Oneg Shabbat Rabbi Frankel welcomed me home and took me aside. 'Dan,' he whispered, 'I saw your mother this week. She's very distraught.'

This was a surprise. 'She came to see you?'

'About that girl,' he said.

This was too much. I simply wanted my parents to know about

my life at Cambridge – as a result Jewish Denver would be gossiping incessantly about my love life.

'And just what did she say?' I asked.

'Look,' he confided, 'you've got a wonderful future ahead of you. Don't spoil it. Take my advice: get yourself a nice Jewish girlfriend.'

Before I could reply, an elderly lady approached Rabbi Frankel and engaged him in conversation about her sister who was in hospital. Clearly there would be no chance to continue the discussion.

On my return to London, I described to Lavinia the miserable reception I had received at home: dinners had been eaten in silence; my father had refused to acknowledge my presence; it had been made clear that I would have to use my own savings to pay for the rest of my studies at Cambridge.

'That's shocking,' she said. 'You're their only child.'

I shrugged my shoulders. 'What can I do?'

'Invite them to come for a visit – it'll make all the difference. Once they meet me and my family, they'll calm down.'

I was doubtful – if anything, my parents would be horrified and intimidated by the Heaths. But I had nothing to lose. Eventually, after pleading with my mother, it was agreed that my parents would come to London at the end of the summer. They had planned to go on a cruise to Italy which was sponsored by the alumni association of the University of Pennsylvania; it was arranged they would make a quick visit to London before returning to Denver. I booked a room for one night at the Oxford and Cambridge Club, which I had recently joined, and Mrs Heath wrote to my parents, inviting them to dinner. I offered to meet them at the airport, but my mother insisted they make their own way. They were to settle in at the club and then come directly to Mrs Heath's flat.

On the day I was full of apprehension. What would they make of Lavinia, the Heaths, Maggers the cat, the imposing portraits? At least this time they couldn't argue that Lavinia was after my money; her family was probably richer than mine. When the buzzer rang, I went to the door to greet them. My mother looked even more anxious than I was. I kissed her and shook hands with my father. Before I had a chance to introduce them, my father marched in. 'I'm Bernie, and this is Ruth,' he announced.

'How nice to meet you,' Mrs Heath said, all effortless charm.

My father brushed by and walked into the drawing room. Chap was standing in thc corner holding a tall glass filled with his mysterious transparent liquid. Again my father asserted: 'Bernie here.' My mother trailed behind, looking distraught. Over drinks my mother recounted, at desperate length, the events of their cruise while the Heaths asked polite questions and my father sat in silence. Eventually we sat down to dinner at the dining table in the passageway. Even her best friends couldn't describe Lavinia's mother as a good cook, but she had done her best: we had tinned mushroom soup, followed by home-made curry. Both my parents pushed the food around their plates and ate little.

Over coffee my father engaged Chap in conversation as we all listened. 'Are you aware,' he asked belligerently, 'that the gross national product of this country is the lowest in Western Europe?'

Chap looked at my father blankly. 'Well, Bernie,' he said, 'what do you expect me to do about it?'

My father shook his head. 'England just can't compete in the world market . . .'

'Dear me,' said Chap. 'I'm sure you're right, I'm afraid. I don't exactly contribute to the gross national product myself.'

'What do you mean, you don't? Everybody contributes.'

'I'm a probation officer,' Chap said.

'You went to Cambridge like Lavinia, and you're a probation officer?' asked my mother. 'Couldn't you do something better than that?'

'Well, I like what I do,' said Chap. 'I try to help ex-prisoners.'

'You help prisoners?' my mother asked.

'Well, I also run a hostel for epileptic ex-lifers. It's very selective. Not everyone can live there, you know.'

'Oh do be quiet, Ruth,' my father said. 'We were talking about England's economic performance. You can't keep on one subject – that's the result of going to a streetcar college.'

'Unfortunately a Cambridge education isn't open to everyone.' Chap smiled at the assembled company. 'Do have another drink, Bernie.'

The next day I went to the Oxford and Cambridge Club to say goodbye to my parents. Lavinia thought I should see them alone, so she stayed behind at her mother's flat. My father was paying the bill as I walked into the entrance lobby. I went up to my mother and kissed her. Her eyes were red – it was clear she had been crying. 'Oh, Dan,' she lamented. 'How can you do this to us?'

I had feared just this reaction.

'They're so different. That big apartment, those spooky portraits and the awful food . . .'

'You really should have eaten something,' I protested.

'And that cat.' She wrinkled her nose. 'The whole flat smells.'

'You're just not used to earth litter,' I said.

'And that red-faced brother. What's he called? Chap. What kind of a name is that? He doesn't even have a proper job.'

'He does. It's a very noble job . . . he looks after people who've been let out of prison.'

'Dan,' she sighed, 'you're just not Jewish any more.'

'Come on, Mom,' I said. 'Of course I'm Jewish. I'm a rabbi.'

'You're not Jewish . . . not any more. You've lost your Jewish heart. You've become . . . English.'

'That's ridiculous,' I said. 'I'm still an American.'

'Look at this place,' my mother said, pointing around the lobby. 'It's so . . . Gentile.' She took out a handkerchief and dabbed her eyes. 'I don't know you any more, Dan.'

I hugged my mother, but my father didn't bother to say goodbye – he hailed a taxi, and they both got inside, leaving me standing alone in front of the noble portals of the Oxford and Cambridge University Club.

The beginning of my second year at Cambridge was much more promising than my first. I saw Lavinia nearly every day, and I was making progress with my work. In addition the President of the College Boat Club was anxious that I rejoin the crew – several previous members had finished their degrees, and there were only six members left who were prepared to row. 'Dan,' he pleaded, 'we need you this year. Please don't let us down.' After my disappointment of the previous year, I was elated. I had also been elected President of the Hort Society – the student theological society of the Divinity School. This too was highly gratifying. The final triumph was the news that I had been given a fellowship from the Rabbinical Seminary in St Louis for my studies; now that I had to rely on my own funds, this was a great relief.

None the less, during the first term, there was a calamity about my housing. Mr Bowen-Montgomery informed me that his wife (who never appeared in public) was distressed about Lavinia's presence in my flat. As I came up the gravel path one day, he put down his secateurs and approached me. 'Ah . . .' he said. 'Could I have a word?'

He looked distressed and anxious. 'Rabbi Cohn-Sherbok,' he said hesitantly, 'I'm afraid my wife . . . ah . . . is unhappy about . . . ah . . . the young lady who comes to see you.'

'What?'

'Yes . . . well . . . am I right that you have a visitor?'

'She's not exactly a visitor, Mr Bowen-Montgomery; she's my girlfriend.'

'I see . . .'

'And quite frankly, Mr Bowen-Montgomery, I don't think it's your wife's affair.'

'Yes, I can see that. But . . . the difficulty is that my wife doesn't see it that way.'

Mr Bowen-Montgomery smelled of drink. He looked bleary-eyed and troubled. 'I'm afraid, Rabbi Cohn-Sherbok, that we shall have to terminate your tenancy.'

I was dumbfounded. 'But why? You never told me I couldn't have visitors. You can't just throw me out!'

Mr Bowen-Montgomery shifted uneasily. 'Ah . . . I do see your point. I am sorry, but you'll have to go.'

I was angry and distressed. 'And what if I won't go?' I asked.

'Then . . . the bailiffs will be summoned,' he replied. So saying, he walked slowly back to his garden and began to dead-head the roses.

Where was I to live? Fortunately, the college had a spare room, and I was able to move in the next week. It was much smaller than my previous flat, but Lavinia didn't seem to mind and it was much cheaper. Since I was living in college, I frequently dined at High Table. The conversation was always interesting and the food delicious. As I sat drinking port and eating fruit and nuts in the candle-lit hall, I thought back to my meals with Max Gold and his wife in Brownsville. They were more affluent than any of those seated in hall, yet life at Cambridge was far richer in every other respect. Chatting to the fellows of the college, I wondered how I could ever go back to the fleshpots of the Jewish suburbs.

Although life at Cambridge was very pleasant, I was haunted by my parents' visit. As I pondered how I might bring about some sort of reconciliation, I received a deeply troubling letter from my mother informing me that my father had resolved to disinherit me. I was their only child! How could they do this? I waited until evening to phone her.

'Mom,' I said. 'I just got your letter. What is this all about?'

My mother sounded distant as she explained that my father had just gone to their lawyer to change his will. 'He's decided to leave all his money to the University of Pennsylvania,' she said.

'But what about you?'

There was a pause. 'Well, actually, I'll receive the interest on the capital if Dad dies. But then at my death it will go to the University of Pennsylvania.'

'So it's locked up in a trust fund.'

'I'm afraid so, Dan.'

'But, Mom, even if you get interest on the capital, that won't necessarily be enough.'

'I know – there is a stipulation that I can take some of the capital if I need it.'

'So you're in fact able to touch the capital?'

My mother hesitated. 'Not directly. I'll have to get permission from the trustees.'

'The trustees!' I exclaimed. 'Just who are they?'

'They're appointed by the bank.'

'I've been disinherited, then?'

'It's not my doing, Dan . . . Dad's very angry about that girl.'

I was furious. 'This is financial blackmail,' I hissed.

'It isn't really, you know. Dad was determined to do this no matter what you did.'

When I told Lavinia about my father's intention, she was deeply distressed. 'It's my fault, isn't it?' she asked.

I tried to console her even though I felt miserable myself. 'It would have happened anyway,' I said. 'Once my father knew I knew that he wasn't my real father, he stopped feeling responsibility towards me. It's the way he is.'

'But if you had found a nice Jewish girl he liked . . . ?'

'He might have liked her at first. But it wouldn't take long for him to develop some dislike. Denver is littered with people he doesn't speak to. Anyway, there's another reason why this has happened.'

'What?' she asked.

'It's a way of saving money. Now that my father feels no responsibility for me – he can do whatever he wants with his money.'

'But what about your mother? Surely she can't be happy about having no access to capital if your father died. What if she needs a nursing home?'

'What can I do?' I asked hopelessly.

Lavinia took my hand. 'I'm sorry,' she said.

'I am too. For me, and for you.'

My second year at Cambridge progressed; I became increasingly involved in my research. By the final term I had written nearly half of my thesis. I gave Lavinia each chapter after I finished it, and she tidied up the style. Eventually, I mustered enough courage to give Professor Rowlandson what I had written. I arrived for my final supervision of the year carrying the manuscript. Once I had settled into his study, I handed it over. Professor

Rowlandson was preoccupied with his pencil sharpener as I put it on his desk. 'Ah, Professor Rowlandson,' I said. 'I thought you might like to look at this over the summer. I've written about half of my thesis.'

'Damn thing,' he said. 'Never works when you want it to.'

'Excuse me, Professor Rowlandson. My thesis . . . I thought you might like to see it.'

Professor Rowlandson looked up. 'Delightful, delightful. Have you finished it?'

'No, not yet . . . only half.'

'Well! Well! Now, what have I done with my pencils? Do you see them anywhere? They're in a green box,' he said as we both stumbled about on our hands and knees, among the papers and books littered on the floor. Eventually I looked into the waste basket: there they were, under a pile of newspapers. 'I've found them!' I announced triumphantly.

'Splendid, splendid.'

I passed them over; he took out two and began to sharpen them. 'You say you've written your thesis,' he muttered. 'Very good. Now let me see, what is it about?'

During the summer I received a letter from Morris – he had returned to Perth the previous August as Barry's assistant. Rabbi Friedlander, he explained, had suffered a heart attack and had decided to retire early; thus he and Barry were anxious to have a third rabbi, and Morris was coming to London to interview candidates at the English rabbinical seminary. He (and Judy) were due to arrive in October, and he suggested we get together. I had written to Morris several times since he started in Perth, but this was the first letter I had received – he apologized for this neglect, explaining that the past year had been overwhelming. I thought back wistfully to the days when I had been in Australia and he was in St Louis. Then, he had written frequently. But then of course he had wanted to know what was going on.

In late October Morris phoned me in Cambridge from his London hotel; we arranged to meet at the Oxford and Cambridge Club and then go to dinner at a Chinese restaurant in Soho. When Morris and Judy pulled up in a taxi, I was waiting in the entrance lobby.

I shook hands with Morris and kissed Judy. 'Welcome to London,' I said.

'Well, Dan,' Morris said, 'you've become an English gentleman at last.'

'Hardly,' I said. 'Come on, let's have a drink.'

Over gin and tonic, Morris related the events of the previous year. Barry, he told me, was thrilled to take over as senior rabbi – this was a long-cherished ambition. However, this posed a serious dilemma for Morris: either he had to secure the senior position in Melbourne or remain Barry's assistant.

'If I have to do that,' he announced, 'I'll leave the rabbinate.'

'But what about Rabbi Goldfarb?' I asked.

Morris fidgeted. 'May his teeth drop out! He's due to retire in a few years. I just hope he does.'

'So you'll just have to hang on?'

'Yeah. . . hang on, and wait.'

'Are you sure there won't be any competition? What about the Finkelstein guy? Are you sure he hasn't got his eye on Goldfarb's congregation?'

Morris winced. 'Of course he has. Solomon's a problem. But he's still got four years to go before ordination – that's a long time. And you never know, maybe Goldfarb will have a heart attack, too,' he added charitably.

After drinks we made our way to Soho to my favourite Chinese restaurant. We all ordered prawns on fried rice, and as we waited for the dishes to arrive I told Morris and Judy about Cambridge. Given Morris's reaction to Jan, I thought it sensible not to mention Lavinia; I didn't relish another lecture about the inadvisability of going out with Gentile girls. Eventually the food arrived, but to Morris and Judy's consternation the fried rice was cooked with pieces of pork. Since they resolutely refused to eat pork products, they attempted to remove the bits of pork with their chopsticks. Watching this spectacle, I smiled.

'Look,' I said, 'what you're doing makes no sense. Pork is no more forbidden than shellfish, and the food is getting cold. Why don't you eat the whole thing?' And so saying I ploughed my chopsticks into the fried rice and ate my prawns. Judy was horrified.

'I just couldn't . . . I mean, it wouldn't be right,' she said.

'You've become a real goy,' Morris said as he struggled with the fried rice.

The next day I told Lavinia about this encounter.

'I wish you'd have let me meet them,' she said.

'Morris is supposed to be a liberal, but he does have principles – at least when it comes to non-Jewish girls.' Previously I had told

Lavinia about my relationship with Jan and Morris's chequered romantic history.

'But what about Victoria?' she inquired.

'Well, he was a liberal when it came to going out with her, but it was against his principles to marry her.'

'That's just a double-standard; it's not a principle,' she pointed out.

'Morris gets his principles mixed up,' I said.

'So it's just prejudice then.'

'Prejudice and prudence all mixed together.'

'I would still have liked to have met them.'

'You will,' I promised. 'But not yet.'

My first supervision with Professor Rowlandson was scheduled a week after my dinner with Morris and Judy. I was anxious to have his reaction to what I had written. Did he like it? Was it of an acceptable standard? I was now in my third year, and time was running out. When I arrived at the Divinity School, I encountered Professor Rowlandson in the hall.

'Ah, Dan,' he said. 'So good to see you. Now, I know you're to have a supervision. I'm so sorry . . . but it will have to be another time . . . see Miss Stelling and she'll make an appointment.'

As Professor Rowlandson swept by, his black gown flowing behind him, I said loudly: 'My thesis . . . is it OK?'

Either Professor Rowlandson didn't hear me, or pretended not to. Despondently I entered the Divinity School office; Miss Stelling was typing and looked up. 'I'm sorry to disturb you,' I said. 'But I was supposed to see Professor Rowlandson. He told me to make another appointment.'

'Oh yes. He's off to London. There was a call this morning from the BBC – I think they're doing a programme on the death of God.'

'What's his schedule like?' I asked. 'Could I see him some time this week?'

Miss Stelling looked into a large appointment book. 'He's free on Friday,' she said. 'He has a supervision at three, but you could see him just after lunch – perhaps at 2.15.'

'That's fine,' I said. 'Will forty-five minutes be enough?'

'I'm afraid it will have to be,' she said.

On Friday I arrived feeling nervous and apprehensive. When I knocked on Professor Rowlandson's door, I heard the familiar greeting: 'Do come in.'

Professor Rowlandson was sitting at his desk wrapped in a black gown. He was reading a paperback book entitled *Theology and Atheism*. 'Ah, Dan,' he said, 'So good to see you. Sit ye down.'

I moved several books from a chair. Professor Rowlandson grimaced and fished into a pile of papers on his desk. 'Your thesis, Dan . . . oh dear, now where have I put it?'

After several minutes of rummaging through stacks of papers, Professor Rowlandson inspected the piles of paper littered around his study.

'That's it,' I said, pointing to a pile of manuscripts under a table.

'How right you are. Now, Dan, I think we shall need to do substantial work on this.'

My heart sank. This was just what I dreaded hearing. How bad was it? How much work was needed?

'Quite good on Jewish prayer,' he mumbled, 'but we shall need to do . . . ah . . . some revision.'

Professor Rowlandson opened the manuscript to the first page, and began dictating. He read out the first line with his corrections, and then the second. I had to admit it was an improvement. But this would take for ever. Could it be done before my time was up at Cambridge? These questions raced through my mind as I fiendishly attempted to keep up with Professor Rowlandson's dictation. As the clock struck three, I looked up – we had done one page. Professor Rowlandson looked pleased. 'I say, it's much better, don't you think?' he said.

'Oh yes,' I replied. 'But we're only on page two.'

'So we are, so we are.' Professor Rowlandson picked up a pile of books and strode out of the room; I followed him into the hall. As he turned the corner, he bellowed: 'We shall meet again!'

Later that evening I told Lavinia about my encounter with Professor Rowlandson. 'Did he say anything about the thesis?' she inquired.

'Not exactly . . . just that we'd have to work on it.'

'Did he think it was good enough for a doctorate?'

'He didn't say, exactly. But I don't think he'd want to go over it in such detail if he wasn't hopeful.'

'And you only got one page done.'

I sighed. 'That's not much progress, is it?'

Lavinia took out a piece of paper and a pencil. She did a rough calculation, and announced: 'The half you've given him is 125 pages plus footnotes. Altogether, it should be about 270 pages. Assuming it takes you forty-five minutes a page, it will take about 200 hours.'

'But I'll never have 200 more supervisions,' I said.
'Dan,' she said, 'I think you've got a problem.'

The rest of the Michaelmas term I spent rowing on the river and finishing my thesis. I had become a regular member of the crew – although the coach still shouted at me from the towpath, I ceased to be upset at his frustration.

Throughout the term Lavinia continued to help me tidy up the second half of my dissertation, and I delivered the manuscript to Professor Rowlandson at the final supervision before the winter vacation. We had completed only twenty pages of the first half, and he looked disconcerted to receive another 120 pages. It was now clear we would never complete the sort of revision he initially intended. None the less, I was determined to submit the thesis after three years. I could not afford to stay any longer.

During the first week of the next term, Professor Rowlandson and I met for further revisions. But this time, instead of launching into dictation, Professor Rowlandson questioned me about my conception of intercessory prayer. 'Ah, Dan,' he said, chewing a pencil, 'your thesis . . . ah . . . it finished on rather a disturbing note.'

'You mean I don't think that petitionary prayer is efficacious.'

'Yes . . . well . . . indubitably there are difficulties. Yes indeed. But I do think there are other avenues . . . that is . . . ways around some of the most insurmountable dilemmas . . .'

Professor Rowlandson's expression was tormented; his face grew red as he tried to explore what he referred to as the 'crucible of prayer'. He was clearly unhappy about the outcome of my investigations. Yet, just as he was about to explain his own view, he hesitated. I could see he didn't want to pressurize me into accepting his own opinions; possibly, too, he wasn't exactly sure what he did think. But in any case it was obvious that my conclusion was less than satisfactory.

But would it satisfy the examiners? And who were they to be? When I described Professor Rowlandson's unease to Lavinia, she looked concerned. 'So he doesn't like it!' she mused.

'He didn't put it exactly like that,' I replied defensively.

'Yes, but he didn't like the conclusion. You must see this, Dan. And it's important.'

'But why? He's not going to be one of the examiners.'

'No of course he isn't. But in all likelihood someone like him will be. They will be Christians . . . in all likelihood, clergy.'

'I don't see that should make any difference.'

'It makes all the difference,' she retorted. 'Like Professor Rowlandson, they will be aware of all the theological perplexities of intercessory prayer, but still they'll believe it works.'

'I won't be judged on my religious opinions,' I insisted.

'Don't be naïve,' Lavinia said derisively. 'Of course you will.'

At the end of the second term, Professor Rowlandson and I had completed only thirty-five pages of my manuscript. I had assiduously taken notes of his revisions, and altered the thesis accordingly. But I was determined to have my viva by the end of the academic year. When I told him, he looked horrified.

'Ah, Dan,' he protested. 'I think this would be most unwise. We haven't completed the task, and there's much work to do. It must be made . . . ah . . .'

'More obscure,' I muttered.

'More . . . ah, more . . . subtle,' he declared.

'I don't want to rush things . . .'

'Yes, just that,' Professor Rowlandson interrupted.

'But I do want to finish. I have to finish the project within three years.'

'I do understand . . . I do indeed. But sometimes these things take time. And in this case, time is required. Patience is called for. And restraint.'

'I'm afraid my money will run out at the end of this year,' I said.

'Yes . . . I see. But we must be careful, Dan. We must be cautious.'

I wondered if I could bring up the topic of my examiners. I was anxious to know who they would be. 'Could I ask about the viva?' I hazarded.

'The viva. Yes, indeed. The viva. Do ask.'

'My examiners, have you decided who they will be?'

'This is a matter of great complexity,' Professor Rowlandson said as he strode about his office. 'Indeed . . . the examiners.' He stopped and looked at me. 'But, Dan, this is not for you to decide.'

I turned red. 'I know. I just wondered . . .'

'Ah, right you are. And so you should. I shall have to give it much thought. Now, let us proceed with the dissertation. Where were we?'

'On page thirty-six,' I said.

Seating himself at his desk, he again began to dictate.

Over the spring vacation my thesis was typed by a professional typist, and two copies were bound for delivery to the examiners who had been approved by the faculty. I knew Professor Rowlandson was unhappy about my decision to submit – but he didn't stand in my way. The faculty informed me of the date of the viva – it was to be held at the end of the Trinity term. For the next two months I read my thesis over and over, attempting to anticipate the questions I might be asked. I was apprehensive and fearful. My eczema was terrible.

Eventually the day of my viva arrived – it was to take place in the college of the internal examiner, who was a lecturer in the divinity faculty; the external examiner was a philosopher of religion who taught in a provincial university in the north. Lavinia walked me to the college, kissed me, and wished me good luck. I asked the college porter where Dr Stoneman's rooms were located. He walked me across the quad and pointed to a narrow staircase. 'Room 5A,' he announced. 'At the top of the stairs.'

Slowly I made my way up a winding staircase and stood before Dr Stoneman's door. I paused, and pondered what might await me. When I knocked, Dr Stoneman opened the door and smiled. He was wearing a dog collar and a Harris tweed jacket. 'Come in,' he said.

Dr Stoneman's room was in the oldest part of the college – it was overlooked by Elizabethan towers and looked down on the college quad. In the drawing room was an elderly clergyman wearing a dark suit. I knew of his work but had never met him before. 'This is Professor Williams,' he said.

Professor Williams stood up and we shook hands. I sat in a comfortable armchair and took my thesis out of a briefcase. Dr Stoneman and Professor Williams were seated at a large oak table covered with papers, plus two copies of my thesis. I expected the grilling to begin immediately, but instead Dr Stoneman handed me a copy of his new book about the problem of suffering. 'Have you seen it?' he asked.

'I must confess I haven't,' I said.

'I suggest you read it,' Dr Stoneman said. 'I think you might find it of interest.'

This was not the most auspicious beginning – I hadn't read the latest book by one of my examiners. I was so absorbed by my own work that I had failed to investigate my examiners' publications. I feared this would prove to be a tragic error.

Professor Williams then asked me if I had read the work of Charles Hartshorne, the process theologian. Professor Williams went on to point out that his concept of God might be of interest in dealing with the problems connected with intercessory prayer. This was more like a seminar than a viva, and I waited expectantly for questions dealing with what I had written myself. Instead, the examiners asked me to amplify my conception of God. I reiterated some of the points I had made in my thesis about God's omniscience and omnipotence.

Professor Williams then rambled on about the nature of divine causality. Still, no questions were forthcoming about the content of my thesis. I couldn't tell if the viva were going badly or well. Why didn't they want to discuss the issues I had raised? And what about my conclusion?

After an hour had passed Professor Williams at last made some critical comments about one or two minor points in my thesis, and Dr Stoneman added a few of his own.

I was still waiting for a deeper probing of the subject when I realized the viva was over. Dr Stoneman thanked me for coming and Professor Williams said goodbye. No mention was made of whether I had passed or not. I was in a complete quandry. As Dr Stoneman led me out, he again reminded me about his own book. 'It's only been out a few weeks,' he said, 'I think you'll find it helpful.' He shook my hand and, smiling, said: 'Goodbye then.'

In a daze I walked down the stairs, through the college, and into the street. I couldn't make out what had just happened. Both examiners were friendly and there was little criticism of the thesis; we had hardly discussed it. And yet . . . no word had been said about whether it was acceptable or not. I knew that some candidates were told straight away if they passed. Why hadn't they told me? Was this an ominous sign? But if they were unhappy about the thesis, why hadn't they given me the opportunity to defend it?

The day after my viva, I made an appointment to see Professor Rowlandson after lunch. When I arrived in his office he was engrossed in another book about death of God theology. I pushed aside a stack of books from a chair and sat down. 'I wanted to let you know about my viva,' I said.

'Yes indeed,' he said, putting aside the book.

'I think it was all right . . . but I'm not sure.'

Professor Rowlandson fiddled with his pencil sharpener. 'Yes, yes,' he mumbled.

'The thing is, I wasn't asked much about my thesis; the examiners wanted to talk about the nature of God. And they didn't tell me anything.'

Professor Rowlandson picked up a pencil and began to sharpen it. There was a silence. He then sharpened another pencil and began chewing on both of them.

'So,' I continued. 'I think I got the degree. But I'm not sure.'

Professor Rowlandson took a pencil in each hand and began wandering around the room muttering to himself. What could this mean? After several minutes he stopped in front of me and looked down. 'You will hear in time,' he said.

'Yes, but . . . what do you think it all means?' I asked.

Professor Rowlandson stood in front of the window and there was again a long silence. Turning around, he grimaced. 'I think we shouldn't speculate,' he said. 'Now, Dan, what are you going to do next?'

'Well,' I said, 'I'll need to earn some money for next year, and I've been hired as a summer replacement in Durban, South Africa. It's only until after the High Holy Days in October.'

'Good, good.'

'And I wanted to ask if you might be willing to write a reference for me; there was a job advertised in *The Times* for a lectureship at the University of Kent at Canterbury. They need someone to teach Jewish studies.'

'Aren't you going to be a rabbi?'

'Well,' I said, embarrassed, 'I've been increasingly thinking I'm more suited to university teaching.'

'Ah, splendid, excellent!'

'Would it be OK to put you down as a referee?' I persisted.

'Of course. Of course. Now, Dan, the Professor there is a very good friend of mine: John Fieldmouse and I were at Cambridge together. You'll like him very much.'

'But I don't know whether I'll even be interviewed,' I said.

'Ah, I'm sure you shall.' Walking over to his bookshelf, he took down a large volume. 'Dan, the first thing you must do is read this.' It was a systematic study of Christian ethics by Professor Fieldmouse. 'Put your application in without delay. This is good news, indeed it is.' Professor Rowlandson then ushered me out of his office and, smiling, shut the door. I felt more confused than ever.

Several weeks later I had a letter from the University of Kent, inviting me for an interview. This was exhilarating, but I was still anxious not to have had any word about my thesis. I phoned the Divinity School and made an appointment to see Professor Rowlandson. He was free for only a few minutes before his 2.15 lecture. When I entered the Divinity School Professor Rowlandson, wrapped in his gown, was reading the noticeboard.

'Ah,' Professor Rowlandson beamed, 'I know. Indeed I do. I've been in touch with Fieldmouse. You are a good candidate, Dan . . . very good, indeed. You must now give considerable thought to your interview. This is most important. When are you going to Canterbury?'

'Next Thursday,' I said.

'As soon as you hear, I want you to phone me. Ring me at home. Now I must go to lecture on Kant – *The Critique of Pure Reason*. A truly magnificent book. I hope you've read it.' And with a flourish, he mounted the stairs to the lecture hall. I wished I could have asked him about the degree.

During the next week I practised answers to questions I might be asked with Lavinia. She was such a good debater, I wished she could take my place. On the appointed day I took the train to Canterbury and made my way to the university, which was located outside the town, a long taxi ride from the train station. When I arrived at the Dean's office, I announced that I was due to have an interview at three. The secretary looked down her list until she came to my name. 'Oh yes,' she said.

I sat in a chair opposite her desk and waited. It was like the dentist's office. At three the Dean, a white-haired gentleman in a grey suit, called my name. I entered another room where about eight academics were assembled around several tables. I sat in a hard chair in the middle. The Dean welcomed me and introduced the members of the interviewing panel. Next to the Dean was a bald-headed man wearing a Cambridge tie: this was Professor Fieldmouse. I was heartened by the tie. However, to my immediate right was a short, moustachioed academic – the Chairman of the Theology Department – who looked glum and unfriendly. By contrast his presence was unnerving.

The Dean began the interview by going over my curriculum vitae. When he finished, he asked me about my research at Cambridge. I explained that I was Professor Rowlandson's research student, and that I had just had a viva. The topic of my thesis, I explained, was petitionary prayer.

'And what was the point of the thesis?' the Dean asked.

'To discover whether such prayer works,' I replied.

'And does it?' the Dean asked with a sly smile.

I swallowed. 'Well,' I said. 'I don't think it does.'

There was general consternation. The Dean giggled. The Chairman of the Theology Department looked even glummer.

'And just how have you proved that?' asked another member of the interview panel.

'I didn't exactly. The thesis is a theoretical examination – it's really a theological analysis of the concept of prayer.'

'Not a scientific examination?' Professor Fieldmouse inquired.

'I'm afraid not,' I said.

For the next half-hour I explained my views. I didn't intend to be funny, but everyone except the Chairman of Theology reacted with much amusement. I could tell that the interview was coming to an end, but before it concluded the Dean asked if I had any questions for the panel.

'Well,' I said, 'I wonder if you could give me some idea of what the purpose of the degree course is – I mean, what are you trying to accomplish?'

This question caused enormous confusion. The Dean gave a long, rambling reply, only to be contradicted by Professor Fieldmouse. The Chairman then disagreed with Professor Fieldmouse. Finally, the Dean called a halt. He guided me out of the room, and shook my hand. 'I say,' he declared, 'you certainly gave them something to think about.' And giggling, he went back to join the panel.

The next day a letter arrived from Canterbury. I ripped it open – I had been hired! I was thrilled; Lavinia was overjoyed. I couldn't believe it. An academic job in a British university. Immediately I phoned Professor Rowlandson.

'Dan, how did it go?' he asked.

'I just heard this morning – they want me to come.'

'How splendid!' he exclaimed. 'This is marvellous news. I'm so pleased.'

'I am, too. Thank you so much for all your help.'

'How was Fieldmouse?' he asked.

'He didn't say much,' I said. 'But I felt he liked me.'

'I'm sure he did; I'm sure he did. Many congratulations, Dan.'

I was unsure whether to ask Professor Rowlandson anything more about my thesis. I didn't want to spoil things in case he had bad news. But I did wonder: why wasn't anyone letting me know how I'd done? I had just been hired as an academic, and yet I was still in the dark about my dissertation. When, I pondered, would I hear?

In just over a week I would fly to South Africa for the summer before starting my job at the University of Kent – I hated to leave Lavinia behind, but I needed to earn some money. Now that I had a proper job, I was in a position to buy a house and begin adult life. There was so much to do, and so little time to do it!

Chapter 7

The English Rabbinical Experience: An American Among Anglo-Jewry

During my years at Cambridge, particularly after my parents disinherited me, my financial situation was somewhat precarious. I was therefore very lucky to be taken on as a part-time rabbi at the Birmingham Temple. One of the oldest synagogues in the country, its membership was made up of affluent Jews who lived in a leafy suburb of Birmingham. The rabbi of the Temple was Harvey Rowbotham. Born in London, he was ordained a rabbi at the Rabbinic Seminary and went to the Birmingham Temple as an assistant. In his first year, he had married the only daughter of one of the richest and most influential members of the congregation. Five years later, the senior rabbi – a much-loved scholar – retired and settled in Israel, and Harvey took his place.

In my second term at Cambridge, I had been invited to preach at the Birmingham Temple. Afterwards, Harvey invited me to lunch; he lived in a lovely Victorian house filled with splendid antiques and oriental carpets. When we arrived Mrs Rowbotham was in the kitchen arranging the meal; the little Rowbothams were playing in the drawing room. Harvey leaned down and scooped up his son. Sitting in a large armchair with a sherry in one hand and his son in the other. Harvey looked the picture of a family man. He was tall, bespectacled and bearded.

'How's Cambridge?' he asked.

'Fine,' I said. 'But I'm not exactly sure what I'm going to write about.'

'No need to rush,' he said soothingly. 'You know, I was at St John's.'

'Were you? What did you read?'

'Philosophy, actually. Wittgenstein was there during my time. He was utterly astonishing.'

'You were fortunate.'

'Yes . . . yes, I was. Now, Dan, before we have lunch I have a proposition to make.'

'Oh yes?' I said, intrigued.

'This summer Heather and I are going to the Caribbean. I'll need someone to fill in for me. I wondered if you'd be interested.'

I was flattered and enthusiastic. I had been in England only for a short time and already I was being offered a job at one of the best synagogues.

'Gosh,' I said. 'That sounds great.'

'The pay won't be that much . . . but it would give you some experience of English Jewish life. I think you'd enjoy it, and I'd be most grateful.'

'I'd really like to,' I replied.

'Good, good. I'll let the secretary know and he'll write to you at Cambridge.'

At lunch Harvey told me about his years at the seminary and regaled me with stories about some of the staff who had also been my teachers.

'Where were your student pulpits?' I asked.

'I only had one,' he said. 'Jonah, Alabama.'

'I was a rabbi there, too,' I said, laughing.

'Were you indeed? That is a coincidence. I liked it so much I went back every year until I left the seminary.'

'And after that you came here?' I asked.

'Not directly. I worked in Washington for a year for a Third World charity and began studying for a PhD at Georgetown University.'

'I didn't know you had a doctorate,' I said.

'I don't, actually. I couldn't see the point. That's why I came to Birmingham.'

'You don't think it's that important in the rabbinate, then?'

'Of course, it looks impressive – there's no denying that. But in fact nobody pays much attention, and it's impossible to keep up with what's going on in the scholarly world if you're a practising rabbi.'

'So you don't think it's that much help?'

'Frankly, no. But don't let me put you off.'

'You haven't,' I said. But I did feel a bit disheartened. If the senior rabbi at the Birmingham Temple didn't need a doctorate, did I?

In July, after I had returned to England from visiting my parents in Denver, I began work at the Birmingham Temple. Lavinia had an aunt in the city and could spend occasional weekends there. On my first day at the Temple, Rabbi Rowbotham introduced me to the secretaries and other members of staff, including the youth director, Marilyn Carlbach. Although she had been at the Temple for only two years, she was a dominating presence. When I met her she eyed me warily. Later I asked Harvey about her.

'A nice girl,' he said. 'She's from Manchester originally – did a degree in Hebrew studies at the university there and then came to Birmingham to make her fortune!'

'In Temple education?' I asked.

'I'm joking,' he said. 'Actually I think she's looking for a husband. Birmingham's not a bad place to look for one.'

'And so far?' I asked.

'So far,' he said, 'nothing's happened. What about you, Dan?' he teased.

'No, no . . . not me. She's attractive; I don't think she'll have any difficulty finding a man.'

'But not an American rabbi in Cambridge?'

'Nope . . . I'm already booked,' I said.

Before he left for the Caribbean, Harvey outlined my duties for the summer and gave me the key to his office. 'Use it,' he said. 'But please don't spill coffee all over my desk.'

'Thanks,' I replied. 'I promise I won't.'

'And let me know if you're in any deep trouble. You've got my itinerary, haven't you?'

'Yeah. But there's just one question: who's in charge while you're away?'

Patting me on the shoulder, he said: 'You are.'

I was pleased, yet apprehensive. What if something did go wrong?

During my first week, I followed the normal routine. Since it was summer there were few congregants at the Temple. But I did have to teach bar mitzvah candidates, see couples who intended to marry, and conduct funerals. I also came into frequent contact with Marilyn, whose office was down the corridor. At the beginning of every day, she exchanged greetings, but when we came across one another subsequently she didn't speak. I couldn't figure out why she had taken such a dislike to me. On Lavinia's first visit to the Temple, I introduced her to Marilyn; she was even more icy than usual.

Sitting in Harvey's office (which had now become mine), I registered my confusion. 'Why's she so unfriendly?' I asked.

'Difficult to tell,' Lavinia said. 'Probably she's jealous.'

'Of me?'

'Well, you're about the same age, and you've taken over from Harvey.'

'But she's not a rabbi.'

'Not yet.'

'Surely you don't think she wants to be a rabbi?'

'Why shouldn't she want to be?'

'There's only one female rabbi in the world,' I replied. 'And she was just ordained this summer at the Rabbinical Seminary in St Louis.'

'That's no reason why she wouldn't want to be one. The rabbinate isn't a male preserve any more.'

I could see Lavinia's point. Yet I couldn't envisage Marilyn in the role. She was short with long, curly blonde hair. I couldn't imagine her dressed in rabbinical gear wearing the female version of a yamulkah.

'And there's another reason,' Lavinia continued. 'You're not interested in her, and it's obvious she's looking for a husband. Instead you've got a brainy Gentile girlfriend. Are you surprised she's not friendly?'

'Well, what am I supposed to do about it?'

'Nothing. Just do your job and stay clear of her.'

'How can I if our offices are on the same floor?'

Kicking off her shoes, Lavinia came to sit on my lap. 'Just keep your door locked,' she said, 'and you won't have any trouble.'

For my first Saturday-morning sermon I preached to a small congregation of about fifty people, including a sprinkling of visitors to the Temple. Marilyn sat in the front row and loudly joined in the Hebrew prayers and the singing. Throughout, she stared at me – I wondered if there might be some truth to Lavinia's conjecture about her aspirations. After the service, I recited the Sabbath Kiddush in the hall and greeted congregants. The men were dressed in well-cut suits and the women wore smart clothes and tasteful jewellery.

I was somewhat disappointed by the turn-out, and I decided I might be able to attract more members if there were a discussion immediately following the service. The next week I preached a sermon about prayer – I wanted to try out some of the ideas I had been developing in my thesis. When the service concluded with the final benediction, I stepped down from the bimah. There was a murmur from the congregation. 'Ladies and gentlemen,' I said. 'Before we break for Kiddush, I'd like to spend a few minutes giving you a chance to respond to what I've said in my sermon. In my view, a sermon should initiate discussion, and I'm anxious to have your views. Of course if any of you need to leave, please do so.'

A few members excused themselves and departed, but the majority remained in their seats. A hand shot up from the back. A middle-aged lady in a navy-and-white dress, wearing heavy make-up, asked whether I thought there was any point in praying if prayers of intercession don't affect the future outcome of events. I explained that I thought prayer was of great importance – it could deeply affect the life of the person praying. There was thus a real point to petitionary prayer. Yet, I stressed that I believed it was a mistake to think it could alter God's will.

An elderly gentleman in the front raised his hand. 'Rabbi,' he said, 'are you implying that God doesn't exist?'

'Not at all,' I declared. 'I believe in God, but not the kind of God who answers prayer.'

A lively discussion ensued for the next fifteen minutes. When the congregation seemed a bit restive, I called a halt. 'Time for Kiddush,' I announced. And we all filed into the hall. After the Kiddush, a number of members came up to thank me for initiating the discussion.

One of the officers of the Temple patted me on the back. 'Well done,' he said. 'Quite a debate we had in there. I enjoyed it.'

A matronly lady wearing a vast hat with feathers shook my hand. 'You're a brave man, Rabbi,' she said.

She was followed by a member of the youth group, who mumbled thanks and disappeared. At the back of the hall, however, Marilyn stood glaring at me. As the last members departed I went up to her. 'Shabbat Shalom,' I said.

'Shabbat Shalom,' she replied. 'I think we ought to talk, Dan.'

In silence we walked up the stairs to my office. I sat behind my desk while Marilyn sat in an armchair opposite. 'What's wrong?' I asked.

'I don't think your sermon was suitable,' she answered.

'Why not? The service went well – and from the reaction I had everybody enjoyed the discussion afterwards.'

'It was completely inappropriate,' she said.

'Oh come on, Marilyn. Several members told me they liked it.'

'It doesn't matter what they said. They're only being polite. This isn't America, you know.'

'Of course it isn't. But members of the Temple should have a chance to respond to the sermon.'

'Well, I wasn't going to mention it, but now that you have I will. That sermon was appalling. This isn't a theology class – it's a synagogue. You're not supposed to tell everybody about your doubts. You should give them encouragement. If you want to express your opinions – about prayer or anything else – you should do it at Cambridge.'

I was insulted and cross. What had I done to provoke such an outburst? 'Listen, Marilyn,' I said. 'I'm the rabbi until Harvey comes back; you're the youth director. Why don't you stick to education rather than tell me how to run the Temple?'

Marilyn turned crimson and stood up. 'It's clear you can't take any advice,' she said. 'It's your neck, not mine. But I think Harvey should know what's going on.' And with that she slammed the door.

Undeterred by Marilyn's criticism, I continued to conclude the Sabbath-morning services with a brief discussion. Although not all the members were able to stay behind, those who did seemed to relish having the opportunity to express their views. I was pleased to see that the numbers attending the service had increased. None the less, two weeks after my confrontation with Marilyn, I received a long letter from Harvey. He and Heather were having a lovely time on the cruise, he wrote. The food was delicious, the other passengers were great fun. But he went on to say that he had been troubled to receive a letter from Marilyn which was sent to their first port of call. Was it true that I had been stirring up religious doubts among the congregation? Marilyn, he explained, had written a disturbing letter explaining that I had introduced a discussion session after the service in which members of the congregation expressed their disapproval of what I said in the sermon. Had I really tried to discourage the congregation from praying? Did I honestly think that prayer was of no use? He was sure that Marilyn was not trying to meddle in Temple affairs; rather she was simply concerned about the welfare of the congregation. Harvey concluded by asking me to desist from introducing any new practices, and simply concentrate on the tasks which he had outlined for me to do.

When I read Harvey's letter to Lavinia, she was appalled. 'What did I tell you, Dan? That girl is out to get you.'

'So what do I write back?' I asked.

'He's the rabbi. You've got to do what he says. But you should defend yourself.'

'That's the end of the Sabbath discussions, then,' I sighed.

'I'm afraid so.'

'So Marilyn's won.'

'The battle,' Lavinia said, 'but not the war.'

The next Saturday I ended the service and announced that Kiddush would take place immediately afterwards. This caused some surprise: what had happened to the discussion? In the hall several members told me they were disappointed; a few cornered me and asked questions about my sermon. Out of the corner of my eye I saw Marilyn smirking.

As Lavinia suggested, I wrote a letter of explanation to Harvey and sent it to him at his next port of call. Within two weeks a reply arrived. He began by telling me that he had been invited by the Cruise Director to lecture on Jewish history to the other passengers on the ship. There were quite a few Jews on board, and he hoped to have a sizeable audience. One advantage of giving lectures was that their cabin had been upgraded – he and Heather now had a large suite and a good table in the first-class dining room. He then turned to my letter. He was glad to receive it and relieved to hear my explanation of the innovation I had introduced. It sounded like a good idea, he wrote, but given that he had not been present for one of these discussions he preferred that I hold off. Regarding Marilyn, he stressed that she was loyal and helpful; he hoped that she and I could establish a good working relationship.

'Some hope,' said Lavinia, when she read the letter.

During the next few weeks Marilyn and I passed each other silently in the corridor; the only time we met was at services. After one Sabbath service Marilyn came up to me smiling; at her side was a short, curly-haired figure. 'Jacques,' she said, 'this is Dan – he's Harvey's replacement for the summer.'

We shook hands. 'Are you visiting England?' I asked.

'Jacques is living here,' Marilyn explained. 'He's in his final year at the rabbinical seminary.'

In a strong French accent, Jacques told me that he was from Paris, but had come to England since there was no Reform rabbinical seminary in France.

'He's writing a rabbinical dissertation about French Jewry since the war,' Marilyn added. 'And he's doing research this summer at the university library.'

I saw Jacques frequently over the next few weeks; he came to the Temple to meet Marilyn after work. I hoped he would provide a distraction for her – if she had a boyfriend, she'd possibly lose interest in undermining me. When I told Lavinia about this new development, she suggested we ask them out for lunch one Saturday after services.

'But why?' I asked.

'If you're planning to work at the Temple after this summer vacation, you ought to bury the hatchet,' she replied.

'But I'm not wielding a hatchet,' I said.

'Well, Marilyn is. And it's better to try to get along.'

Following Lavinia's advice, I took Marilyn aside after the Kiddush the next Sabbath morning. Jacques, as usual, was at her side. 'Look,' I said, 'why don't you both join Lavinia and me for lunch? We can go to the little Greek restaurant near the Temple.'

Marilyn looked surprised. Turning to Jacques, she asked: 'Is that OK?'

'But yes, of course,' he said.

So it was arranged. After everyone left the Temple hall, I went upstairs to put away my rabbinical gown; Lavinia stayed behind chatting to Marilyn and Jacques. We then set off for the restaurant. When we arrived I was greeted in Greek by Constantine, the waiter – I answered in Greek and we took a table near the window. Looking down the menu, Jacques looked apprehensive. 'I hope you won't mind if I have something vegetarian,' he said. 'You see, I try to avoid non-kosher meat.'

'There's plenty to choose from,' I said. 'Why don't you try the dolmades – they're delicious.' When Constantine arrived, I gave our orders in Greek.

'Where did you learn that?' Marilyn inquired.

'I studied in Greece for junior year in college,' I said.

Jacques looked impressed; Marilyn stared at Lavinia.

'And how did you two both meet?' Marilyn asked.

'At Cambridge,' I said. 'Lavinia and I sat next to each other at a meal before a debate in the Cambridge Union.' I glanced at Lavinia. 'We disagreed over dinner and we still don't agree now.'

'About what?' Jacques asked.

'About God's omnipotence,' Lavinia said.

'Good grief!' Marilyn sighed.

'I say, Marilyn,' Jacques said as he sipped a glass of retsina, 'didn't you want to go to Cambridge?'

Marilyn looked sour. 'I did, but I didn't get in.'

'Ah yes,' Jacques said. 'It's different in France – everyone can get in.'

During lunch Jacques told us about the rabbinical seminary. There were, he mentioned, only two women students. 'And . . . well, you know how it is,' he said. 'They probably won't finish.'

'And just why not?' Lavinia asked.

'It's not because of any prejudice, but so far all the female students have got married to other students. They've become rebbetzin, rather than rabbis.' He grinned.

Lavinia then asked about converts. 'Are there any students who have been converted to Judaism?'

Jacques shrugged his shoulders. 'I don't know of any,' he replied.

We had all ordered dolmades and Greek salad. When the food arrived, Lavinia expressed her views about converts. I listened with some trepidation, since I had heard her opinions before. 'I thought they were meant to be treated like born Jews,' she said. 'But there seems to be extraordinary prejudice.'

Jacques listened, but Marilyn butted in: 'That's not true,' she asserted.

'But it is,' Lavinia countered. 'Why are there no convert rabbis?'

'Well, it's not so in Reform Judaism,' Marilyn asserted. 'I teach the Conversion class at the Temple, and nobody has ever complained to me about it.'

'Probably too scared that you won't give the Temple stamp of approval,' Lavinia giggled. 'Jewish law is full of negative feelings about converts. Take a cohen, for example. He's not allowed to marry someone who is faulty . . . like a divorcee, or a harlot, and a convert is specifically mentioned in that category. It's obvious that converts are looked down on.'

'I'm aware of all these laws,' Marilyn said coldly. 'I do teach the Confirmation class, you know. I suppose you're going on to point out that the child of a cohen and a convert is a mamzer . . . But we've abolished all those distinctions in the Reform movement.'

Lavinia interrupted: 'But even the Orthodox wouldn't consider the child a mamzer in those circumstances.'

'Look,' Marilyn said. 'I do know about these things . . . he or she would be a mamzer, because the union was forbidden in the first place.'

'Yes, the marriage is prohibited,' explained Lavinia patiently, 'but if it does occur it's valid. It's a matter of "L'hathila d'avad" – it shouldn't happen in the first place, but if it does, then it's OK. It's a special category.'

Marilyn looked confused and angry. 'That's not right,' she said.

'Ah, Marilyn,' Jacques interjected. 'She is right. That's the halakhah.' Jacques was clearly impressed. 'Do you mind if I ask you,' he said admiringly, 'how you know that?'

Lavinia responded as she finished her salad. 'I'm a lawyer's daughter – I always think Jewish law is rather ingenious.'

Marilyn sat in silence for the rest of the meal.

The next day we went to London to Lavinia's mother's flat for tea. Chap was also there. Once we had all settled down to tea, biscuits and cake in the drawing room, Mrs Heath asked me about my summer job.

'Well, I like it. But I'm having a bit of trouble with the youth director. I don't think she likes me.'

'But why not, Dan?'

'Because she's jealous, Mummy,' Lavinia said. 'She wants to be the rabbi.'

Stroking Maggers, who was sitting on her lap, Mrs Heath looked puzzled. 'But surely she isn't ordained.'

'Of course not, Mummy. But she still would like to be in charge.'

'And I don't think she likes Lavinia either,' I continued. 'Particularly after yesterday.'

'Yesterday?' Mrs Heath asked.

'Well, we went out to lunch with Marilyn – the youth director – and her boyfriend . . .' Lavinia explained.

'She has a boyfriend? How nice.'

'Do listen, Mummy. We were discussing Jewish law, and she didn't know what she was talking about.'

'And Lavinia told her so,' I added.

'Oh, darling. You shouldn't have. The poor girl.'

'Really, Mummy. She should take a refresher course. After all, she is in charge of education in the Temple.'

In the corner, Chap put down the *Sunday Times*, 'Hey, Rabs,' he said. 'Isn't it time for a little drink?'

At the end of the summer Harvey returned from his cruise. When he came to the Temple, everyone complimented him on his tan. Over lunch in a nearby restaurant he recounted his exploits. Not only was his cabin upgraded on the ship, but he was given a generous honorarium and asked if he would lecture again on a different cruise the following summer – he was clearly delighted and flattered. We then discussed what had happened at the Temple while he was away. Both of us avoided the subject of Sabbath discussions as well as my relationship with Marilyn. But I thought he would be interested to know about Jacques.

'I remember him,' he said. 'He was one of the students in my practical rabbinics course at the seminary.'

'I didn't know you lectured there,' I said.

'Just one course in the final term of the third year – I like to keep my hand in.'

'He seems like a nice guy,' I said.

'Very quiet. Never said a thing in class.'

'Marilyn will be quite a handful for him, I think.'

Harvey looked thoughtful. 'Yes, but it might just be the making of Marilyn,' he mused.

'But if it's serious . . . then she might have to go and live in Paris.'

'I doubt it. Marilyn can't speak French, and she's devoted to the Temple.'

'Then Jacques will have to become an English rabbi.'

Harvey smiled. 'An English rabbi with a French accent – very chic!'

At the beginning of my second year, I returned to Cambridge. One afternoon, I had a phone call from Harvey. After asking me about my research, he told me why he had telephoned: the Temple board had agreed that he could have some rabbinical help at weekends and he wondered if I might like to come to Birmingham once or twice a month. This was very good news: I had hoped I might be asked back since I needed to earn some money.

'I'd love to,' I said.

'Great. Twice a month, then?'

'That would be fine,' I replied. 'If it's on the weekends, I'm sure my supervisor won't mind.'

'Then I'll ask the Temple secretary to get in touch. We'll pay for your hotel, food and travel. Plus an honorarium. I'll leave it to you to negotiate the amount.'

'That's good of you, Harvey,' I said.

'There's just one thing, Dan. Um . . . Marilyn . . . I think she's a bit upset about this.'

'She is?'

'I thought I ought to let her know.'

'What did she say?'

'I don't think we need to go into it.'

'But I really should know,' I persisted.

'Well, her final words were: "What about Jacques?" But I told her he wasn't yet ordained. The thing is . . . I'd be grateful if you two could try to get along.'

'Really, Harvey, you ought to be talking to *her* about this.'

'I already have. And now I'm talking to you.'

'Yeah, OK. I promise.'

'Good. I'm glad. Once you hear from the secretary, let me know which weekends would suit you best, and then we can sort out the details.'

'Thanks, Harvey,' I said.

'My pleasure . . . glad to have you on board.'

When I told Lavinia about our conversation, she was delighted but apprehensive about Marilyn. 'Look,' she said, 'you're still a threat – but for a different reason.'

'Oh yes?'

'Marilyn's interested in the senior position in the Temple – she'll be pushing for Jacques, and you're in the way.'

'But they're not even engaged,' I objected.

'Not yet,' she said. 'But wait . . .'

When I began work at the Temple, Marilyn was much friendlier than before. Clearly she had taken Harvey's advice. But I became increasingly disturbed about Harvey. With considerable charm, he told stories which were difficult to believe. On one occasion, for example, when we were discussing the hymns for the Sabbath-morning service, he proudly announced that he had been in the choir at St John's College as an undergraduate.

'You were actually part of the choir?' I asked incredulously.

'I won a choral scholarship,' he stated.

'To St John's?'

'As well as my academic scholarship,' he declared.

But this was inconceivable: Harvey could hardly sing in tune. How could he have possibly sung with one of the best choirs in the country?

It also became harder and harder to accept what Harvey said about his academic prowess at Cambridge. His sermons lacked any philosophical sophistication – they were usually incoherent ramblings touching on the Torah portion. Delivered with considerable gusto, they appealed to the emotions rather than the reason of the congregation. Could he possibly have won a scholarship to St John's to study philosophy? I couldn't believe it.

My doubts about Harvey's truthfulness deepened when I heard

him converse with visitors to the Temple about his participation in the Israeli War of Independence. As he described his exploits, they listened with admiration. But it was obvious to me that Harvey couldn't have been old enough to fight in the war – in 1948, he would have been only thirteen. An English thirteen-year-old boy simply wouldn't have been allowed to engage in the operations he depicted. Was Harvey perhaps falsifying aspects of his life to impress those who heard him? I worried about it. When I told Lavinia of my suspicions, she suggested I check the details of his Cambridge career. 'If he really was at St John's, you'll find his name in the listings of former students of the college,' she suggested.

'But I don't really want to go to St John's to look,' I said.

'There's no need to do that – you'll find all the information in the university library.'

Following her advice, I searched in all the reference books I could find in the reading room; I checked all the years when he might have matriculated, but there was no Harvey Rowbotham. I then asked the librarian for help – together we studied the relevant records, yet found nothing. Perhaps I had missed something. Possibly Harvey had spelled his name differently, or even registered under a different surname. I was determined to know, and wrote a letter to the registrar of the Rabbinical Seminary in St Louis. I explained that I was doing some research about Harvey, and I needed to know a few details about his academic career. I asked if she could fill me in. Several weeks later, I received a note – Harvey, she explained, had graduated from London University, and subsequently studied at the Rabbinical Seminary in St Louis. When I told Lavinia what I had found, she warned me to be cautious. 'You mustn't let him know that you know about him,' she said.

'But how can I know when he's telling the truth? If I'm to work with him, I've got to have some idea.'

'Don't be too hard on him, Dan,' she said. 'Everyone exaggerates a bit.'

'This isn't just an exaggeration. These are lies,' I protested.

Over the next few months, my worries about Harvey became even more acute when a number of congregants expressed concern about the relationship between Harvey and a recent convert to the Temple, Patricia Franklin. Allegedly, Harvey was spending an inordinate amount of time with her and during services it appeared that they exchanged glances. In addition, Patricia was spotted driving Harvey's car. When I heard the gossip, I tried to maintain that Harvey was happily married.

As agitation grew about this relationship, I came down with flu. The landlady where I stayed at the weekends kindly undertook to nurse me back to health before I returned to Cambridge.

As I languished in bed, the President of the Temple came to visit. 'Dan,' he said, 'I'm sorry to bring this up while you're ill, but I need to talk to you about Harvey.'

Bleary-eyed, I sat up and tried to concentrate.

'Do you know Patricia Franklin?' he asked.

Fearing what might be coming, I nodded that I did.

'This is all confidential,' he continued, 'but I have to ask you about Harvey and this girl. It has come to the attention of several board members that Harvey seems to be spending a lot of time with her. I'm sure this is entirely innocent – but has anybody talked to you about it?'

'Yeah,' I said. My eczema began to itch.

'Oh dear . . . Well, we do have a problem. The Temple can't afford to have this kind of gossip circulate.'

'I quite agree,' I said.

'Ah . . . Dan . . . is there anything I ought to know?'

'If you're asking if Harvey has said anything to me about Patricia, he hasn't.'

'No, no. I'm sure he wouldn't.'

'Look,' I said. 'I don't know whether there's any truth to these rumours, but I think you ought to talk to Harvey.'

After I recovered, I went back to Cambridge; two weeks later I returned to the Temple to conduct the Sabbath-morning service. During services Harvey eyed me with hostility, as did Patricia, sitting in the front row. Clearly something had happened, but I had no idea what. At the Kiddush I spotted the President and took him aside. 'Can I talk to you?' I asked.

'Not now,' he said. 'Call me after lunch.'

Later in the day I phoned him at home. 'What's been going on?' I asked. 'Harvey is clearly upset and so is Patricia.'

'It's a long story. I hoped I'd have an opportunity to talk to you about it, but I didn't think it would be a good idea for Harvey to see us together.'

'So what happened?' I asked.

'Well,' he began, 'some of the officers got together for an informal discussion. I told them that I had spoken to you. I'm afraid none of us felt we could speak directly to Harvey about Patricia.'

'But if you didn't, why was he so upset?'

'We thought it would be better to ask someone else to discuss this with him – so we asked Marilyn.'

'But why? – she's just the youth director.'

'She's been at the Temple for some time now and she and Harvey have a good relationship. We didn't want it to seem as though this was an accusation.'

'And what was Marilyn instructed to say?'

The President hesitated. 'We wanted her to put it as delicately as possible. She simply agreed to tell Harvey that a rumour about him and Patricia was going around the Temple.'

I felt sick. 'Did she mention me?' I asked.

'We did tell her that we had spoken to you first, and that you had told us that you had heard the rumour too.'

'How exactly did Marilyn put this?' I inquired.

'I don't know, Dan. You'll have to ask her.'

'And what did Harvey say?'

'Obviously, he was very distressed. But he told Marilyn that there was absolutely no substance to what people were saying. He admitted that he had been spending a lot of time with Patricia, but that's because she needs it. According to Harvey, she's a very troubled person.'

'And that was the end of it?'

There was a silence. 'Dan,' he emphasized, 'this must be confidential.'

'It will be,' I reassured him.

'I then spoke to Harvey, and stressed that he must make sure this gossip ceases. He promised that he would spend less time with Patricia and in the future be more careful.'

'Did Harvey mention me?'

'The only thing Harvey said was that he wished you had talked to him first.'

'But how could I? I didn't think you wanted me to interfere.'

'That's what I said. But Harvey didn't seem convinced.'

The next day I saw Marilyn at the religion school; she tried to avoid me, but I insisted we talk. After school finished I went to her office; when I arrived she was sorting books.

'Listen, Marilyn,' I said. 'I spoke to the President yesterday about Harvey. He told me the officers asked you to talk to him. What did you say?'

Marilyn glared at me. 'I don't think it's really your business,' she declared.

'I think I have the right to know what you said about me.'

'You weren't the main subject, you know.'

'I'm well aware of that. But did you mention me?'

'If you must know, Harvey was furious that you'd been gossiping about him.'

'Look, Marilyn, I haven't been gossiping. The President asked me if I'd heard any rumours about Harvey and Patricia – the truth is that I have. And I told him so.'

'That's not what Harvey thinks. He's convinced you're the one who's been spreading them.'

'And is that what you said to him?'

'What I said to Harvey isn't your affair. The point is that you shouldn't talk about Harvey behind his back.'

Reeling with this accusation, I stormed out of Marilyn's room. What was I to do? On her mission from the Temple officers, Marilyn had no doubt accused me of disloyalty: how could I redeem the situation?

When I told Lavinia what had happened, she looked apprehensive. 'I fear that's the end of your employment at the Birmingham Temple,' she said.

'Do you really think so?'

'Harvey will never forgive you. And the officers will want to look for a scapegoat.'

'But all I did was tell the President what I'd heard – after all, he was the one who asked me about it.'

'It won't make any difference. They'll support Harvey, and Marilyn will urge Harvey to get rid of you. And honestly, Dan, I don't think he'll need much urging.'

'This is hardly fair,' I complained.

'Who said life was fair?' Lavinia countered.

Although Harvey and I had to work together, our discussions were always brief and cool. How long, I wondered, could this situation continue? The answer to this question was provided by the next edition of the *Newsletter* from the Progressive Movement. In the column listing rabbinical jobs, there was an advertisement for an associate rabbi at the Birmingham Temple. Clearly Harvey had decided to terminate my employment and hire someone else without telling me.

When I was next in Birmingham I confronted him after the Sabbath-morning service. Holding a copy of the *Newsletter*, I asked him why the advertisement had appeared.

'It's a mistake,' he said.

'Come on, Harvey, things don't get into the *Newsletter* by accident.'

'This is no time to discuss this, Dan; come and see me later in my office.'

After everyone left the Temple, I knocked on Harvey's door. Icily, he told me to come in and sit down. I sat opposite his desk while Harvey stood looking out of the window at the street beneath. 'As a matter of fact, Dan,' he began, 'I didn't put that advertisement in the *Newsletter* – quite frankly, I don't know how it appeared. But I'm glad it did. I think we won't be needing your services in the future.'

'What have I done wrong?' I asked.

'You've done your rabbinical duties – but it's your attitude. Particularly towards me.'

'Look,' I said defensively. 'I think Marilyn has given you entirely the wrong picture . . .'

Harvey cut me off: 'I'm not interested in talking to you about Marilyn. The point is that the Temple will be needing someone else. The board has agreed to appoint a full-time associate rabbi.'

'And there's no point in my applying for the job?' I asked.

'You'd be better off finishing your thesis – and then looking for a congregation in the States. That's where you belong, Dan. Not here.'

Before we had finished speaking, the telephone rang – it was Harvey's wife asking when he was coming home to lunch. As he signalled me to leave, he gave me an envelope containing notice of the end of my tenure at the Temple. 'You can continue here,' he said, 'until we find someone . . . I'll let you know.'

A month later, when I returned to the Temple, I heard from several members that Jacques had been appointed as the associate rabbi. He was to take over from me after his ordination. In addition, Jacques and Marilyn were to be married in June; the marriage was to take place in the Temple with Harvey as the officiating rabbi. When I saw Marilyn at the religion school, she looked radiant. Just before I was to take my class, she stopped me in the corridor. 'Have you heard about Jacques?' she asked.

What could I say? I congratulated her on his appointment and her forthcoming marriage.

'We're so thrilled,' she gloated. 'The Temple is providing a flat for us, and I'll be staying on as youth director. Everything's worked out so well.'

'I hope you'll both be happy,' I said as I made my way to the classroom.

'Oh we will,' she declared, 'we will.'

By the end of the academic year I was anxious to leave the

Birmingham Temple. Decorators had started to repaint my office, and new furniture for Jacques was stacked up in the corner under dust sheets. Whenever I saw Jacques he looked in the other direction and I felt an unwelcome presence. When Harvey and I took Sabbath services together, he refused to talk to me about anything other than details concerning the Torah reading and the preaching schedule. It was agreed that I should preach at my last service; on the final day I arrived early and put all the belongings from my desk into a bag. I took down my diplomas as well as Cambridge rowing pictures from the walls, and packed up my books.

Just before the service began, the janitor came in to say goodbye. 'Ah . . . Rabbi . . .' he said, 'I just wanted to give you my best wishes.'

Tony had been the caretaker for over thirty years; although not Jewish himself, he always attended services wearing a yamulkah.

'Thanks, Tony,' I said sadly. 'It's nice of you to drop in.'

Tony looked around the room. 'There's still a lot of work to do here. It's going to be nice for the new rabbi.'

'They're doing a good job,' I said.

'Sorry it couldn't be you, Rabbi.'

'Me too,' I said as I shut the door for the last time.

Before the service began I saw Harvey talking to Marilyn and Jacques in the corridor. When I passed by they all looked at me in silence. During the service, Harvey led the prayers and read the Torah portion. As I joined in, I felt a wave of sadness. I hadn't been fired from the Temple – I was simply being replaced by someone who would work full-time. Yet this was my first serious failure in the rabbinate, and it made me unhappy.

Just before the sermon Harvey announced that this would be my last time at the Temple. He briefly thanked me for serving the congregation, and then launched into an extensive profile of Jacques who, he explained, would be taking my place. As I listened I looked at Marilyn and Jacques who were sitting near the front – Marilyn held his hand and looked joyful. When Harvey finished, I began my sermon. A few seconds later there was a loud moan from the back of the congregation. Then another. Everyone turned around as two men carried a frail gentleman out of the synagogue. What could have happened? Did he have a heart attack? Had he simply fainted? I struggled to go on, but as I looked at the stunned faces in the congregation, I realized it was better to omit the sermon and continue with the service. When I finished, the congregation looked relieved. At the

Kiddush, it was announced that an ambulance had been summoned to take Mr Stein to hospital. When the congregants left, I went up to my office to collect my possessions. Marilyn and Jacques had already left for lunch at Harvey's house and there was no one in the building except the Temple cat, who followed me into my office. I picked him up and he settled in my lap when I sat in my chair. The room was filled with paint pots, brushes and a ladder. Nimrod purred as I stroked him. Morosely I told him this was my last day at the Temple. 'Well, Nimrod,' I said, 'that's it. The end of a promising career at the Birmingham Temple.'

Nimrod continued to purr as I watched the rain through my window. It was a grey, English day, and I was filled with gloom. There was no party to say goodbye; no presents; not much thanks.

When I stood up, Nimrod got back in my chair and went to sleep.

Clutching my bag, I walked down the street to say goodbye to the landlady who had always let me stay in her flat. When I arrived she was making tea. 'Hello, dear,' she said. 'Do you want some tea?'

'Thanks,' I said.

'It's your last time then, is it?'

'I'm afraid so. I'm very grateful to you for having me on the weekends.'

'It was a pleasure, dear. A pleasure. So, you'll be going back to Cambridge now?'

'To finish my thesis . . .'

'Well, that's a good thing. And then I expect you'll be going back to America to have a synagogue of your own.'

'Yes . . . I guess . . .'

'That's good, dear. Now you just sit down and have a nice cup of tea. You'll feel a lot better.'

After leaving the Birmingham Temple, I had no opportunity to serve as a congregational rabbi in my third year at Cambridge. But during the first term of the year I was asked to lead a seminar at a weekend retreat for provincial Jewish congregations – I was to be their scholar-in-residence. I was flattered by the invitation, and excited at the prospect of testing out my ideas. The conference was to take place at the end of the winter vacation in a historic house which had been converted into a conference centre.

When I arrived at Mulgrove Hall near Oxford, the organizer,

sitting behind a registration desk in the entrance, handed me an identification badge, a folder of material, and my room key.

'It's good of you to come, Rabbi,' he said. 'Your room is at the top of the stairs; tea will be served at four. In the meantime you might want to walk around the grounds.'

'How many are you expecting?' I asked as I looked down the list of participants.

'About sixty. That's quite a good number: we only had thirty-five last year.'

After unpacking my bag, I walked in the gardens. Occasionally, I came across other visitors who were obviously at the conference. I was surprised to see that some of the men wore yamulkahs – clearly there would be a smattering of Orthodox Jews at the gathering. At tea I mixed with the participants, who appeared to be largely retired. For many the conference served as an inexpensive annual holiday, and they greeted friends from previous retreats with enthusiasm.

At the opening session following dinner, the organizer introduced me as an American research student at Cambridge who was completing a PhD dissertation about Jewish prayer. He explained that I had been ordained as a Progressive rabbi at the seminary in St Louis. I then spoke for about forty-five minutes: the question I asked was whether prayers of intercession could possibly work, and I outlined the central arguments of my dissertation. I concluded by asserting that prayer is important in Jewish life, but that Jews are mistaken in believing that prayers could actually affect the future outcome of events. Such prayers, I explained, might have subjective value, but could not be objectively efficacious.

When I had finished, there was a hush – no one dared ask a question. Eventually the organizer asked me if I myself prayed. I explained that I did, but I emphasized that I didn't believe the prayers I recited could actually alter future events.

From the back of the room, an elderly woman raised her hand. 'Rabbi,' she said, 'you've given us a lot to think about. But it's discouraging to think that prayers to God are of no benefit.'

There was a ruffle of unease among the audience. Several members whispered to one another. In response I stressed that I had not come to cause distress, but rather to pose challenging questions about prayer. An elderly gentleman wearing a yamulkah stood up. 'I can't accept all this,' he said with irritation. 'You're a rabbi; it's your job to support the tradition. Even Progressive rabbis believe in prayer,' he insisted.

In response, I explained that the title 'rabbi' means teacher – I saw my role as teaching about the Jewish faith, and this involved raising questions, even if they were uncomfortable. For the next half-hour I was besieged with hostile responses, accusations and criticisms. No one came to my defence. As the session drew to an end, the organizer meekly thanked me for my contribution which, he pointed out, had led to a lively discussion.

During the break coffee was served, and several members of the audience accosted me. One heavy-set, middle-aged woman berated me for my views. I tried to soothe her, but to no avail. Continually she interrupted me and poked her finger at my chest. 'If I were you,' she spat out, 'I would think again about being a rabbi. Rabbis are supposed to help people, not destroy their faith.' Such a response was profoundly discouraging: at rabbinical seminary we were encouraged to see ourselves as educators. But what this audience clearly wanted was reassurance rather than stimulation. Instead of facing theological challenges, they preferred easy solutions.

Such a perception was further reinforced when I was asked to preach one Sabbath at the largest Progressive synagogue in London. As I was completing my thesis, I was phoned by Rabbi Morganstern whom I had briefly met; since he was going to be away at a bar mitzvah, he asked if I would be able to take his place.

When I arrived at the synagogue, I was greeted by the cantor, who went through the service with me. I was to read the Torah portion and preach later in the service. The synagogue itself was much larger than the Birmingham Temple; the architecture was Moorish in character, and the windows filled with brightly coloured stained glass. In the front row, officers from the synagogue were dressed in morning coats and top hats, and a magnificent choir sang from behind an elaborately decorated screen. When I carried the Torah around the synagogue, I glanced at the congregants: the men were dressed in perfectly tailored suits, and the women were elegantly attired. As I slowly made my way back towards the ark, I was very aware of the odour of expensive scent.

In attempting to avoid the outrage that my lecture had caused at the winter conference, I decided to preach about Jewish law rather than petitionary prayer. I stressed that, as Progressive Jews, we were not bound by the prescriptions found in the Bible or in rabbinical literature. It was impossible, I argued, to have a Progressive Code of Jewish Law. Rather, each Progressive Jew is free to select those parts of the tradition which are personally meaningful. Unlike Orthodox Judaism, the Progressive Movement allows for individual conscience and free decision-making. It would be a mistake, I continued, for Progressive rabbis to legislate for others. I concluded by citing the case of Job, who challenged God. Like Job we must challenge received tradition.

After the service, I stepped down from the bimah and announced that I wished to give congregants an opportunity to respond to what I had said in my sermon. I explained that I had adopted this approach at the Birmingham Temple. Immediately several congregants put up their hands. The first questioner was extremely hostile: he declared that it was the duty of the rabbi to give a firm lead on moral issues. My approach, he said, would lead to utter chaos. 'Our children need guidance,' he insisted, 'and if they don't get it from the rabbi, where will it come from?' The second questioner was a gentleman in a top hat. 'What is the point of Judaism,' he asked, 'if it doesn't lay down standards? Rabbis,' he maintained, 'are there to give a strong lead in all spheres of life.' The third questioner was a young woman wearing a multi-coloured silk dress. Angrily, she denounced me as an anarchist. As the congregation grew restive, I announced that Kiddush would take place in the synagogue hall.

Once I had recited the appropriate blessings, the President of the synagogue introduced himself. Sir Israel Lewis was a high-court judge, and a descendant of one of the founders of the congregation. After thanking me for taking Rabbi Morganstern's place, he asked me about my future plans. I told him that I hoped I would hand in my thesis soon and then look for a congregation.

'Have you thought about academic life?' he asked.

Uneasily, I explained that I had always planned to be a congregational rabbi. In all likelihood, I said, I'd be returning to the States to look for a job.

'Yes . . . yes,' he replied. 'But you might think of lecturing in a university.' Glancing at the congregants milling about, he hummed almost to himself. 'A rabbi's lot is not a happy one.' And with that, he wandered off to greet the members of the synagogue. My eczema itched intolerably.

After I completed my thesis, I went back to Denver for a short visit during the spring vacation. As usual, my mother collected me from the airport. I was anxious to discuss my future plans with my parents; after the last visit, I feared there might be a similar hostile response, but I was determined to let them know that I had serious reservations about being a congregational rabbi. My mother served my favourite food for dinner; I could tell my father wanted to leave the table as quickly as possible. Hence, before we finished dessert, I began my prepared speech – 'I want to tell you straight away that I've been thinking a lot about the rabbinate . . .'

My mother looked distressed; my father stared at his cherry pie.

'We were expecting this,' he said gruffly.

'You know I've had quite a few jobs as a rabbi now; quite frankly the rabbinate isn't what I expected.'

'It's that girl, isn't it, Dan?' my mother interrupted.

'Lavinia has nothing to do with this . . .'

'You don't really expect us to believe that, do you?' my father said.

'Do let me finish: I've served congregations in the States, in Australia and in England. I know they've all been part-time, but being a rabbi isn't what I thought it would be.'

Angrily, my father glared at me. 'It cost a lot of money to send you to Tewksbury, and the Rabbinical Seminary. I could have bought two Rolls-Royces for what it cost! And now you tell us you don't want to be a rabbi. You might have thought about it a bit earlier.'

Defensively, I tried to explain that I couldn't have known what the job was like.

'But, Dan,' my mother argued, 'you always wanted to be a rabbi – ever since your bar mitzvah. You wouldn't consider anything else. What's changed your mind?'

'It's not any single thing,' I explained. 'It's the job itself. I never knew how difficult congregations could be. I had no idea what sort of expectations congregants have. And the rabbinate is filled with intrigue.'

'I don't see how you can tell at this stage,' my father objected. 'You've never been a rabbi full-time.'

'Look, I've had jobs on three continents. It's always the same. And rabbis continually quarrel with one another instead of teaching about Judaism. I've had to take children to the circus, take part in a fashion show, be a bingo announcer, play tennis with ladies in the congregation . . .'

My father looked disgusted. 'I don't want to hear any more of this,' he announced.

'But I haven't finished,' I said. 'I've come home to tell you what I want to do.'

'What you want to do is quit being a rabbi and play with your shiksa.' My father scowled.

'I'll always be a rabbi. But I want to teach about Judaism in a university.'

'Oh, Dan,' my mother said, 'it's very hard to get an academic job – and they don't always give tenure. You haven't even got your PhD yet.'

'Yes, but I've finished my thesis. And I'll know the result soon. Then I'll be in a position to apply for jobs.'

My father stood up. 'I think I've had enough of this. You've been a student for thirteen years now. Before you've even started as a rabbi, you want to give up. I know it's only because of that girl. This is what comes from going to England!'

After my father stormed out of the room, my mother looked tearful. 'I don't see the point of coming home to tell us this,' she said. 'It's all so upsetting. How can you do this to me, Dan?'

That evening I phoned Lavinia. When I told her about my parents' reaction, she was angry. 'Will they tell you to go and stay in a motel as a result?' she asked.

'No, not this time. I'm only here for a few days.'

'Didn't they want to know how you reached this decision?'

'I tried to tell them, but they wouldn't listen. My father thinks it's all because of you.'

'But that's not true, is it?'

'Of course not,' I replied.

When I returned to Cambridge after several fraught days in Denver, a letter was waiting for me from the senior rabbi of the Temple in Durban, South Africa. He was an old friend of Joshua Friedlander in Australia who, several years ago, had mentioned that I had worked with him in Perth. Since he needed some help over the High Holy Days, he wondered if I might be free for the summer. Despite my reservations about entering the active rabbinate, I was delighted to be invited, but I was loath to leave Lavinia for three months.

However, when I showed her the letter, she urged me to accept. 'You must, Dan,' she said. 'It's only for three months – it will be a marvellous experience, and you'll need the money for next year.'

'But I don't want to go without you.'

'Don't be silly. You'll do fine.'

'But three months is a long time.'

'Honestly, Dan, it's a wonderful opportunity. You should go.'

The next day I phoned Rabbi George Saltzman as instructed.

I told him I would be pleased to come, and we discussed the travel arrangements. I was to fly to Addis Ababa, and then travel through East Africa. He insisted that the congregation pay for my trip. In addition, I would be paid the equivalent of £900 for three months; I would be housed by the secretary of the Temple in her flat and provided with a car. Given these arrangements, I was determined to save my entire salary if possible. When I told Lavinia, she was delighted. 'Look, Dan,' she said, 'you'll need somewhere to live when you get back to England. If you can save that much money, you could easily put a down-payment on a house.'

While I waited for my PhD viva to take place, Lavinia helped me purchase a large trunk and pack. In addition, I organized for all my books and other things to be put into storage. I also made several trips to London to obtain visas for the countries I planned to visit.

During all this activity, I had my PhD examination as well as an interview for the job at the University of Kent which would start after my summer employment in South Africa. When I heard that I had been hired to teach Jewish studies, I was overjoyed. I arranged to have all my belongings sent to the university, and Lavinia accompanied me to Canterbury to look for a house. On my return, I hoped I'd be able to buy something I liked. Since I had decided not to enter the congregational rabbinate and had secured an academic job, I no longer felt the same constraint about marrying someone who was not born Jewish. I could marry whomever I liked. Yet I was reluctant to broach the subject with Lavinia. Given her background, I wasn't entirely convinced she would want to marry an American rabbi. Because of my family's attitude, I was no longer likely to be rich and I didn't feel I had much to offer. And I also had some reservations about my own motives. Lavinia was from an established English family. Did I find her attractive for the same reasons I was drawn to Tewksbury, Cambridge and the Oxford and Cambridge University Club? Was she a symbol of the Gentile world I was so keen on being part of?

On the day I was due to catch my flight to South Africa, Lavinia took me to the airport. As we waited in the passenger lounge, she looked severe. 'I think it's about time you asked me,' she said.

'Asked you what?'

'Come on, Dan, don't be silly, asked me to marry you.'

I took a deep breath. 'Oh, Lavinia. Not now.'

Quoting the Jewish sage, Hillel, she said: 'And if not now, when?'

'Must I?'

'Yes. You must.'

'But what if you say no?'

'You'll just have to take your chances, won't you?'

'Aw, come on, Lavinia.'

'Nope. Now.'

'OK. Would you care to marry me?'

'Of course. Now let's get your plane.'

Chapter 8

Serving the Jews of South Africa: Rich Jews and Poor Blacks

When I arrived in Addis Ababa, soldiers with machine guns had surrounded the airport. The few tourists who disembarked filtered through immigration as the military looked on suspiciously. It was clear that something was happening – but what? A group of us boarded a bus for the city; en route guards were everywhere on the roads stopping cars, checking papers, and searching passengers. When I arrived at my hotel – a modern building with plush carpets and lavish decorations – there was considerable consternation. Later in the day, I walked through the streets and saw hundreds of black men and women who looked as though they had come into Addis Ababa from other parts of the country. There were beggars everywhere.

Because there was a curfew in the city, I returned early to the hotel: there I encountered an American family having drinks in the bar. Anxiously, I asked why there was such agitation.

'You don't know?' the father inquired.

'I've just arrived. Why is there a curfew?'

'There's a coup.'

'A coup? Against whom?'

'Against Haile Selassie,' he responded.

I gasped. 'You mean there's a revolution going on?'

As he sipped his drink, he explained that he had been told the government was being overthrown by a left-wing revolutionary group. But, he assured me, it was a bloodless revolution – no shots had been heard anywhere.

Anxious to avoid being caught up in this conflict, I rearranged my travel plans and left the next day. My next stop was Nairobi,

Kenya, where I stayed at a hotel on the outskirts of the city. On my first day I went to a travel agency to book a trip to see a lake inhabited by thousands of flamingos. Together with several other tourists, I crowded into an old car driven by our guide. The park was about 100 miles from Nairobi; on the way the car died. It refused to move any further – the driver was utterly perplexed by this predicament. We became increasingly irate. Eventually one of the passengers opened up the boot, extracted a tool kit, and after an hour's labour, managed to fix the car. We crawled along the rough African roads to see the flamingos, and in the evening limped back to Nairobi.

I spent several days visiting other game parks, before flying to Dar-es-Salaam on the Tanzanian coast. As I passed through the city, I saw only black faces; it appeared I was the only white person around. With some trepidation I booked into my hotel; I was plagued by fears that I would be murdered in the street in this utterly foreign place. Such anxiety, however, was groundless – everywhere I encountered friendly, smiling people. As I walked through picturesque markets, I was fascinated by the sounds and smells, but felt empty without Lavinia beside me. My loneliness became increasingly acute on the final stage of my journey. After booking into my hotel in Lusaka, Zambia, I took a day trip to Victoria Falls. There in this romantic setting – with water cascading down gigantic waterfalls – I felt sad that Lavinia couldn't have been with me.

Eventually I arrived at the airport in Johannesburg. At passport control, I was grilled about my intention to stay in South Africa. I explained that I had been hired to be a rabbi for the summer in Durban, and that I was sure my employers had made all the necessary arrangements. The immigration officer shook his head. 'I'm afraid we have no papers for you,' he said.

Taking out the letter I had received from Rabbi Saltzman, I reiterated that I had been assured that everything had been sorted out. The officer carefully studied the letter, and handed it back to me. 'We have no papers,' he repeated.

'Look,' I continued, 'I've been travelling through Africa for over a week; I was supposed to be met by Rabbi Saltzman. Why don't you announce his name – I'm sure he'll have all the relevant documentation.'

Several minutes later, I heard an announcement for Rabbi Saltzman, and across the immigration barrier, I saw a rotund, harassed-looking figure barrelling towards us. Taking several sheets of paper out of a black briefcase, Rabbi Saltzman looked flustered.

'I'm sorry I'm late, here are the documents,' he puffed. The immigration officer perused the papers and shook his head. 'The visa's not been signed by the Home Office; he can't come in until it is.'

'That's ridiculous,' Rabbi Saltzman protested. 'We've been through all the official channels and we have the necessary approval.'

The immigration officer stroked his moustache. 'Sorry,' he continued, 'he can't enter. You'll have to get it signed by the right person.'

Rabbi Saltzman rolled his eyes. Across the barrier he apologized. 'This is stupid,' he said. 'You'll have to stay at the airport hotel – there's one on your side. Make yourself comfortable, and I'll be back for you tomorrow.'

'Tomorrow?' I asked.

'The immigration office closes at five. It'll be shut by the time I get home. I'll come back in the morning.'

'I'm sorry to cause all this trouble,' I said.

'It's not your fault. Just get a good night's rest, and I'll see you before lunch.'

Despite my polite remarks, I was furious. Why hadn't the synagogue sorted out my entry visa? After I checked into the airport hotel, I went into the dining room for dinner. As I looked over the menu, I decided I'd have exactly what I wanted, regardless of cost – if the Temple was so inefficient as not to ensure that I could enter the country, they could pay for a lavish meal. The speciality of the restaurant was Chateaubriand: I told the waiter I'd like to have it along with the best South African red wine on the menu. He nodded and disappeared. After several minutes the wine waiter arrived with a bottle of wine. He poured a glass and let me taste it. As I ate my steak and drank the entire bottle, I felt much better. I only wished Lavinia had been with me to enjoy my imprisonment.

The next day Rabbi Saltzman arrived as planned. He presented the necessary papers, signed by the appropriate authority, and I was whisked through passport control and customs. On the way into the city, he cursed the immigration office. 'It's like the Gestapo,' he declared. 'A bunch of little Hitlers.' After a long drive, we arrived in Durban and I was taken to the flat of Mrs Blintz, the secretary of the Temple. She lived in an elegant suburb of the city in a large apartment. Rabbi Saltzman rang the bell: the door was opened by a black maid wearing a white uniform.

'I've brought the rabbi,' he announced. The maid took us down a long passageway which led to my room. Rabbi Saltzman and I entered, and I unpacked my bags.

After I finished, I sat on the bed across from Rabbi Saltzman who had settled into an armchair. 'Dan,' he began, 'I think there's one thing I should mention before you meet any of the congregation. They're very sensitive about apartheid.'

'But I thought the Jewish community was very liberal.'

'They are on the whole, but they're touchy about race.'

'Don't they want the political system to change?'

'Most do. Not all, of course. But the thing is . . . they would rather not be reminded too much about it.'

I was puzzled. Why had the subject come up so quickly? 'Why are you telling me this now?' I asked.

'I don't want you to misunderstand, Dan. But I think you'd be wise not to discuss the issues at all. And certainly not preach about it.'

Hearing this, I was reminded of my conversation with the President of the congregation in Jonah, Alabama. On my first night there, I had been cautioned not to get involved in civil rights. Clearly the same situation applied here.

'As a matter of fact,' Rabbi Saltzman continued, 'I'm afraid the Temple board will insist that you don't discuss the subject in public. And if I were you, I'd be careful what you write home. It's not unknown for letters to be opened.'

'I hope not by the congregation,' I said indignantly.

'Of course not. But you can never be sure what the authorities are up to.'

Later in the day Esther Blintz arrived home. A middle-aged woman of German origin, she was the owner of the largest and most fashionable clothing store in Durban. As a refugee from Hitler's Germany she had emigrated to South Africa in the 1930s; she had settled in Durban, and had had a successful career. Several years previously, she had been divorced from her husband and she currently lived with her elderly aunt, Ida Graftsman. Before Rabbi Saltzman left, he told me that Mrs Blintz would take me to a dinner party which would be held in my honour at the home of the President of the Temple.

After Mrs Blintz had introduced herself and her aunt, we all piled into her car – a large Mercedes-Benz. The President, Dr Glickstein, was an affluent dentist who lived in a vast modern house set in acres of lawn with a swimming pool and a tennis court. In the drive were already parked a Rolls-Royce convertible, several Jaguars and a Bentley. When we rang the bell, a black butler answered the door and led us into the drawing room. Mrs Blintz introduced me to the other members of the Temple board and their spouses: all the women were deeply tanned and bejewelled. The men were more informally dressed – most in safari suits.

Handing me a cocktail, Dr Glickstein smiled. 'Welcome to Durban, Rabbi.' Raising his glass, he said: 'Here's to three fruitful months with us.' He clinked my glass, and I mumbled a response.

I was then set upon by a tall, balding figure – the treasurer of the Temple – who roughly put his arm around my shoulders. 'Good to have you here, Rabbi. It's not always easy to convince the Yanks or the Brits to come out to South Africa.'

'No . . . probably not . . .' I stammered.

'Well, they don't understand the situation. And they judge us too harshly.'

Remembering Rabbi Saltzman's advice, I forebore to say anything.

'The thing is, Rabbi, they can't see the situation with their own eyes, and they believe whatever they read in the papers.'

I glanced at the rabbi who was standing nearby; he gave me a knowing look.

'Now, Rabbi,' the treasurer continued, 'we hope you won't be giving us any political advice during your stay here.'

'I hadn't planned to,' I replied.

'Good, good. You see, foreigners come out here and tell us how to run the country. They have no idea what the real problems are.'

'I don't intend to do that,' I said. 'But to be honest, I don't approve of apartheid.'

'Of course you don't. And frankly, neither do I. But things can't change overnight. It's got to come gradually. And you'll learn, Rabbi . . . South Africa needs its white population. If the black boys were to take over, it'd be chaos.'

At dinner I was seated next to Mrs Glickstein, a plump blonde with extraordinarily long red fingernails. Throughout dinner, she told me about the problems with her black help. 'I tell them what to do,' she complained, 'and then they do the opposite. They're like spoiled children.'

'Spoiled?' I asked.

'I know that doesn't sound right,' she confessed. 'But they live in their own accommodation in the back of the house. They're well fed, and paid a good wage. Compared to the homelands, this is paradise. But they're lazy and obstinate.'

As I watched the black servants wait on us, she continued

her complaints. But I couldn't understand: these maids looked obedient and subdued; they appeared to be working extremely hard. Obviously Mrs Glickstein had had a trying day.

The next day Rabbi Saltzman took me to the Temple, introduced me to the staff, and went through my duties. Afterwards he took me home for lunch. Unlike Mrs Blintz and Dr Glickstein, Rabbi Saltzman and his wife, Betty, lived in a relatively modest flat. South African by birth, he had studied at the Rabbinical Seminary in St Louis and had returned to Durban to take over the Temple. He had served the congregation for over twenty years. During lunch he confessed that the South African Jewish community was not so very different from the non-Jewish white population.

'There are ardent Jewish liberals,' he explained. 'But the majority are quite content to leave things pretty much as they are. Life is easy here.'

'Most of the women in the congregation have black servants,' Betty broke in. 'A lot don't even know how to cook.'

A Jewish woman who couldn't cook! – I had never come across one before. 'Not even chicken soup?' I asked.

'They've got a lot of Jewish recipes,' Betty went on, 'but why stand over a hot stove if you don't have to? The blacks do everything – cook, clean, fetch groceries . . .'

'That's why there's little point in trying to change people's opinions; it's not in their interest to do away with a system that benefits them,' George said.

'But what about you, George?' I asked. 'You grew up here – but you don't feel this way, do you?'

'No, I don't. But, listen, Dan, until things do change, we've got to protect ourselves. Life can be dangerous.'

'What do you mean?' I asked.

George fidgeted. 'I've got a gun . . .'

'What?'

'Most families do,' Betty interjected. 'Just in case.'

George got up from the table and went to the living room. He returned with a black, shiny revolver. He emptied the bullets from the chamber and handed it to me. I wasn't sure what I was to do with it.

The next morning I had breakfast with Mrs Graftsman; Mrs Blintz always rose early and left the apartment before eight. We were served by a black maid who hovered nearby in case we wanted more coffee. Mrs Graftsman told me that she had come to South Africa with her niece after the Nazis had gained power

– the rest of her family perished in the Holocaust. 'We were lucky,' she said. 'But I had no idea I'd be coming to a place like this.'

'What do you mean?' I asked.

'It's just like the Nazis, the way they treat the black people.'

'But you must have known something about the political situation?'

'Yes, of course. But it's different when you actually live here.'

'Did you ever think of going somewhere else?' I asked.

'I've thought about it. But Esther has such a good job. And it's not easy to start all over again.'

As she spoke there was a loud scream. We both looked at each other. Again, the same scream. Ceaselessly the screaming continued. It was hard to tell where it was coming from.

'It must be one of the servants in another apartment,' Mrs Graftsman conjectured.

Again, there was the same piercing, frightening sound.

Mrs Graftsman motioned to the maid. 'What is it?' she asked.

'It's from the apartment down below. I know the girl . . . the police have come for her.'

I gasped. 'The police?'

'I've lived here for over thirty years,' Mrs Grafstman said, 'but I'll never get used to it.'

'Would Master like some more coffee?' the maid asked.

During my first weeks in Durban I was invited for dinner at the houses of several members of the Temple. Invariably, the food was cooked and served by black maids who addressed me as 'Master'. In Denver my mother had had a black cleaning lady whom she treated with consideration; here black help was taken for granted and frequently abused. Often I watched Jewish housewives treat their servants as belligerent children: they shouted at them if they made a mistake, and ordered them about with no consideration for their feelings. No wonder the white population protected themselves with guns!

One of the members who had invited me to dinner was a criminal lawyer. Knowing I was interested in the racial problems of South Africa, he asked if I would like to visit a black township. After making the necessary arrangements, we set off through the lush suburbs of Durban. The township was a stark contrast. Black men, women and children roamed dirt-paved streets – there were no trees or shrubbery anywhere. Occasionally dogs with protruding ribs appeared, scavenging for food. The houses – one-storey cement bungalows – were arranged in straight rows. At one end of the township were two large apartment buildings facing each other. Parking in front, we got out to look.

'Who are these buildings for?' I asked.

'They are for men who've come to work in Durban,' he said.

'Just men?'

'It's really a dormitory – these workers are from other parts of the country. They've come here because of jobs. The work in Durban pays well, and they send as much as they can to their wives and families.'

'They're separated from them?' I asked, incredulously.

'It's the way of life in South Africa. It happens in all the cities. Most of the black maids you've seen in people's homes are far away from their families too.'

'But why?'

'Because the money is good. That's what foreigners never understand: the black population in our country has a higher standard of living than in any other country in Africa. We don't make these people come to work here – they do it voluntarily.'

When I arrived in Durban, I changed into a jacket and tie – Mrs Blintz had asked me to join her bowling party at her country club. As we drove in her Mercedes-Benz through Durban, I was even more unhappy at the difference between the leafy streets of the city and the dirt-paved roads of the nearby township. When we arrived, Esther introduced me to her friends. One moustachioed gentleman, wearing a white suit and a bow tie, bowled first; an elderly lady in a pink cotton dress followed. Then it was my turn. I was handed a silver ball and told what to do. It was generous of the group to include me, but I was a disaster: either my bowl was far too short or much too long.

Afterwards we sat on the veranda overlooking the golf course, drinking Pimm's. Esther and the others animatedly discussed the game as I listened. The gentleman with the moustache patted me on the shoulder. 'Don't worry,' he said, 'it was your first time. I'm sure you'll do better once you get the hang of it.'

'You really weren't too bad,' Esther added. 'It just needs practice.'

Later, as the wind came up, we went inside for dinner. I was encouraged to order the speciality of the day: grilled giant prawns. I looked at Esther to see if she'd mind. She smiled and ordered the same. Clearly, eating prawns wouldn't get me into trouble in South Africa.

When I arrived back in the flat, I went to my room. Lying on the bed was a stack of clean laundry. I went into the kitchen, opened up the refrigerator, and took out a jar of freshly squeezed orange juice. No doubt the oranges had been purchased that morning and squeezed by the maids. I went back into my room, and sat at the desk. As I wrote a letter to Lavinia, I pondered the day's events. How easy it would be to be seduced by the comfort of life here: but the image of the township continued to haunt me.

The next Sunday I was sitting reading a book on Esther's patio: I had just finished teaching in the Temple Sunday school and had returned to the flat. All at once Esther burst in; she looked distraught. 'Dan,' she said, 'something terrible has happened.'

I put down my book. 'What is it?' I asked.

'It's Jack.'

'Jack?'

'You remember – he was with us last week when we played bowls. The one with the moustache.'

'Oh yes – he was very nice about my pathetic attempts.'

'This is terrible . . .'

'Has he had a heart attack?'

Shaking her head, Esther looked confused. 'Look, Dan, I don't know how to explain this to you. But Jack and I have had a relationship for some time. I do feel awfully guilty. You see, Jack's married. Actually he's a grandfather. Anyway, that's how it is. And now . . .'

'He's broken it off,' I conjectured.

'No. Oh God, no, it's worse. His wife has just found out about it and thrown him out.'

'How old is Jack?' I asked.

'He's seventy-two, but it doesn't matter. The point is, he's got to pack his bags and come and live here.'

'Here?'

'He has nowhere else. And I want him here, Dan. Look, I hate to ask you this, but would you go and help him?'

I swallowed. 'Help him?'

'Help him pack. He's coming over to get some bags, and then he's got to return for his clothes. His bags will be very heavy . . .'

Jack arrived looking even more distraught than Esther. Together we drove to his apartment. From inside I heard screaming. With a trembling hand Jack opened the door. Sitting on the sofa was Jack's wife – an elderly woman with tousled white hair and smudged make-up wearing a dressing gown. By her side stood an attractive woman in a tennis dress. Jack introduced her to me as his daughter.

'You son of a bitch!' the older woman yelled. 'How dare you do this to me?'

Jack tiptoed into the bedroom as a stream of abuse echoed from the living room. Quickly he packed his bags, stuffing shirts, ties and shoes inside. We filled one bag and then another. Pointing to his golf clubs in a corner, he asked if I would carry them as well.

As we re-entered the living room Jack's wife stood up and accosted me. 'You're the rabbi, aren't you?'

'Well, yes . . .' I mumbled.

'How can you do this? You're supposed to stand for Jewish values. And here you are helping this old windbag commit adultery. And that woman's supposed to be a big macher in the Temple. I just don't understand it. I could spit.'

'Sorry,' I said.

' "Sorry!" ' she yelled. 'Is this what you mean by "sorry"? Coming in here where you're not welcome; helping Jack pack his stuff. This is "sorry"?'

'Come on, Mother,' the lady in the tennis clothes said, 'you'll have a heart attack if you go on like this.'

Jack's wife produced a handkerchief from her bathrobe and wiped tears from her face. She tried to speak but sobbed instead.

Jack kissed his daughter, picked up a bag and I followed behind, lugging another bag and the golf clubs.

As Jack drove to Esther's, he began to relax. 'That's the worst of it over,' he said. 'Thanks for helping me.'

I wasn't sure what to say and so remained silent.

'You know,' Jack went on, 'I've been married for over forty years. But this is the first time I've ever been in love.'

'Really?' I said.

'No kidding. I've got three grandchildren, but I feel like a new man.'

I wasn't sure whether I was meant to be congratulatory or censorious. I sat in silence for the rest of the journey.

Despite the conservatism I experienced in the congregation, the Temple was officially liberal in its attitude towards apartheid. As part of its educational programme, Rabbi Saltzman invited a prominent African chief to give a lecture in the Temple. On the night, the Temple car park was full, and the hall was completely packed. Before the lecture a small party had been arranged for the chief, his wife and the Temple officers. As we stood drinking cocktails in Rabbi Saltzman's study, I was impressed. In the context of the undercurrent of resentment against the black population I had experienced, this was a major step forward.

The chief spoke for nearly an hour about the problems facing South Africa, and the evils of apartheid. Movingly, he recounted stories about blacks in the homelands and the townships. Racist attitudes, he emphasized, were contrary to biblical teaching: it was the duty of the Jewish community to ensure that scripturally-based values were put into practice. When he finished, Rabbi Saltzman asked for questions. There was a hushed silence – no one dared speak. Since I was the guest rabbi, I thought I ought to start the ball rolling. When George called on me, I stood up. 'Chief,' I began, 'I think many of us are very sympathetic to your views. As you know, there are Jewish activists in South Africa who are fighting on your side. But if there is a bloodbath, as you indicate there might be, will blacks give any thought to those Jews who support political change?'

The chief shook his head. 'If my brothers and sisters descend upon the white inhabitants of South Africa, there will be no mercy. Do you think a black man with a knife will pause to ask if his white victim is Jewish? His knife will spill the blood of anyone he perceives as having oppressed and exploited the black nation.'

The answer caused a chill in the audience. If the black populace would not spare the lives of Jewish supporters, what was the point of advocating racial tolerance? Other members of the congregation then pursued related topics, and after half an hour of discussion, the evening came to an end. I joined Rabbi and Mrs Saltzman in his study where we thanked the chief. On the way out, he took me aside. 'You're American?' he asked.

I nodded.

'Let me give you some advice. Things may not improve in our country. This is not going to be a safe place for someone who is white. You'd be wise to get out while you can.'

'I wasn't planning to stay,' I replied. 'Actually I've got a job teaching in an English university next year.'

'Good,' he said. Looking down the street, he continued: 'One day tanks are going to come down this street. They will flood the streets of South Africa. And there will be nowhere to hide.'

When I arrived back at the flat, Esther and Jack were on the patio. They asked me to join them. After Esther poured me some coffee, she apologized for not coming to hear the chief. 'I thought it might be better not to appear at the Temple with Jack for a while . . . at least until this thing calms down.'

'Well, it was quite an experience,' I said. 'Very good to have it at the Temple.'

'Now, Dan,' Esther began. 'Jack and I have been planning a holiday. We both need a break, and we're intending to go to Botswana next weekend. We wonder if you'd like to join us? Jack is very grateful for the help you gave him when he moved out of his flat.'

Jack smiled wanly. 'Do come,' he said. 'There's swimming, and the best casino in Southern Africa.'

'We're going to drive there,' Esther continued. 'I'll speak to Rabbi Saltzman about it – I'm sure he'll give you the weekend off.'

After this conversation, I spoke to George about going away for the weekend; he had already been approached by Esther and was happy to cover for me.

'You're going to Botswana, then?' he asked.

'It was Esther's idea,' I replied. 'Ah . . . George,' I began. 'I've been meaning to ask you about this: did Esther mention Jack?'

We were sitting in George's office; coffee and biscuits had just been brought in by one of the black servants at the Temple. It was just after eleven. George thoughtfully stirred his coffee. 'I know all about it,' he said.

'You do? Did Esther bring it up when she asked if I could go?'

'I knew about it anyway,' he answered. 'Jack's wife came to see me.'

'Is she a member of the Temple?' I asked.

'An old member . . . actually her grandfather was one of the founders. He made his money in real estate, but the family has fallen on hard times since. Anyway, she was very upset. Very.'

'Did she mention me?' I inquired.

'Well, as a matter of fact, she did. She said you went with Jack to collect his clothes.'

'I didn't have much choice,' I said defensively.

'No. Of course not. Well, these things happen in life; she did take it badly, though. I just couldn't console her.'

'Did you tell Esther about it?'

George paused. 'I didn't see any point in upsetting her too.'

'And what do you think?'

George fiddled with his spoon. 'Esther's been an active Temple member for a long time, she's a big donor and a conscientious secretary of the board . . .'

'Is it true Jack's been married for over forty years?'

George sighed. 'I married his children, and did the bar mitzvah for his grandchildren.'

'You know Jack said he'd never been in love before?'

George whistled. 'At seventy-two that's quite something.'

'But George . . . Esther is an important member of the Temple. What are people going to think? And what do you think?'

George looked up. 'I think it's a tragedy.'

'You didn't express your opinion to Esther, I mean as a rabbi?'

'What's the point? She's going to do what she wants. And she didn't ask me.'

'I know. But shouldn't we express a bit of disapproval . . . ?'

George looked at me harshly. 'Dan, Esther's been very generous to the Temple. She's made a lot of money over the years, and the Temple has benefited. And she's also dedicated a lot of time to Temple projects.'

'Doesn't that apply to Jack's wife, too?' I asked.

'Not really,' he replied. 'Her family lost most of its money. Anyway, that's nothing to do with it. Esther was kind enough to house you for the summer; I don't think it's for us to stand in judgement.'

'I didn't mean to sound ungrateful.'

'The best thing,' George concluded, 'is to ignore it. After all, it's Esther and Jack's problem.'

That night at dinner Esther, Jack and I discussed the travel plans. In the course of our conversation, I mentioned that I had some friends from Cambridge who were from Botswana. Esther looked surprised. 'Who?' she asked.

When I told her their names, her eyes widened. 'That last person,' she said, 'is he related to the President?'

'I think the President's his cousin,' I said. 'We both rowed in the same boat for the college – he was a better rower than I was, but our crew was the worst on the river.'

'And he's back in Botswana?' she asked.

'I think so,' I replied.

'Why don't you ask him to dinner, then?'

'That's very kind of you,' I said. 'Are you sure?'

Listening to our conversation Jack looked uncomfortable. 'Uh, Esther,' he said, 'I've never eaten at the same table with a black man.'

Esther smiled. 'There's a first time for everything, Jack.'

The next Friday Esther, Jack and I set off for Botswana in Esther's car; I sat in the back seat as Esther drove. En route we stopped for lunch at a plush hotel which served an enormous smorgasbord. I marvelled at the capacity of white South Africans filling their plates with mountains of food. Late in the afternoon we arrived at our hotel in Gaberone, Botswana. When we checked into the hotel, I tried to locate my Cambridge friends. I didn't have their phone numbers, but I hoped the operator might be able to help me. I explained that I was visiting Gaberone, and I was trying to get in touch with several people who had been research students at Cambridge University in England the previous year. I then mentioned the name of my rowing friend who was the cousin of the President of Botswana. Somewhat awestruck, she said she wasn't allowed to give out his number.

'Well,' I said, 'there's someone else I know: his name is Adebajo.'

'You mean Adebajo, the government minister?'

Adebajo had never told me he was such a high-ranking minister; I knew him simply as a jolly, beer-drinking fellow who was usually in the college bar. As a mature student he had been sent by the government to study at Cambridge, but he never discussed his job at home.

'Yes,' I replied. 'That must be the same person.'

Eventually, after speaking to several secretaries at the ministry, I was put through to my friend.

'Dan, what are you doing in Botswana?' he asked.

'It's a long story . . . but I'm working in Durban for the summer as a rabbi, and I've come here for the weekend on holiday.'

'Ah . . . ministering to the rich in the fleshpots,' he teased.

'Something like that – but look, Adebajo, the people I'm with wonder if you'd like to join them for dinner at our hotel. And Rexford too, if he's free.'

'How very kind . . . I'd love to. I'll phone him and get back to you as soon as I can.' A half-hour later, Adebajo's secretary phoned to say that both he and Rexford would be delighted to come. When I told Esther, she was thrilled. 'A minister and a cousin of the President. That's quite impressive, Dan.'

'At Cambridge no one ever talked about it,' I said.

At eight Adebajo and Rexford arrived at the hotel, and I went to meet them in the lobby. I explained that my hosts were from South Africa, and that Esther was the secretary of the Temple. Jack, I said, was her boyfriend.

'How old are these people?' Adebajo asked.

'Actually, Jack is seventy-two. And I don't know how old Esther is.'

Hearing this, Rexford laughed. 'A boyfriend of seventy-two – that's a record.'

'And you're their chaperone?' Adebajo asked, grinning.

'Come on, you guys,' I said, 'let's go in for dinner.'

Throughout the meal Esther kept up an animated conversation about trading links between South Africa and Botswana. Jack, however, ate his food without speaking. I tried to engage him in the discussion, but he inaudibly muttered a reply and sank back into silence.

After we finished coffee, Adebajo and Rexford thanked Esther and Jack for their hospitality, and I walked them back to their car. 'Thanks, Dan,' Adebajo said. 'It was good to see you. But I hope you're not planning on being a rabbi with those people.'

'It's just for the summer,' I explained. 'Actually, I've just been appointed to a lectureship in theology at the University in Canterbury starting in September.'

'Canterbury's the place to be if you're a rabbi,' remarked Adebajo and slammed the car door behind him. My last glimpse was to see them giggling as the car skidded out of the car park.

The week after we arrived back in Durban there was a meeting of the Temple board. Because I was only visiting, I had never been invited to attend board meetings before. But since one of the major topics of discussion was the principle behind conversion to Judaism, I was asked to be present to give rabbinical weight to the proceedings. I sat next to Esther, who furiously took notes. When we came to the subject of conversion, George outlined the normal procedure, and then launched into a discussion of typical cases. He was concerned about the growing number of instances where a Jewish and non-Jewish partner were living together. The Temple, he believed, would implicitly be seen to condone such situations if the non-Jewish person was allowed to convert. George's stance had been to refuse to allow the non-Jewish candidate into the conversion class. Turning to board members, he asked if they agreed with him. All the members nodded sagely, including Esther. What, I wondered, could Esther be thinking? She was secretary of the Temple and she was living openly and adulterously with Jack. And yet we had just decided not to allow someone even to participate in Temple conversion classes if they were living in sin – it was extraordinary! And what about the rabbi who had so strenuously sought to distance himself from Esther and Jack's situation? How could he reconcile such caution and tolerance with this unequivocal condemnation of young couples living together? Was there simply one rule for the rich and powerful, and another for the poor and vulnerable?

The next item on the agenda concerned the High Holy Days. George was anxious to take a strong line against those who kept their stores open on Yom Kippur. Again, all the board members nodded agreement. George then proposed that in the next Temple bulletin he would reiterate the Temple's policy about this matter. But before he finished, I put up my hand. 'Uh, George,' I said, 'I think there's a problem about this.'

George glared at me. 'And just what is it?'

'The thing is,' I began, 'that a lot of Temple members keep their shops open on Saturday – like Esther. But according to Jewish law, it's actually more serious to do this than stay open on Yom Kippur . . . because the Sabbath is the most important holy day, even though it happens every week.'

Esther put her pen down. 'I resent this,' she sputtered. 'I keep my shop open like everyone else because that's the busiest day of the week. And quite frankly, Dan, I don't think it's any of your business telling us what we can do and what we can't do. As far as I'm concerned the Day of Atonement is the most important day of the year, and I come to the Temple then just like everybody else should.'

My eczema began to itch. Meekly, I hinted that if the Temple adopted such a position, we would be inconsistent and look ignorant.

At this point the President called a halt. 'I think we've discussed this matter quite enough. The Temple has always discouraged members from keeping their stores open on the High Holy Days, and we should continue to do so. The Sabbath is just a red herring.' And with that we moved on to other business.

One of my tasks in Durban was to officiate at the weddings of those who were not affiliated to the Temple. Frequently couples who wished to have a Jewish wedding requested that they be married in the synagogue. In such cases, I met the couple beforehand, discussed the details of the service, and made the appropriate arrangements. In some instances the engaged couple asked for modifications to the traditional service. On one occasion, the bride – a hefty opera singer – demanded that she be allowed to sing to the groom. Since George had never expressed reservations about altering the wedding service, I complied. When the day arrived, I stood under the huppah as she boomed out an aria – her voice was shattering and I nearly dropped the wine cup. At another ceremony the groom was so nervous that he kissed me as well as the bride, much to the amusement of the gathering. Frequently grooms had enormous difficulties breaking the wine glass at the conclusion of the ceremony; to facilitate this matter, I put a lightbulb in a handkerchief. The glass would then be broken without anyone knowing that there had been a substitution. At one wedding, however, the lightbulb exploded as the groom stamped on it and he nearly fainted.

On one Sunday, George sat in the congregation to listen as I conducted a wedding service; afterwards he offered a critique. 'Listen, Dan,' he said. 'You've got to do better than that.'

'You didn't like it? What did I do wrong?'

'You've got to slow down – you rushed through the prayers . . . and the sermon was far too short.'

'But I hardly know the couple,' I protested.

'I know. But the whole ceremony only took twelve minutes.'

'Did it? It seemed a lot longer to me.'

'I timed it. When I do a marriage, it takes nearly half an hour.'

'Half an hour! But what do you do?'

'For one thing,' George went on, 'I welcome everyone, and make a little speech about what a happy occasion it is for both families.'

'I don't do that. Anyway, both families disapprove of each other in this particular instance.'

'Well, then you must smooth it over between them. And then I read the prayers much more slowly, at about half your pace. And I take my time over the rest of the ceremony. People have to have their money's worth, you know.'

'I'm sure they don't think of it in those terms,' I said innocently.

'You'd be surprised. Anyway, I also say something much more personal about the bride and groom. I spin it out, and talk about how important marriage is in the tradition.'

'Well that pair have nothing to do with the tradition. He learned his bar mitzvah from a tape-recorder and she doesn't even know the blessing over the candles.'

'Never mind,' said George. 'You've got to make the right noises.'

'Uh, George, I don't think this is exactly my style,' I countered.

'That's what's required, Dan. After all, it is a marriage, not a funeral.'

'I think I prefer funerals,' I said.

Paradoxically, funerals were much more fun than weddings. As the visiting rabbi, it was my responsibility to officiate at all funerals for non-affiliated members – throughout the time I was at Durban,

Jews who did not belong to synagogues phoned the Temple when their relatives died. The Temple secretary took all relevant details, and then passed the information on to me and contacted the funeral director. It was the normal custom for the funeral director to collect me at the Temple: he parked his Rolls-Royce in the car park and came directly to my office. Soberly dressed in a black suit, Jack Weiss was in fact riotously funny. Every time I let him in, he told me the latest joke before we set off. From the time we left the Temple until we arrived at the cemetery, Jack kept up a monologue of Jewish humour. Sometimes he took a Groucho Marx nose and moustache out of his glove compartment and wore it en route. One time he put on an eye patch. But as we drove into the cemetery grounds, Jack assumed a serious expression, and we silently shook hands with the mourners. Jack then supervised his men who had brought the coffin, and ushered those who had come to the funeral into a small chapel. He then accompanied me as well as several of his assistants into a separate room at the back of the chapel. As soon as he closed the door, his expression changed, and another flood of Jewish humour was unleashed, but this time Jack's men told the jokes. As the mourners settled into their seats, the pallbearers broke into hysterical laughter, which was drowned out by the organ. However, once the organ stopped, Jack and his assistants became totally silent and serious. I tried to match their expressions as I led them into the chapel.

Although I never knew the person who died, I was always moved by the prayers and the tears of the mourners. By the time I recited the Twenty-third Psalm, I too used to cry as the organ played. Usually the mourners gave me a short speech to recite, and I was always choked with emotion as I read it. At the conclusion of the service, I recited the Kaddish prayer as though I were a close relative. Following the service, I led a procession to the grave for another brief graveside service. Again, I used to be overwhelmed by sadness as I recited the appropriate prayers and watched the coffin descend into thc grave.

On the way back to the Temple, Jack always congratulated me on my performance. 'Hey, Rabbi,' he said, 'that was tremendous.'

'Come on, Jack,' I said.

'No. Honestly. The relatives loved it. You broke their hearts.'

'Jack . . .'

'I mean it – I've been to thousands of funerals. You're the best . . . all those tears, and the crying. It was real Hollywood stuff.'

'Those tears were for real, Jack. I find it terribly sad.'

'Real or not, they really did the trick.'

'Listen, Jack, these funerals wear me out. I'm really drained by the whole experience.'

As we drove through the suburbs of Durban, I looked at the blacks waiting for buses.

'I'm telling you, Rabbi, you ought to think about specializing in funerals. Forget this congregational business. You don't want to deal with Temple boards – they're full of politics. Take it from me, I've seen enough of it in my time. You could make a good living just doing funerals. People would die just to have you take the service.'

'Very funny, Jack,' I said.

'Honestly, Rabbi. I'm not fooling. You'd be the Laurence Olivier of the funeral business.'

'Cut it out, Jack . . .'

As he manoeuvred his Rolls into the car park, he looked at me. 'You really want to be a rabbi with a congregation?' he asked.

'No, Jack. I don't. I'm going to become a university lecturer.'

As he parked the car, he shook his head. 'You'd make a lot more money burying people, that's for sure.'

As the High Holy Days drew near, I was anxious to return to England. I missed Lavinia terribly, and I was excited about my new job in Canterbury. As I worked feverishly on my sermons, I had a phone call from the President of the Temple. He explained that he and some of the officers wanted to talk to me; he asked if they might pay a visit to Esther's flat one night. My eczema began to itch. What had I done wrong this time? Hesitantly I asked what they wanted to see me about.

'Actually,' the President said, 'we wanted to discuss the possibility of your working here as an associate rabbi. But it's best to discuss the details when we meet.'

This was very flattering. But there was simply no way I could stay in South Africa: Lavinia and I were to be married, and I had decided to give up the congregational rabbinate. During the summer I hadn't revealed my future plans to anyone in the congregation because I was reluctant to face the complicated questioning which would inevitably ensue. What was I to say now?

At the arranged time the President arrived, along with the Vice-President and the treasurer. Esther apologized that she couldn't come as well, since she had to work late at her store. The black maids served coffee and cake as we chatted in Esther's living room. I had never known the President to be so affable. After a rambling discussion about the High Holy Day arrangements, he finally got down to business.

'Dan,' he began, 'the board members had an informal discussion last week, and we would like to make you an offer. We're pleased with your work, and we wonder if you might consider staying on – at least for a few years – as George's associate.'

'What does George think of this?' I asked.

'We've discussed it with him, and he's happy with the idea – as you know, he needs some help. The congregation is growing, and it's really too much for one rabbi.'

'It's very kind of you to ask me,' I replied, 'but I've got to go back to England: I haven't heard about my PhD.'

'But why would you need to return?' the President asked.

'Well, if I get the degree, I won't need to,' I hedged, 'but I might have to revise the thesis if my examiners recommend that it be resubmitted.'

'Let's not worry about that now. All things being equal, we'd like to have you here.'

'Thanks,' I said meekly.

The treasurer then took a calculator out of his pocket, did several computations, and announced how much the Temple would be willing to pay.

'How much is that in American dollars?' I asked.

Again the treasurer did a calculation and told me the amount.

I cleared my throat. 'Uh . . . I must tell you, that's actually only half of the normal starting salary that the seminary currently recommends for newly-ordained rabbis. And I've been a rabbi for three years.'

The officers looked at one another. 'You must remember,' the President began, 'that the cost of living is much lower here than in the States. You can have a good flat, or even a house, for much less. And you could easily afford to have black help on this salary. In addition, we'd pay your travel expenses, plus moving costs. And I think we might even be able to help you with the cost of furniture. Don't forget, too, that we'd provide you with a car.'

'I realize that,' I said. 'It's very nice of you to ask me. But I'll need time to think about it.'

'Of course you will,' the President said. 'It's a big step . . . we understand. But it would be best if you could let us know after Yom Kippur. That's officially when your contract with us ends anyway. Will that give you enough time?'

Throughout the summer I had followed George's advice not to discuss apartheid, but I felt the time had come to express my view. Since I knew I would be leaving South Africa for good, I resolved to broach the subject in my sermon for Rosh Hashanah. On the day I arrived early at the Temple, and waited for the congregation. From my office I watched the car park fill up – I had never seen so many members before. By the time the service was due to begin, there must have been over a thousand people present. George was to conduct the service and read from the Torah; my responsibility was to preach. When my turn came, I took out my notes and waited for silence. I began by explaining that I had been cautioned not to speak about apartheid, but I believed the time had come for me to face this issue. As I spoke, I observed that the congregation was becoming increasingly uncomfortable. I then told them about an experience I had had in a car park in Durban – when I got out of my car, the door lightly touched the car next to me – it was a Jaguar. The owner got out and angrily abused me even though I hadn't scratched anything. This, I asserted, was a perverse preoccupation with material objects. I then proceeded to tell them about the accident I had had in my own Austin Healey in Brownsville: I emphasized that I had been distraught then because I had felt that my self-image had been dented when my car was demolished. But, I went on, this was an illusion. My identity was the same with or without the car.

All this was an introduction to my theme. I went on to tease the congregation about its materialism: I said I was blinded by their diamond rings, and amazed to see so many expensive cars in the car park. I joked that I had never seen so many Mercedes-Benzes, Rolls-Royces and Jaguars in one place. Such a concentration on material goods, I argued, was misguided, given the economic deprivation I had experienced in Durban and elsewhere. It was not enough to be rich Jews among poor blacks. Our ancestors were slaves in Egypt; in each and every generation Jews are obliged to struggle for the liberation of those who are oppressed and persecuted. As Jews, we must not become the Pharaohs of the modern world; instead the Jewish community must stand shoulder to shoulder with their black brothers and sisters and oppose all forms of racism and exploitation.

When I had finished, there was a stunned silence. I glanced at George – he looked away. At the end of the service, George gave the priestly benediction and together we walked down the aisle to the back of the Temple. There, we greeted congregants and wished them a good new year. From their expressions I could tell they were displeased – many avoided me. Finally, when the sanctuary was empty, I accompanied George to the room behind the bimah where we put our robes. I could tell George was furious. When we were alone, he shut the door. Eyes blazing, he castigated me for breaking my word.

'But, George, I never actually promised I wouldn't talk about apartheid.'

'That was a really stupid thing to do,' he said. 'I mean . . . the congregation was set to offer you a job. Do you really think they will now?'

'I didn't agree to stay, George . . .'

'Well, it's too late.'

'I believe what I said, George.'

'That's not the point. You're new here; you're a guest. You've insulted your hosts.'

'I'm also a rabbi . . .'

'That was the most unpolitic sermon I ever heard,' George protested.

'Sermons aren't supposed to be politic – we're supposed to speak the truth.'

'Look, Dan. Do you know what kind of car the President's wife drives?'

'No,' I said innocently.

George glared at me as he took off his robe. 'It's a brand-new Mercedes convertible.'

'I hope she's ashamed of herself,' I said, determined to stand my ground.

When I arrived back at Esther's flat, I ran into Esther's aunt in the hall.

'Dan,' she whispered, 'come with me.'

I followed her on to the patio. 'What is it?' I said apprehensively.

Ida smiled and took my hand. 'That was a wonderful sermon,' she said.

'Did you think so?'

'It's about time somebody spoke out like that. You were very brave.'

'But, Ida,' I said. 'George just told me off. And I think it'll cause a lot of trouble.'

'Of course it will,' pronounced Ida. 'Esther complained all the way home. But you're right about the blacks.'

'This is kind of you, Ida. I really appreciate it.'

'Esther said they'll never offer you a job now – do you mind?'

'Don't tell Esther, but I've already got a job for next year. I'm going to teach at an English university.'

Ida was relieved. 'This isn't the place for you, Dan,' she said. 'You'll be much better off in England. I wouldn't have stayed here myself if it weren't for Esther.'

The next day I was awakened by one of the maids. 'Master,' she said. 'It's the President of the Temple on the phone.'

Half-asleep, I padded into the drawing room and picked up the phone. 'Hello,' I said.

'It's about time you were up! I've practically done a day's work and you're still in bed.'

'What time is it?'

'It's half past eight. Now, look here, Dan, all day yesterday people kept telephoning me about your sermon. It was a disgrace – I can't imagine what you were thinking of. Anyway, the point is you should forget about the job offer we made to you.'

'I never said I'd stay,' I said.

'No. I know. But you can forget about it. I just wanted to get that straight.'

'I've got the message.'

'And there's one more thing: no more comments about the South African situation in your Yom Kippur sermon. I mean it, Dan. We've had quite enough.'

'I haven't written it yet . . .'

'Well, when you do, just stick to something spiritual. No more politics.'

Before I could reply, he hung up.

During the next week George ignored me. However, a few days before the Day of Atonement, he called me into his office. After discussing the details of the service, he took out a pack of cigarettes, lit up and leaned back in his chair. 'So what are you going to do when you get back to England?' he asked.

'I've got to find out about my thesis . . . I might have to revise it,' I said.

'And then?'

I paused – I was disinclined to tell George the whole story. But, before I said anything, he continued: 'Look, Dan,' he said, 'you've done a good job here. But quite frankly, I don't think you're suitable for the congregational rabbinate. That sermon of yours caused more trouble than anything I can ever remember. People are still fuming about it.'

I listened as George continued to lecture me about my career.

'I'm sure this isn't the only time you've had difficulties with congregations. Am I right?'

'You're right, George,' I replied.

'To survive in this business, you've got to be practical. And you need common sense. Honestly, Dan, you have no instinct when it comes to the rabbinate.'

I continued to remain silent as George carried on. 'You could have had a good job here, Dan. But you messed things up – the situation is irredeemable.'

I stood up to go. 'Thanks, George,' I said. 'But I don't really need your advice – I've already made up my mind not to enter the congregational rabbinate.'

'Then what are you doing here?' George demanded.

'Actually, George,' I said as I closed the door, 'I came to make some money.'

Anxious not to create another storm, I avoided the subject of apartheid in the sermon I prepared for the Day of Atonement. I decided I would appeal to the children in the congregation. My idea was to represent broken promises – made for the new year – by pricking a balloon with a pin. Each balloon was to represent a specific promise. This was to be my final appearance at the Temple, and I vaguely hoped I might be able to redeem myself. When I started out in the morning, I collected together my rabbinical gown, prayer book and sermon. But to my horror, I realized I had forgotten to buy balloons. What was I to do? I asked the black maids if they had any – they shrugged their shoulders. There was only one solution – I'd had to buy some on the way to the Temple. But it was Yom Kippur! What if someone saw me?

There was no alternative, however, and I drove as fast as I could. There was a shopping centre on the way, and I parked in the lot. I walked past several shops, and quickly entered a toy store. Surely no one from the congregation would be there! I asked if I could buy a packet of balloons, and departed as speedily as I could. I got into my car, started the engine, and sped away. Yet, as I turned into the main road I looked in the rear view mirror. In the car behind me was someone who looked familiar; she was wearing a hat. Next to her were two children dressed in their best. Could they be members of the congregation? Had they spotted me?

When I arrived at the Temple, the parking lot was nearly full and I had difficulty finding a place. I ran all the way to the entrance, and shot up the stairs. I still had about ten minutes before the service was due to begin: I changed into my robe, and made my way to the sanctuary clutching my prayer book, sermon and balloons. The sermon proved to be a great success; afterwards many of the parents thanked me for doing something so entertaining. The children smiled when they saw me; this was quite a different reaction from Rosh Hashanah.

At the end of the day, I was exhausted: George and I shared the service, but it was still tiring to be on one's feet the entire time without anything to eat. I was due to go to George's flat to break the fast with his family. But before we started out, he indicated he wanted to speak to me about something important. I swallowed, and my eczema itched as I sat across from him in his office. 'Dan,' he began. 'I heard something very troubling today from one of the parents.'

Fearing the worst, I listened without saying anything.

'Did you go shopping today?' he asked.

So I had been seen – but I had only bought a few balloons for my sermon. How was I going to defend myself? 'Yes, George. I did. But it wasn't really shopping – I simply forgot to buy the balloons, and I got some on the way to the Temple.'

George shook his head in disbelief. 'You bought balloons?'

'For my sermon. That's all. It's been a busy time with all the packing. I just forgot.'

'On Yom Kippur?'

'Is it such a sin, George? After all, we are Progressive Jews.'

'Not that Progressive.'

'Look, I simply forgot. But a lot of people congratulated me on my sermon. They said it was great.'

'I don't understand you, Dan. You're a rabbi. You can't go and spend money in a shopping mall on the most holy day of the year.'

'Well, George, I did. And it's done. And that's the end of it.'

'So is your tenure here at the Temple,' he replied.

'Well at least I went out with a bang,' I said.

Chapter 9

An Ivory-tower Rabbi: In the Groves of Academe

When my plane from Durban landed at Heathrow, I stood in the queue for aliens. On the other side of passport control, I saw Lavinia waiting for me – but I had to negotiate immigration first. The officer looked at my picture, scrutinized me, and then thumbed through a massive book. I assumed this ominous volume contained a list of undesirable characters. In the distance Lavinia look anxious. Finally, after a long exchange about my job at the university, I was let through. Home at last!

The next few weeks were hectic. Lavinia and I had a small wedding arranged by Lavinia's mother. We purchased a tiny terraced cottage in the centre of Canterbury and filled it with furniture Lavinia had inherited from her family. In the sitting room we arranged small portraits of Lavinia's ancestors; on the floor we put an old Persian carpet which was a wedding present from my grandmother. The rest of the house was decorated with objects both of us had accumulated during our days at Cambridge.

Marriage to Lavinia also involved the acceptance of Digger – her ginger cat, who was rumoured to have a very distinguished pedigree. He was said to be descended from one of the earliest Burmese in England. I didn't like him and he didn't like me. On the first night in our house, he curled up on Lavinia's side of the bed and when I turned towards her, he bit me. For weeks he regarded me as an invader of his sacred territory. He used to sit on our dressing table, glaring at us both in bed and then knock my watch off on to the carpet. Eventually, I could bear his hostility no longer. He sat blinking at me from Lavinia's lap while we had our first major quarrel.

'That beast has got to go,' I declared.

'He's not going!' she said indignantly.

'He's horrible – and he hates me too.'

'We're a package deal,' Lavinia announced, tickling him under his tiger-striped chin. 'It's both of us or neither.'

'Come on, Lavinia,' I said. 'Be reasonable.'

'I am reasonable,' Lavinia stated, and continued reading her book. Digger closed his eyes and purred provocatively. He knew he was safe.

What was I to do? We would simply have to get used to each other. Several days later, I fell asleep in the sitting room reading the newspaper. Lavinia had gone out shopping – when she arrived back, she found Digger draped over my knee, also enjoying a little nap.

'Well, well . . .' she said, putting down the groceries. 'I see you've made friends.'

Digger and I looked sheepishly at one another. There didn't seem to be anything either of us could say.

Term had just begun when we moved into our house. My main responsibility was to teach an introductory course on Judaism and a seminar for a joint course on comparative religion. At my initial meeting with Professor Fieldmouse, he had explained what my duties would be. When we had gone over all the arrangements, I anxiously brought up the subject of my thesis. 'I haven't heard anything yet,' I complained. 'I've phoned the Cambridge Graduate Office several times, but they won't say anything. They simply say I'll have to wait, and they refuse to tell me how long it will be.'

'Look, Dan,' Professor Fieldmouse began, 'I'm not supposed to tell you. But I think you ought to know there are some difficulties. That's why it's taken so long. You're going to have to revise the thesis.'

This was just what I had feared. 'How bad is it?' I asked.

'I'm not sure. There seems to be a problem about your conclusion. I mean . . . are you definitely persuaded that intercessory prayer doesn't work?'

'That's what the whole thesis is about.'

'I thought so. I want to give you some advice – but you don't have to take it, of course.'

'I would appreciate some help,' I said.

'It's not that kind of advice. You might consider submitting the thesis as it stands to an academic press. If you can get it published, and can include other material with it, you could resubmit all your published work for a PhD some time in the future. This would be an alternative to rewriting. You'd then be spending your time on publishing rather than revising. Think about it.'

When I discussed this suggestion with Lavinia, she urged me to follow Professor Fieldmouse's advice. 'You're busy enough preparing for your classes,' she said. 'See if you can get it accepted as it stands.'

To my astonishment, the first firm I submitted it to – an academic press which only produced books for research libraries – expressed interest in the manuscript. After only a short negotiation, they took it for their list. I was about to become an author!

Teaching at the university was a delight – in contrast to those of Temple religion schools, the students were actually interested in the subject and wrote down every word I said. What, I wondered, would they do with this written record? To my astonishment some of the students even brought tape-recorders to class – it was beyond comprehension that they would want to listen twice to what I had said. How different this all was from my experience in the rabbinate, where I had struggled to attract anyone to adult study groups!

Sprinkled among the undergraduates were a handful of friars who were simultaneously studying at the Franciscan Study Centre located next to the university campus. Occasionally, they came dressed in their habits to my Judaism class. The cleaning lady, who was a Catholic, was thrilled whenever she saw them with their black rosaries hanging from their belts; before class she chatted to them in the corridor. On one occasion I was explaining about tefillin. These, I said, are small leather boxes which contain passages from the Torah; they are worn by Orthodox male Jews on their arms and heads in fulfilment of a biblical commandment. Their purpose, I went on, is to remind the wearer to keep God's law. Listening to my explanation, one of the Franciscans held up his rosary. 'Uh, Rabbi Dan,' he said. 'We have something similar, you know – the rosary is supposed to aid concentration in prayer.'

I had never made the connection. I couldn't help but wonder what the rabbis I had worked with or the congregants I had served would make of this scene: I was lecturing to Christians about Judaism, and they were teaching me about their own faith in relation to mine. This was so utterly different from what I had expected to do in those years I was a congregational rabbi and infinitely more satisfying.

For me such teaching was bliss – yet I did feel guilty. It had been my aspiration to serve Jews – but there were no Jews in my classes. Was this in some sense a betrayal?

When I told Lavinia about my self-doubts, she laughed. 'But you don't like synagogues,' she said. 'And quite clearly the members don't like you.'

'That's true,' I admitted. 'But I have a conscience about this. Do you think I'm doing any good?'

'Of course you are. You're countering anti-Semitism.'

'I am?' I asked, puzzled.

'Do you think any of your students will end up pushing Jews into gas chambers after they have taken your class?'

'I never thought about that,' I admitted.

'Come on, Dan. As a congregational rabbi, you'd just end up making everybody angry. But here you're helping the goyim feel better about Jews. That seems a far more useful activity than driving your board President into premature apoplexy.'

'Do you think so, really?'

'You're doing a mitzvah, Dan. That's the way to look at it. What do you want for supper?'

I felt a great deal better and demanded a hamburger.

Frequently Lavinia and I went to parties at the university; at these events academics mingled with people from the town. On one occasion I met the wife of a new Canon of the Cathedral. When I told her I was a rabbi, she grabbed my arm. 'Come with me – you must meet William.' I was led across the room to a tall, bearded figure who was holding forth to a group of women admirers. 'William,' the Canon's wife said, 'this is the new rabbi from America. He teaches Jewish studies at the university.'

The Canon shook hands and took me aside. 'You know,' he said, 'my mother was Jewish.'

'That means you're Jewish, too,' I said. Despite the large cross he wore around his neck, he did look like a patriarchal character out of the pages of the Bible.

'When she married my father,' he explained, 'she converted to Christianity. And I was brought up in the faith.'

'Do you know much about Judaism?' I asked.

'Not as much as I'd like . . .'

Brushing her long red hair from her face, William's wife turned to Lavinia. 'Come for lunch this Saturday – we always like to have guests then.'

On Saturday Lavinia and I arrived at one. The door to the Canonry – a vast mansion in the Cathedral precincts – was wide open. We walked inside, to be greeted by three cats. Lavinia, in her element, was enchanted. Down the corridor, we heard William and his wife Elizabeth's voices. 'Come on into the kitchen,' William shouted. As we walked down the hall, we gazed at magnificent portraits of previous Canons that lined the walls. In the kitchen Elizabeth was making lunch as several of their children ran in and out of the room. When we sat down at the kitchen table, two of the cats joined us while the other fell asleep on a basket in the corner. Over lunch William and Elizabeth asked us where we met. I explained that we had been adversaries at a debate at the Cambridge Union.

'William and I met at Cambridge, too,' Elizabeth said. 'I was a librarian at Newnham and William was a chaplain at Selwyn.'

After lunch, we had coffee in the drawing room, which was lined with more portraits. Just before we were about to leave, William told me that he was anxious to continue teaching theology; previously he had been the canon theologian at Chelmsford Cathedral.

'Would you consider teaching an adult education course for the university?' I asked.

Stroking his beard, he nodded. 'That's just the kind of thing I had in mind.'

'Well,' I went on, 'I'm supposed to teach a course about worship. Would you like to do something together – maybe something about Jewish and Christian prayer?'

'Oh, William,' Elizabeth interjected, 'that would be wonderful. Do say yes.'

'Well, that would be most kind. Are you sure?'

As the university rabbi, it was somewhat incongruous that I should be teaching together with a Christian clergyman, but our course attracted a sizeable number of students – for convenience's sake, we decided to meet at the Canonry. Every Wednesday evening, a dozen elderly ladies, William and I sat around the dining table. One week it was William's turn to lead the class; I took over the next week. Beginning with biblical origins, we traced the development of Jewish and Christian ritual to the present.

As the course was nearing its end, we arranged an outing to a nearby convent of Anglican Benedictine nuns. William had previously been in contact with the Mother Superior, and she readily agreed to have our group. The purpose of the trip was to give our class an insight into the contemplative life. It was to be a day of silence. When we arrived we were ushered into a hall where the Lady Mother addressed us. An impressive figure in her late seventies, she was dressed in black. Silence, she pointed out, is fundamental to the religious life – it is in stillness that the voice of God can be heard. Citing Scripture, she emphasized that the prophet Elijah experienced the divine presence as a still small voice rather than through the tempests, fire and general cacophony that accompanied the revelation on Mount Sinai. For the Christian, she continued, it is in the mysterious depths of silence that Christ can be found.

After her talk, William said a short prayer as we all bowed our heads. This was followed by a long period when no one said anything. I looked at some of our students – most had shut their eyes and folded their hands as they meditated on what we had been told. Finally, the Lady Mother brought us to order and announced that lunch would take place in the dining hall. She instructed us not to say anything during the meal, since one of the nuns would be reading to us from *The Little Flowers of St Francis*.

When we took our places, the Lady Mother said grace. There was a scraping of chairs, and then a clattering of dishes as food was served. The meal consisted of a home-made pizza with salad. Unfortunately the jug of water had not been passed down to our end. Was it acceptable to ask that it be handed down? In the background one of the nuns droned on about the adventures of St Francis and his brothers. I looked at one of the nuns near the water jug. I smiled; she smiled back. Could I whisper instructions to pass the water? This was too perplexing, and I decided to keep quiet. As I ate lunch, I looked at those across from me who munched their pizza as the nun continued reading. How different this all was from a Jewish household! It was simply unthinkable for Jews to eat without talking. Unused to the overpowering quiet – except for the incessant reading – I concentrated on the food.

After lunch the students were taken on a tour of the grounds, but the Lady Mother asked that I join her for a brief chat. As we entered her study, she urged me to sit across from her in an overstuffed armchair. 'William tells me you're a Progressive rabbi', she began. 'Do you know that our Lord was a Progressive rabbi, too?'

'I'm not sure "Progressive" is the right word,' I replied.

'Ah . . . but he was, you know. He was critical of the Pharisees, and I dare say you and he would have had more in common than you think.'

'Perhaps,' I mused.

'Now, Rabbi. May I ask you an impertinent question – have you ever thought about accepting Jesus as Saviour?'

I hadn't expected to be faced by such an onslaught on my first visit to a convent – the purpose of our trip was to give our students a taste of the Benedictine experience. Hesitantly, I explained that I couldn't possibly accept the central tenets of the Christian faith.

'Why not?' she said, smiling.

'To begin with,' I stated, 'the doctrine of the Incarnation is unbelievable – at least to me.' I went on to say why I thought it was theologically incoherent.

'Is it more unbelievable than what you Jews believe about God?' she asked.

'Well, yes . . . frankly. We don't think that God could become man. For us that's impossible.'

'You know,' she continued. 'That's just what one of our most famous fathers of the Church said about the Incarnation. He thought it was impossible, too. But that's just why he was so convinced it was true.'

'I don't think I understand,' I said.

Picking up the train of her habit, the Lady Mother stood up. 'Faith is the greatest of all mysteries. You mustn't try to understand with your mind. You should reach out to God with your heart. I will pray for you, Rabbi. Now, let us go and find your students.'

Once we had settled into Canterbury, Lavinia was hired to teach religion at King's School. Located in the Cathedral precincts, King's is an ancient foundation, dating back to the sixth century. The boys at the school wear wing collars and black jackets with striped trousers; prefects are entitled to purple gowns. On speech day those leaving the school wear court dress consisting of tails, knee-britches with black stockings and buckled shoes. At the first speech day I attended, the masters donning academic gowns and hoods sat together in the school hall; I was placed near the front among ladies with hats. As we filed out afterwards into a grass quadrangle facing the Deanery with the Cathedral in the background, a brass band played. Boys in court dress mingled with their teachers and parents in a large, striped tent. Eventually, after collecting tea and cakes, everyone sat down at small tables scattered on the lawn. Tourists gaped at this extraordinary sight as they passed by on their way to the Cathedral.

As I ate my chocolate cake, the Headmaster approached our table. Canon Firestone was a clergyman as well as head of the school; he was dressed in a dark suit, dog collar and academic gown. 'Well, well,' he teased, 'I see the rabbi is enjoying himself.'

Standing up, I muttered an inaudible reply.

'Don't get up,' he said. 'Look, I've got a proposition for you, Dan.'

'For me?' I asked.

'What about teaching some theology to our Oxford and Cambridge candidates next year?' Looking at Lavinia, he smiled. 'I'm sure the head of religious studies won't mind.'

'But are you sure? I mean . . . I'm not a Christian. And this is a Church of England school.'

'That doesn't matter a bit. What you need to do is get them thinking. Make them ask some questions. That sort of thing. It goes down a treat with the Oxbridge dons.'

'Are you sure?' I queried.

'The bursar will get in touch about expenses. But don't expect to make a fortune.'

'Thanks,' I said as the Headmaster strode off to greet parents.

At the first session, older boys as well as sixth-form girls flooded into the classroom. I cleared my throat and explained that I was Lavinia's husband. From the back an athletic youth shouted out: 'Do we call you Rabbi, sir?'

'Well, yes, I guess. But for the purpose of this class you mustn't make any assumptions about what I believe.'

'Right on, Rabbi,' nodded another youth.

For the next half-hour I lectured about the nature of religious truth. I outlined various theories and discussed the view of logical positivists who maintain that religious statements have no factual content. The pupils took extensive notes. When I had finished, I asked if there were any questions. About ten hands shot up, and for the next half-hour I was grilled about what I had said. Some of the conservative-minded pupils attacked the logical positivists; the sceptics counter-attacked. When the bell rang, I excused the class but a few remained behind to continue the discussion.

Later in the day, I went to meet Lavinia in the Senior Common Room of the school. On the way I came across the chaplain. Smiling, he told me that he had heard about my class from several of the pupils. 'You caused quite a storm among the evangelicals,' he said.

'Oh dear; did I?' I felt nervous.

'Very good, if I may say. They need a bit of stirring up. It comes better from you than from me.'

After teaching in the school for some time, the chaplain asked if I would like to preach at one of the school services. He explained that no rabbi had ever preached in Canterbury Cathedral, and permission would have to be sought from the Archbishop. I was flattered and readily agreed. Several weeks later, he phoned to say that the Archbishop had given his consent, and a date was set. It was also arranged that Lavinia and I would have lunch afterwards at the Headmaster's house.

On the day, I arrived early at the Cathedral; the chaplain met me in the nave, showed me where I would be sitting, and explained how the microphone worked. A few minutes before the service was to begin the Cathedral began to fill with pupils in Sunday best and masters in academic gowns and hoods. I was then ushered into one of the chapels where the choir and the clergy had already assembled. The Headmaster asked if I would like to say a prayer; not sure what was required I recited a traditional Jewish formula: 'Blessed art Thou, O Lord, our God, King of the universe, who has preserved us, sustained us, and brought us to this day.' No doubt this prayer had never been used in such a context!

I then filed into the Cathedral, following the Headmaster and the canons. I sat next to William, who helped me follow the service. After a reading from the New Testament, I was led to the pulpit by one of the stewards and I mounted the steps. Before me sat six hundred pupils, plus all the masters; in the front row Lavinia was placed next to the Headmaster's wife. When the hymn ended, I began my sermon. The topic I had chosen was 'failure', and I began by describing my catastrophic career in my Cambridge college boat; I hoped the congregation might be able to identify with that. I went on to explain that in both the Jewish and Christian traditions failure is recognized and accepted – it is symbolized in Christianity by Jesus on the cross, and in Judaism by the image of God's suffering servant. In conclusion, I emphasized that success should not be the ultimate goal in all our endeavours – rather by sharing in failure and suffering we are able to grow in compassion.

After the service the Headmaster congratulated me. But as he led Lavinia and me to his house, he teased me about what I had said. 'Well, Dan,' he stated, 'that's the end of any attempt to get the boys to study for their exams – what am I going to do about my Oxbridge results?'

The Headmaster's house was located opposite the Cathedral; as we entered the door a maid handed us glasses of champagne. Mrs Firestone – an elegant willowy woman – greeted us and showed us into the drawing room. Seated on a sofa was the Archbishop of Canterbury: no one had bothered to mention he was coming for lunch! The Headmaster introduced Lavinia and me, and we stood talking before the fireplace. Disconcerted by this encounter, I accidentally spilled champagne all over my suit. In horror I watched it fizz and bubble. The Headmaster handed me a handkerchief and kept talking. I mopped up as best I could and tried to hide my embarrassment.

At lunch Lavinia was seated next to the Archbishop; I was placed at the opposite end, next to Mrs Firestone. The lunch was delicious and the talk fascinating. It felt a long way from Jewish Denver. We then had coffee in the drawing room. On the way out, Lavinia took my arm. 'Dan', she said, 'I've got something to tell you: the Archbishop needs your help.'

'My help? Come on . . .'

'That's what he said. He's got to make a speech to a group of rabbis. And he's not sure what to say. He wants to talk to you about it.'

'Are you kidding?'

'Honestly. He told me to tell you. I gave him our phone number, and he said he'll give you a ring.'

Several weeks after I preached at the Cathedral, Morris came to stay with us in Canterbury. He was on his way home to Australia from the United States, where again he had been interviewing candidates for the position of assistant rabbi at the Temple in Melbourne. With the retirement of Rabbi Goldfarb, Morris had fulfilled his life-long ambition and had been appointed rabbi there. We picked him up from the airport and drove to Canterbury; all the way he regaled us with tales about life in Australia. Barry, he said, was thrilled to be in charge of the Temple in Perth now that Joshua had also retired. Solomon Finkelstein, he went on, was due to take Morris's place as Barry's assistant in Perth once he finished at the seminary.

After Morris had settled into his room, he closed the door. 'Does Lavinia know about Margie?' he asked.

'I told Lavinia all about her,' I replied. 'We don't have any secrets.'

'You might be interested to know that she married the son of Henry Goldstone, the treasurer of the Temple.'

'Did she?' I asked wide-eyed, 'so she really was ambitious.'

'And I just did her son's circumcision.'

'She had a son?'

'She said I should send regards,' Morris smiled.

'Well . . . well,' I muttered. 'What about you, Morris? Have you kept up with Victoria?'

Morris reddened. 'How do you know about her?'

'I met her at your wedding – didn't you know?'

'I haven't seen her since then,' he said. Reaching into his wallet, he took out a crumpled piece of paper and unfolded it. 'But I've kept her address.'

'Still holding the torch, are you?' I teased.

'I suppose so . . .' he mumbled. 'I've never told Judy about her.'

'Does Lavinia know about Jan?' he asked.

'Of course,' I said. 'She married a Jewish psychiatrist and the four of us are planning to meet up when we go to Boston.'

Morris shook his head in amazement.

That evening we had dinner at home; I was carving roast chicken as the telephone rang – Lavinia was busy in the kitchen. 'Could you answer it, Morris?' I shouted. Morris picked up the telephone. 'Yes, he's here,' he said. 'Can I ask who's calling?'

Morris laughed as he handed over the phone: 'It's some guy pretending to be the Archbishop of Canterbury.'

'Hello,' I said. 'Oh, yes, Archbishop – Lavinia mentioned you might be ringing.'

When I hung up, Morris asked who I was speaking to.

'It really was the Archbishop,' I said.

'Cut it out, Dan!'

'Honestly. He wants me to help him with a speech he's got to deliver to a group of rabbis. I've got to write it in the next few days.'

'Ha, ha,' Morris said.

'Do you want to come?' I asked.

Dinner was uproarious; Morris had never been a quiet person, and over the years he had become more voluble and outspoken. Digger did not enjoy the noise; he continually glared at Morris from Lavinia's lap. When Morris went upstairs to bed Digger padded up behind him. Suddenly we heard a shriek. 'It's your damn cat!' Morris screamed. 'He's peed in my wastebasket.' Digger shot downstairs and out of the cat door. Lavinia and I went up to investigate. It was true: Morris's wastebasket was dripping and it smelled of cat pee. We were both highly amused. Digger was the most fastidious of cats – he had never done anything like this before. But he certainly knew how to express his disapproval when the occasion demanded it.

Over the next few days Morris stayed in London, where he interviewed more candidates for the position in Melbourne, and we arranged to meet for dinner before the Archbishop's talk. The three of us went to a small Italian restaurant in Soho; over spaghetti I told him what I had written for the Archbishop.

'Look, Dan,' he interrupted, 'you can't really expect me to believe this.'

'It's the truth, Morris.'

'We'll see,' he jeered.

The talk was to take place at Lambeth Palace, the Archbishop's official London residence. When we took our place in the hall, several London rabbis came over to say hello. Finally, the Archbishop entered accompanied by the Chief Rabbi, who introduced him. As I had told Morris, the topic was to be the Christian attitude to the poor. The Archbishop began by quoting from Scripture, and then gave a long discourse about the traditional Christian attitude to the underprivileged. In conclusion he delineated common ground between Christian and Jewish teaching on social responsibility. As the Archbishop spoke, Morris glanced at me – the speech was exactly as I had described at dinner. At the end the Archbishop quoted from something I had written: several heads turned around and Morris closed his eyes.

Afterwards we went to a pub; Morris was unusually silent.

'A bit shocked are we, Morris?' Lavinia asked.

'That was incredible,' he said. 'I mean . . . what are you doing, writing speeches for the Archbishop of Canterbury?'

'He asked me to,' I replied.

'But it was all about Jesus! Just whose side are you on?'

'I'm ecumenical,' I said.

Morris shook his head. 'You're a rabbi, not a Christian.'

'But the Archbishop's a Christian, not a rabbi – so that's what I wrote.'

'And what do you think the Chief Rabbi would have thought if he knew that a Reform rabbi had written the Archbishop's speech?'

'I think it would confirm his view on the heretical nature of Reform Judaism,' I replied.

‘And what were you doing getting the Archbishop to quote from something you’d written?’ Morris grew more and more agitated.

‘I thought I ought to get a bit of credit,’ I said.

Morris rolled his eyes. ‘Nice Jewish boys don’t write Archbishop’s speeches,’ he pronounced.

‘This one does,’ responded Lavinia.

My article, which the Archbishop had referred to in his speech, had appeared in a leading British journal of religion. William had read it and was impressed. As a result, he asked if I would be interested in being proposed for membership of the British Society of Religion. The organization, he explained, had been founded at the beginning of the century and was composed of forty elected members who met three times a year at the Pantheon Club in London. I was thrilled at the suggestion. Several months later, I received a letter from the secretary of the society, inviting me to join.

On the day of my first meeting, William and I travelled up together from Canterbury. I had never been inside the Pantheon Club before – located in the heart of London clubland, it was the haunt of bishops, high-court judges, top civil servants and distinguished academics. On the way in, I spotted the Archbishop of York talking to a famous television presenter; he waved at William as we made our way to the library where the meeting was to be held. At the top of the stairs, William showed me a large volume containing photographs of members of the club who had won Nobel Prizes. How different this all was from Jewish Denver!

In the library a queue had formed for tea, and William introduced me to several members. Later we took our seats in comfortable leather armchairs, and the chairman – a tall, stooped Oxford professor – called us to order. The secretary read the minutes of the last meeting, which included my election; the chairman then introduced the speaker, a well-known Anglican bishop, who read a long paper about the nature of divine revelation. Afterwards there was a wide-ranging discussion lasting for over an hour; this was followed by sherry. We then filed down the stairs (the more elderly taking the elevator) to an elegant private dining room. At dinner I was seated between a bearded Orthodox patriarch and one of the most famous British sociologists of religion.

‘Was that a normal meeting?’ I asked.

The patriarch stroked his beard. ‘Quite typical,’ he said. ‘Most people were on form, weren't they?' He turned towards the sociologist.

'I never say anything,' the sociologist replied. 'I'm far too frightened.'

At the next meeting, I was reluctant to speak during the discussion, but I resolved to make a contribution at the third paper. At dinner I was seated next to a venerable Catholic bishop who was well known in Christian–Jewish affairs. Over port we discussed the future of inter-faith encounter. Just before he left, he leaned near me. 'Dan,' he whispered. 'Would you like to join the Pantheon – a number of us in the society belong, and I'm sure you'd have support. Would you like me to put you up?'

'I'd be delighted,' I gulped. 'But . . . I'm not sure I'm grand enough.'

The bishop laughed. 'I'll see what I can do.'

In the weeks that passed, I heard nothing further; I wondered if the bishop had forgotten his offer. However I eventually received a brief note saying the process of election was under way. He urged me to be patient. 'It can take a long time,' he wrote.

At the next meeting of the Society, the bishop was absent. After three more months of hearing nothing further, I gave up hope. 'That's it,' I said to Lavinia. 'There's a problem . . . I can tell. I better forget about the whole thing.'

'Don't be impatient,' she assured me. 'You'll hear.'

Several days later, as I went through my post at the university, I came across a large envelope with a Pantheon seal. I ripped it open: inside was the announcement of my election, a request for membership dues and material about the club. Anxious to tell Lavinia the good news, I drove to King's School and parked in the precincts. Mounting the steps, I heard Lavinia's voice echo down the corridor; she was in the middle of a lesson. None the less, I knocked on the door. Opening it, she looked distraught. 'What is it, Dan?' she said. 'Is something wrong?'

I handed over the letter from the Pantheon Club. Excitedly I told her the good news.

'Dan, I'm in the middle of a class.'

'But I wanted you to know. Isn't that great?'

'So you've become one of the immortals,' she teased.

'Come on . . .' I protested.

'I'm terribly pleased – but I've got to get back to my class.' And with that she shut the door.

During the next few months, I frequently went up to London

to dine at the club, and became a regular at the club table. The talk was always fascinating, and I didn't hesitate to join in. As a consequence I met several gentlemen who belonged to a dining club that met once a month at the club. The Pantheon Discussion Group had been going for nearly twenty-five years, and was made up of about a dozen members. Often I saw them gathered together at a long table in the dining room. To my surprise I received a letter from their secretary asking me if I would care to join them.

When I showed Lavinia the letter she sniggered. 'Dan, those men are awfully old! Are you sure you want to belong? You'll be the baby of the group.'

'But they're so interesting – and it's flattering to be asked.'

'That place is nothing more than an upper-middle-class geriatric day-care centre,' she pronounced.

Lavinia was right about the age of the Pantheon group – nearly all of the members had retired, and some were over eighty. This, however, did not impede their appetites. At dinner most ordered a full meal consisting of a starter, main course and dessert plus half a bottle of wine. Afterwards they went upstairs for coffee and then retired to the library where one of the members gave a paper. At the first gathering I attended, I watched in astonishment as one member after another fell asleep during the presentation. A few snored loudly as the speaker droned on. When he finished, everyone woke up, and fulsome thanks were given for such an interesting talk. For the next forty-five minutes, there was a probing examination of the paper; those who had snored loudest asked the most difficult questions. It was most mysterious.

When eventually my turn came to give a talk, I was unsure about the subject. When I asked Lavinia, she suggested I read the conclusion to my thesis which had just come out as a book; I wondered what they would make of my views and followed her suggestion. On the evening I read out selected extracts; throughout I stressed that in my opinion there were no grounds for thinking that prayers of intercession could be efficacious. Everyone was apparently asleep. When I finished, the chairman thanked me for my presentation, and then the questions began. One of the oldest members of the group – a prominent member of the House of Lords – apologized in advance; his hearing aid had not been working well, and he was afraid he might not have understood everything I said. None the less, he began to probe some of the central difficulties of my position: in the end I had to confess he had a point. This was followed by a demolition of some of the major assumptions of my book by a retired civil servant.

At ten the discussion ended and my head was spinning. As we marched down the stairs most of the members congratulated me for stimulating such a good discussion. Thinking back to my viva, I wished that my examiners had been so acute.

Every year Lavinia and I travelled to the United States to see family and friends. On one trip we booked into the Tewksbury Club in New York; during our stay I had made an appointment to see the editor-in-charge of Orbis Books, the major publisher of liberation theology. Over lunch he suggested I write a book about Judaism and Christian liberation. 'Nobody's done this before,' he said. 'If you produce it, I'll publish it.'

But what was I to say? I had no idea. As we walked down Fifth Avenue, I discussed the project with Lavinia. En route we went inside Tiffany's – the jewellery shop. As we strolled down rows and rows of diamonds, she stopped. 'Look,' she said. 'I'll make you a deal; I'll tell you what to say as long as you buy me something from Tiffany's with the royalties.'

I looked at the jewellery sparkling under the lights. 'OK,' I said.

'What you need to show,' Lavinia said, peering into the show-cases, 'is that Christian liberation theology has gone back to its Jewish roots. It's become less spiritual and more literal in its approach. It's no longer the poor in spirit who'll inherit the Kingdom of Heaven, it's the plain poor.'

'That's good,' I said.

'. . . and then you ought to sketch out those areas where Jews and Christians can work together . . . boy scout prospects – urban renewal and so on.' Calling out to the sales girl behind the counter, Lavinia asked to see an antique ring with an enormous marquise diamond.

'What do you think?' she asked as she tried it on.

'I hope the book sells well,' I replied.

Over the next six months I read everything I could about liberation theology; I discovered that most liberation theologians were ardent Marxists. Some had participated in revolutionary struggles in South America and advocated violence – there were nuns with guns and priests with pistols. All this was far removed from my experiences in the leafy Jewish suburbs of four continents. As I began writing the book, I discussed this obvious discrepancy with Lavinia.

'Don't worry about it,' she advised. 'Just keep writing.'

'But look,' I protested, 'you can't imagine my aunt standing shoulder to shoulder with those in the urban ghettos, working for social justice.'

'I can't even imagine her driving through the ghettos in her Cadillac,' Lavinia replied.

'Well, then, what am I doing? Nobody's going to accept these theories.'

'Some of the Christians might like it . . .'

'But what about the Jews? They'll think I've lost my marbles.'

'I doubt if they'll bother to read it, so I don't think there will be a problem. They'll just think it's very admirable and have a fundraising dinner at the country club to combat urban illiteracy.'

'Are you sure about this?' I queried.

'Of course. They'll love it. I'm very hopeful – I've been looking through the Tiffany catalogue.'

When the book appeared, it caused something of a stir – liberation theology had become a fashionable subject, and this was the first study of its kind. On both sides of the Atlantic I came to be regarded as something of a radical theologian. In consequence, I was invited to write and lecture about the importance of integrating the insights of liberation theology into the inner city. And because the book sold well, I was able to keep my promise to Lavinia; she bought a lovely diamond ring which she ostentatiously announced was purchased from the sales of a work of revolutionary thought.

In classes at the university my students read seminar papers about liberation theology in which they frequently referred to my book. On one occasion a conservative undergraduate challenged my views. 'Uh, Rabbi Dan,' he asked, 'do you put this stuff into practice? I mean do you live in the urban ghetto?'

'There aren't any ghettos in Canterbury,' I admitted. 'But we do live in a mixed community in the centre of town – there are poor people as well as those who are better off.'

'But it's not exactly an area of urban deprivation like you describe in your book?'

'No,' I said. 'But . . . you could call it a social experiment.'

An even greater challenge to my endorsement of social activism, however, came from next door. One of our neighbours, an elderly lady, had recently died; the person who bought her house when it came on the market was a loud, abrasive, beer-drinking lout. The first night he moved in he gave a party that lasted until three in the morning; the next day Lavinia and I were awakened by loud rock music at eight. Bleary-eyed, I got dressed, and knocked on his door. He answered it wearing only his underwear. 'Yeah?' he grunted.

'I'm from next door,' I said.

'Can't hear what you're saying . . . let me turn this thing down.'

'The thing is,' I continued, 'your party went on awfully late last night, and we'd be very grateful if you could . . .'

Eyeing me contemptuously, he interrupted. 'As far as I'm concerned, you can just piss off. I'll have my friends over when I want.'

'Look,' I said. 'We're going to be neighbours, and the least . . .'

'Mind your own business,' he yelled and slammed the door.

That afternoon our new neighbour put up a target in his back yard, and shot at it with an air rifle. Digger was terrified, and refused to go outside. From the kitchen we watched in horror.

'There's only one thing we can do,' Lavinia said. 'We've got to phone the police.'

After a long explanation of our difficulties, Lavinia hung up. 'The police officer said he'll come round.' Half an hour later a police car pulled up in front of our house, and an officer knocked on the door. Over coffee, we explained our predicament. 'I'll see what I can do,' he said and went next door. Anxiously we waited for his return. Eventually he reappeared, sat in our drawing room and told us the bad news. 'Gordon Boom,' he announced, 'is well known to the police: he has recently been in prison; when he was released his mother bought him the house next to yours. Gordon's quite a familiar face at the station,' he went on. 'Last time, he was up for drug dealing. We'd be grateful if you could keep an eye on him.'

'But what about the air pistol and the late-night parties?' I asked.

'I'm sorry, sir. But he's got a right to use an air pistol as long as he doesn't fire into your garden.'

'But what about our cat?' Lavinia objected.

'Let us know if it gets shot,' he said.

'But that's just the point,' she said in desperation. 'We don't want him to get shot.'

'Sorry, ma'am. But that's the law.'

'And the parties?'

'Oh yes. I've told our friend Gordon that they must end at midnight. And I've cautioned him to keep down the noise.'

When the officer left, I slumped on to the sofa. 'That's it,' I declared. 'We're moving to the best part of Canterbury; I'm not living next to a drug dealer!'

‘But this is our house,’ Lavinia protested.

‘That guy is a complete menace. You’re the daughter of a successful solicitor, and I’m the son of an orthopaedic surgeon – I’m not going to be the next-door neighbour of an ex-convict who insults me and shoots at our cat.’

‘Dan, Gordon’s a symbol of the inner city . . . and you’re supposed to be a Jewish liberation theologian.’

‘It’s all very nice in theory,’ I said angrily, ‘but I can’t cope in practice. I’m quitting. My liberation theology doesn’t stretch as far as Gordon.’ And with that I picked up the telephone to call the estate agent.

Despite our constant protests, Gordon continued to hold wild late-night parties and shoot his air rifle. In desperation we put our house on the market; at the end of the summer we bought an equally small terrace cottage in one of the best parts of Canterbury. Georgian in style, it was built of mellow red brick and had a Kent-peg tile roof. Out of the study window there was a splendid view of the Cathedral, and the front of the house overlooked a lovely garden. Most important, the neighbours were respectable and middle-class – at least there would be no more drug dealing or rowdy drunks!

While these domestic changes were taking place, the issue of test-tube birth was hotly debated in the media; anxious to keep up with this development, I discussed artificial insemination with my students at the university. In one seminar a female traditionalist delivered a stinging attack on any kind of artificial birth technique. Such procedures, she maintained, were contrary to God’s will and sinful in nature. I was surprised and somewhat taken aback by her vehemence; afterwards I asked her to stay behind.

‘Your paper,’ I began, ‘was very interesting, but why do you hold such strong views?’

‘Because it’s contrary to the Bible,’ she insisted.

‘But why do you think that?’ I asked. ‘In these cases couples really want babies and love them.’

‘It doesn’t matter,’ she stated. ‘If God had wanted them to have babies, they would have been able to have them.’

‘And those children born of artificial insemination?’

‘They’re like the products of Frankenstein,’ she declared.

That evening I told Lavinia about our conversation. ‘You know,’ I said, ‘there are thousands of people like me – and there’ll be thousands more in the future. We’re not freaks.’

‘Why don’t you write an article about it?’ she suggested. ‘It would be very suitable for the *Sunday Times* – you could call it:

"My Birth was a Miracle of Science". Just the type of schmaltz they like.'

The next morning I composed an article along these lines and sent it off, along with a photograph. Several days later I received a telephone call from the head of features, telling me that they liked what I had written and planned to publish it. On the day it appeared, I rushed to the newsagent's and bought several copies. During the next few days I received a stack of supportive letters; in addition, several anxious parents requested advice about the wisdom of going ahead with the procedure.

'You've become famous,' Lavinia pronounced.

'Hardly,' I said.

'Honestly, Dan. Over a million people read the *Sunday Times*. Fame at last!'

'You know,' I said, 'I couldn't possibly have written that piece if I were a congregational rabbi. Imagine the outrage.'

'But even they couldn't fire you just because you're the product of artificial insemination.'

'In the rabbinate,' I sighed, 'anything's possible.'

Now that I had become more established as an academic, I thought it might be a suitable time to submit my published work for a PhD. As advised by Cambridge, I bundled up a package of books and articles and sent it off. After a lengthy process of waiting, a viva was arranged. Together with Lavinia, I travelled to Cambridge: as before, she walked me to the college where my examination was to take place. This time I had been assigned a new set of examiners, and unlike my previous viva they asked me a great many searching questions about my work. At the end they informed me that I had passed. While this ordeal was taking place, Lavinia had gone shopping; we arranged to meet for tea in a student snack bar near King's Parade. Lavinia was seated among stacks of purchases in a booth when I entered. From my expression, she could see that the viva had gone well. 'Were you a triumph?' she asked.

'I'm not sure . . . but I got the degree.'

'Whoopee!' she hooted.

'It's a relief,' I said.

'Well, at long last – Dr Cohn-Sherbok.'

'It took a bit of time,' I asserted.

'Yes . . . but it was worth waiting for.'

'Uh, Lavinia,' I said hesitantly. 'What about going to look at PhD gowns after tea?'

At the time these events were taking place, the Archbishop

of Canterbury announced his retirement. I had been asked to contribute to a collection of essays in his honour – mine was to depict his contribution to inter-faith relations. When I told my publisher about this, he had an idea: 'What about publishing a festschrift for him?' he asked.

'You don't think it would compete with this other collection?'

'We'll do something very different,' he stated.

'What about a volume of sermons written by distinguished admirers of the Archbishop?' I asked. 'We could ask the Archbishop of York, the Bishop of Durham, the Lord Chancellor, Archbishop Desmond Tutu . . .'

'Don't forget the Pope?' he said.

'But I don't know the Pope,' I confessed.

'The Archbishop does – just give the Vatican a ring.' Refilling his glass, he toasted the project. 'Here's to big sales!' he proclaimed, and downed his claret.

Over the next month I sent out over fifty letters – to my delight I had an overwhelming response. Most wrote by return of post and enclosed a sermon for the Archbishop along with a brief introductory paragraph. The list of contributors was a *Who's Who* of significant spiritual leaders and theologians. When the book came out, we held a party at the Pantheon Club. On the night, I stood at the door welcoming all the guests at a table stacked with books and the publisher handed out copies to all the contributors. When the Archbishop arrived, he was besieged by those wanting his autograph. Out of the corner of my eye I watched the throng. From afar I spied the Vice-Chancellor of my university hopping from one important person to another with his wife in tow; in the corner of the room the Chief Rabbi was conversing with the Dean of Westminster Abbey. It was all certainly ecumenical!

Eventually I prised the Archbishop from his admirers and put him next to the Lord Chancellor, who had written an introduction to the book. I welcomed everyone, and then the Lord Chancellor spoke warmly about the Archbishop – whom he had known for years. The press took photographs, and then everyone made a dive for more drink and refreshments.

After it was over, Lavinia and I went upstairs for dinner. Over a candle-lit meal in the Pantheon dining room, Lavinia congratulated me on the event. Thumbing through the collection, she smiled. 'Well, you seem to have joined the ranks of the British Establishment. Made it in the end, Rabbi!'

'Shut up, Lavinia.'

'What's a nice Jewish boy like you doing in a place like this?' she asked.

'He's enjoying his beef bourgignon,' I replied.

Once we had settled into our new house, I assumed that there would be no reason to move again; that, however, was not to be. One afternoon Lavinia came home from King's clutching the latest edition of *The Times Educational Supplement*. Enthusiastically she announced that she was going to apply for the Headship of a girls' boarding school.

'But why?' I asked. 'We're happy here; you have a splendid job at King's.'

'I need a new challenge,' she replied.

Looking at the advertisement, I questioned her about the school.

'You'll love it,' she insisted. 'The Princess of Wales was a pupil there, and so were her sisters – it's full of posh little girls. Absolutely your kind of thing. And it's in a lovely Regency house in over thirty acres of grounds.'

'But I like it in Canterbury,' I objected.

'You'll like it there, too,' Lavinia declared as she took out writing paper to draft her application.

After several weeks, Lavinia received a letter from the school requesting she attend an interview with a management consultant who had been hired to screen candidates. We travelled up to London by train, and I waited for her at the Pantheon. Her interview was arranged for noon, and I expected her to arrive at the club for lunch. Anxiously I paced back and forth in the library. Finally, at two, I was summoned by the porter – Lavinia had arrived at last! She was smiling when I saw her.

'How did it go?' I asked.

'It was fine. But he wants to meet you, too.'

'Me. But why?'

'Because you're part of the deal. And he wants to see you this afternoon at four.'

'But I haven't had lunch,' I protested.

'Neither have I, but we can grab a sandwich on the way.'

At the arranged time, I was ushered into a small office overlooking Green Park. The headhunter stood up and shook hands. On the way to his office, I had practised answers to the sorts of questions I thought he might pose. To my surprise he asked none of them. He was interested in Lavinia rather than me. He was anxious to know if she really wanted the job. Would she be fulfilled by being a Headmistress? What were her strengths and weaknesses? I answered as best I could. As we approached the elevator, I cleared my throat. 'Mr Hancock,' I said. 'I really ought to ask you – won't the parents mind having a rabbi around the place? I mean . . . it's not exactly a Jewish environment.'

Looking me over, he laughed. 'Don't worry! You haven't scared me, and you won't scare them either!'

This interview was followed by another with the appointment committee, and a final interview with the governing body. On the day, Lavinia dressed the part. She wore a tweedy, country outfit; I put on my best suit from Marks and Spencers. Over a buffet lunch the governors were extremely affable; most told me about their latest trips to America. While Lavinia was being interviewed I waited with the bursar and the current Headmistress. After an hour, Lavinia appeared, flushed and amused. 'It was hilarious,' she said.

Just as we were saying our goodbyes, the Chairman knocked on the door. 'Mrs Cohn-Sherbok,' he said, 'we'd like to make you an offer.' And she was swept away to meet the governors once again.

The first week after Lavinia took up her appointment at the school, a new Sports Hall – built in honour of the retiring Headmistress – was to be dedicated by the Princess of Wales, she being a famous old girl of the school. There was much excitement. Parents, governors and hordes of journalists and photographers waited outside for the Princess to arrive. At eleven a red helicopter hovered above the lacrosse pitch; several minutes later it landed, and the Princess of Wales emerged, followed by her two sisters. The Chairman of the governors was the first to greet her. He bowed as he shook her hand; then other governors bowed and curtseyed. Lavinia and I watched this scene from the Headmistress's study; the Princess was to come there first to meet us and then go to the Sports Hall to give her speech.

'Uh, Lavinia,' I said as the entourage headed in our direction. 'I'm not supposed to bow like that, am I?'

'Of course,' she replied, 'she is the Princess of Wales.'

'But I'm an American,' I objected, 'the land of the brave and the free. We don't go in for that sort of thing.'

'Just do it – a little bow will be quite sufficient.'

'And you're going to curtsey?' I inquired incredulously.

'Certainly,' she said, 'I know how to behave.'

'This is ridiculous,' I replied.

When the Princess entered the room I was introduced as the new Headmistress's husband, and I bowed as instructed.

'And what are you going to do here?' she asked.

'Well, I'm writing a book on Holocaust theology, Your Royal Highness.'

'How very interesting . . .' she replied with a polite smile. She turned to speak to her lady-in-waiting.

When the Princess was taken away to meet some of the distinguished guests, I took Lavinia aside. 'You know,' I said, 'I don't think the Princess of Wales has ever heard of Holocaust theology. Did you see her reaction?'

'What do you think – of course she doesn't know about it.'

'Maybe I ought to send her a copy when I finish it,' I suggested.

'Good grief,' Lavinia sighed as we followed the party into the Sports Hall.

During the Princess's speech, I was put next to one of the sisters, and Lavinia was seated on the stage – throughout, flashbulbs went off and video cameras hummed. At the end of the proceedings, we led the throng into the school hall for lunch. In the evening, Lavinia and I joined the girls in one of the common rooms to watch the television news; halfway through the newscaster announced that the Princess of Wales had visited her old school to dedicate a Sports Hall in honour of her former Headmistress. There followed various scenes of the school, the Princess and the gathering in the Sports Hall. When Lavinia and I appeared on the screen, there was giggling and general applause.

Later that night I was having a bath, and Lavinia came in to talk to me.

'What a day,' she said. She sat on the edge of the bathtub.

'Wasn't it fun?'

'Did you ever think all those years ago that you'd be entertaining the Princess of Wales in a posh girls' boarding school?' She smiled at me. 'There you were on television, a celebrity!'

'Come on, Lavinia . . .' I said.

I started soaping my leg and stopped in astonishment. 'Look at this! I don't believe it. My eczema. I've had it since I was thirteen years old. It seems to have completely disappeared.'

Lavinia laughed. 'Mens sana in corpore sano. A healthy mind in a healthy body,' she said.

Epilogue

One summer, on the way to a theological conference in San Francisco, Lavinia and I stopped off in Denver. By this stage my father did not even pretend to be cordial and had retreated to a local hotel. Lavinia and I stayed in the basement of my parents' house, and ate our meals with my mother. A number of my mother's friends who were aware of the family friction invited the three of us out. On one occasion, we were asked to join a couple for lunch at the Jewish country club. The plan was that we would eat first and then go swimming.

After we had finished lunch Lavinia and I changed and went into the pool. My mother sat with our hosts under an umbrella. Lavinia, who was not a very good swimmer, borrowed a large rubber ring and floated in the deep end as I swam to and fro. Eventually I climbed out of the pool and flopped down by the water's edge. Sitting nearby was an attractive red-head wearing large sunglasses. I spread out on a towel, picked up a paperback novel, and started to read.

'Excuse me,' the red-head said. 'I wonder if you could hand me my suncream.'

'Sure,' I replied.

As she covered herself with lotion, she asked me if I was new to the club.

'I'm not actually a member,' I explained. 'We're the guests of the Feldbergs.'

'My name is Jackie Goldshmidt,' she said.

'I'm Dan Cohn-Sherbok.'

'Cohn-Sherbok . . . is your father a bone doctor?' she asked.

'Yes – how did you know?'

'Well, your father once operated on my grandmother. She was devoted to him – thought he was a genius. I think my grandmother was a friend of your mother's mother, too. She's passed away now, but her name was Hannah Schwartz.'

'You're not going to believe this,' I said. 'But I met your grandmother once, and she suggested I meet you. It was in a jewellery store downtown.'

The red-head took off her sunglasses. 'No kidding.'

'Didn't you go to the University of Arizona to study something like music?'

'It was dance, actually.'

'And then what happened?'

'I got married to someone from Denver: Jerry Goldshmidt.'

'Really?'

'We had two kids: a boy and a girl. He's a dentist. But we're separated now.'

'I'm sorry.'

'Believe me, it's much better. What about you? Do you live in Denver?'

'No – I'm visiting my mother. I live in England.'

'Gee, that's a long way from here.'

'It is,' I said.

'And what do you do there' she asked, sitting up.

'Well . . . I'm a rabbi,' I began.

'A rabbi?' She laughed. 'I'd never have guessed. I always thought that wasn't a job for a nice Jewish boy.'

I sat up. 'That's exactly what your grandmother said when I met her.'

'She didn't,' said the red-head.

'She did,' I replied. 'And do you know, she was absolutely right.'

Glossary

Aliyah: Immigration to Israel
Ark: The place in the synagogue where the Torah Scrolls are kept
Bar Mitzvah: Jewish ceremony for thirteen-year-old boys at which they take their adult place in the congregation
Bimah: Dais in a synagogue
Cantor: Synagogue chanter
Cohen: Priest
Frummer: Traditional Orthodox Jew
Haftarah: Reading from the Prophetic books of the Hebrew Bible
Goyim: Non-Jews
Haggadah: Passover prayer book
Halakhah: General term for the Hebrew oral or traditional law
Hasidim: Pious Orthodox Jewish sect
High Holy Days: Period between and including the New Year and Day of Atonement
Huppah: Marriage canopy
Kabbalah: Jewish mystical writings
Kaddish: Funeral prayer
Kiddush: Blessing over wine and bread
Kipah: Skullcap (same as yamulkah)
Kol Nidre: Service on the eve of the Day of Atonement
Kosher: Ritually prepared food
L'hat hila d'avad: Rabbinic formula: it should not take place, but if it has occurred it is valid
Macher: Important person
Mamzer: Illegitimate child (the product of a forbidden marriage)
Midrash: Rabbinic commentary on Scripture

Minyan: Minimum number of men for a Jewish worship service
Mishnah: Early codification of Jewish law
Mitzvah: Commandment (or duty)
Nu: Ejaculation expressing various emotions
Purim: Feast of Esther
Rosh Hashanah: Jewish New Year
Sabra: Native-born Israeli
Shabbat: Jewish Sabbath
Shabbat Shalom: Sabbath peace (a greeting)
Shiksa: Derogatory term for a non-Jewish female
Talmud: Sixth-century compilation of Jewish law and lore
Tefillin: Small leather boxes containing passages from the Torah
Temple: Reform Synagogue
Torah: Five Books of Moses
Torah Scroll: Scroll of the Torah used in the synagogue
Yamulkah: Skullcap
Yeshivah: Orthodox Jewish seminary
Yeshivah bocher: Yeshivah student
Yom Kippur: Day of Atonement